EMPLOYMENT DISPUTES AND THE THIRD PARTY

Employment Disputes and the Third Party

Pat Lowry

M
MACMILLAN

First published 1990

Published by
THE MACMILLAN PRESS LTD
Houndmills, Basingstoke, Hampshire RG21 2XS
and London
Companies and representatives
throughout the world

Typeset by Footnote Graphics,
Warminster, Wiltshire

Printed and bound in Great Britain by
WBC Ltd, Bristol and Maesteg

British Library Cataloguing in Publication Data
Lowry, Pat
Employment disputes and the third party.
1. Great Britain. Industrial relations. Disputes.
Arbitration
I. Title
331.89'143'0941
ISBN 0–333–49372–9

Contents

List of Tables

List of Abbreviations

ACAS	Advisory, Conciliation and Arbitration Service
AEU	Amalgamated Engineering Union
AFPRB	Review Body on Armed Forces Pay
ASLEF	Associated Society of Locomotivemen, Enginemen and Firemen
BT	British Telecom
CAC	Central Arbitration Committee
CBI	Confederation of British Industry
CCSU	Council of Civil Service Unions
CIR	Commission on Industrial Relations
COHSE	Confederation of Health Service Employees
COIT	Central Office of the Industrial Tribunals
CSAT	Civil Service Arbitration Tribunal
DDRB	Review Body on Doctors' and Dentists' Remuneration
DE	Department of Employment
ECA	Electrical Contractors' Association
EAT	Employment Appeal Tribunal
EC	European Community
EEF	Engineering Employers' Federation
EETPU	Electrical, Electronic, Telecommunication and Plumbing Union
GEC	General Electric Co. Ltd.
LRT	London Regional Transport
NACODS	National Association of Colliery Overmen, Deputies and Shotfirers
NALHM	National Association of Licensed House Managers
NAPRB	Review Body for Nursing Staff, Midwives, Health Visitors and Professions Allied to Medicine
NAT	National Arbitration Tribunal
NCB	National Coal Board
NGA	National Graphical Association
NHS	National Health Service
NUM	National Union of Mineworkers
NUPE	National Union of Public Employees
NUR	National Union of Railwaymen
OME	Office of Manpower Economics
POAT	Post Office Arbitration Tribunal

POAMT	Post Office Arbitration and Mediation Tribunal
PRP	Pharmacists' Review Panel
RSNT	Railway Staff National Tribunal
SJIC	Statutory Joint Industrial Council
SOGAT	Society of Graphical and Allied Trades
SRB	Special Review Body (TUC)
STUC	Scottish Trades Union Congress
TGWU	Transport and General Workers' Union
TSRB	Review Body on Top Salaries
TSSA	Transport and Salaried Staffs Association
TUC	Trades Union Congress
UCW	Union of Communication Workers
UDM	Union of Democratic Mineworkers

Preface

This book covers more than just the ACAS involvement in industrial disputes. My thanks are therefore due not just to those former ACAS colleagues who have assisted me so enormously but also to all those others – in employers' associations, trade unions, nationalised industries and private sector companies – on whose time I have so shamelessly trespassed and whose patience I have so sorely tried. To them all, as well as to officials in the Department of Employment and the Office of Manpower Economics, I am most grateful.

I am particularly indebted to Jean Hiltrop, David Burrill and Alice Brown for allowing me to quote some of the results of their research work for ACAS into certain aspects of the Service's conciliation and arbitration activities. At Warwick University Linda Dickens offered me some much needed help and advice in the area of individual employment rights in which she is so widely acknowledged an expert.

As a result of all this assistance I have tried to be as factually accurate as a rapidly changing scene permits. Needless to say, the conclusions and opinions are my own. In a book which dwells, in part, on matters concerning equal opportunities in employment, it is particularly important to stress that I have observed the convention of using 'he' and 'him' to cover both genders, save of course where the context is so obviously concerned with one sex only.

PAT LOWRY

Introduction

For generations the independent and neutral third party has played a vital but sometimes misunderstood role in keeping the industrial peace. Neutrality doesn't just take the present, well-known form of the Advisory, Conciliation and Arbitration Service (ACAS) or of arbitral bodies like the Central Arbitration Committee (CAC). Important responsibilities are also discharged by members of commissions and courts of inquiry (relatively rare these days), by members of pay review bodies and the independent members of wages councils (now a threatened species). Trade unions and employers' associations, in addition to their representational role, sometimes play the part of conciliators in the operation of their grievance and negotiating procedures, and the Trades Union Congress (TUC) itself provides independent conciliation and arbitration for handling inter-union disputes that often have to be settled quickly if the public reputation and credibility of the trade union movement is not to be harmed.

This book seeks to trace the evolution of the third-party role in both dispute resolution and its avoidance.

From even before the days of the Taff Vale case the judgements of the courts have exercised a powerful influence over industrial relations behaviour. Indeed, the judiciary probably exercises the most powerful neutral and independent role of them all, but in an age in which employment law and its application daily become more complex, it is safer for the layman to refer to this role but marginally – in other words to comment on the content of the law and its implications and the decisions of the courts (including industrial tribunals) only when it is necessary to complete a particular picture.

Conciliation and arbitration were a logical consequence of the development of collective bargaining during the second half of the nineteenth century. Even in an age when the primacy of the managerial right to manage was regarded as unassailable, there were some employers and some industries that were prepared to admit that there was a role for the independent third party either during the bargaining process or after direct negotiations had broken down.

Professor Henry Phelps Brown has described how collective

bargaining gave rise to a new institution generally known as the board of conciliation and arbitration:

> one of the few inventions that have been made in industrial relations, a device, it seemed, which would make them run more smoothly than, with the same men and problems, they ever could without it. It was to be the characteristic form of organised British industrial relations for the thirty years from 1860 to 1890, then to be taken over by government in Australasia, and to return thence to the British statute book.[1]

The best known early examples were in the Nottingham hosiery industry and in the North of England iron industry. In Nottingham A. J. Mundella, an employer, took the initiative in 1860 in setting up a board which not only brought to an end one particularly difficult dispute, but helped afterwards to settle a number of other strikes and lock-outs. In the North of England David Dale, a Quaker ironmaster of Darlington, joined with a trade union leader, John Kane, in 1869, to set up a board for the iron and steel industry in the North of England. Numerous boards were set up elsewhere, for example, in the building industry, and in the boot and shoe and hosiery industries in Leicester. Conciliation boards in the coalmining industry did not arrive until 1893. Again it was Mundella (by this time President of the Board of Trade) who was responsible. Mundella must have been an interesting character. The son of an Italian refugee and a Welsh mother, he was apprenticed as a hosier and by the age of 23 was himself a manufacturer. He was an MP for 29 years and, as President of the Board of Trade, set up its Labour Department in 1886. Despite the present-day belief that pendulum arbitration is a modern development, the 'invention' seems to have been his.

The boards normally comprised equal numbers of representatives of employers and employed together with an independent person. In some boards the third party acted as a conciliator trying to help the other members to reach their own agreements. But in other cases the independent member might be authorised, if conciliation failed, to assume the role of umpire or arbitrator as well and hand down a binding award.

The fact that these boards got off to a good start was probably due to the circumstances of conflict in which they had been set up and the desire for something better in future. But in some industries they declined relatively rapidly and this seems to have been because the issues that arose began to impinge on the prerogatives of management;

the feeling of mutual trust diminished as bargaining moved from the local to the national level; and as memories of the circumstances in which the boards had been set up began to fade, the motivations of the participants became suspect. Some disputes never came to the boards at all, and in others where they did, failures to agree, as distinct from decisions, were recorded. Even in some cases when decisions were reached, they were subsequently disowned or repudiated.

In the strong, developing engineering industry, boards were never established. Employers in this industry were implacably opposed to any development which might impinge on their right to manage – and they would certainly have regarded the establishment of a joint board presided over by an independent conciliator or arbitrator as doing just that.

In 1891, faced with an industrial relations situation that was deteriorating, the government of the day set up a Royal Commission on Labour 'to enquire into the relations between employers and workmen and to report whether legislation could be directed to remedy any faults disclosed'.[2] The Commission was clearly impressed by the work of the joint conciliation and arbitration boards for, in its report, it drew attention to them and to the desirability of the government encouraging their development.

The Commission's recommendations were reflected in the Conciliation Act of 1896. Mundella's special section of the Board of Trade (which lasted until the Ministry of Labour was established after the First World War) was given the task of fostering these agreements. Additionally, this section was granted powers to inquire into the causes and circumstances of a dispute; to appoint a conciliator or board of conciliation on the application of employers or workers; and to appoint an arbitrator on the application of both parties. Thus was born the state's conciliation service.

During the period of parliamentary debate that preceded the passing of the Act, the possibility of wider powers for the state was canvassed but was resisted by employers and trade unions. Three virtually defunct arbitration acts were repealed. It was, in fact, the Act of 1896 which confirmed the essentially voluntary framework on which British industrial relations were to be based and on which indeed, despite the changes of the 1980s, they are largely based to this day.

Neither side was exactly enthusiastic at the prospect of accepting government intervention in its industrial disputes, and so the new powers were used sparingly. All the emphasis was placed on voluntary development.

By the 1890s, under the pressure of public opinion, the government had felt obliged to take action in another direction. In an attempt to check the evils of 'sweating', the first Fair Wages Resolution was passed in 1891. And in Parliament, and in the country, Sir Charles Dilke was actively campaigning for the establishment of trade boards. The statutory protection for which he was pressing (his first draft bill was printed in 1900) would have applied to any trade in any district that after inquiry, the Home Secretary might determine. A board would consist of an independent chairman and representatives of employers and employed appointed by the Home Secretary. After a board had fixed minimum rates for the trade they would be binding on all employers and enforced by inspectors.

It was to be 1909 before Winston Churchill piloted the first Trade Boards bill through Parliament. The act which emerged bore striking similarity to Dilke's proposals, and for the next 90 years a new breed of independent was to fill a vital and much criticised role in the work of the Trade Boards (re-titled Wages Councils in 1945).

But in 1906 there had already been another development which for nearly 80 years was to have not only a tremendous impact on British industrial relations but also an incalculable effect on the conciliation and arbitration workload. In that year the Trade Disputes Act was passed.

In 1901 the House of Lords, flying in the face of widespread views to the contrary, had held in the Taff Vale case that a trade union could be held liable for any injury or damage caused by any person considered to be acting as its agent. As a result the union involved in the case (the Amalgamated Society of Railway Servants) had to pay £23 000 in damages. Of much greater significance was the fact that in any lawful strike in which it was engaged in future a trade union could be held liable for heavy damages.

There was an enormous outcry, and in 1906 the majority of a Royal Commission appointed to report on trade disputes and trade combinations recommended that some immunity should be restored, but not to the extent that had applied prior to the Taff Vale judgement. The Royal Commission reported just before a general election swept the Liberal Party into office. The new government tabled a bill based on the findings of the Commission but under great pressure not just from the 29 newly elected members of the Labour Representation Committee (the embryo Labour Party) but also from Liberal party members who had pledged themselves on the hustings to the return of complete immunity, the government threw in the towel. The Trade Disputes Act of 1906 laid down, among other things, that any act done by a person in contemplation or furtherance of a trade dispute should not be actionable on the ground only that it induced another person to break a contract of employment. It went on to enact that no action in tort should be brought against any trade union.

Trade union immunity against civil actions in the courts (the so-called golden formula) was thus complete and despite occasional attempts by the courts to dilute the principle, it remained virtually unchanged until the employment laws of Mrs Thatcher's government were put in place nearly 80 years later.

From 1907 until the outbreak of war in 1914 the country was beset by one serious industrial dispute after another. One contributory factor may well have been this newly restored and extended immunity. The laws certainly did not act as any spur to the trade unions to seek a peaceful resolution of their differences with employers through direct negotiations. At one time or another the railwaymen, coal miners, cotton spinners, seamen, dockers, engineers and shipyard workers were all locked into disputes. For a large part of this pre-war period it seems in retrospect that the industrial peace was either maintained or restored by the efforts of just one man, undoubtedly the greatest industrial conciliator of them all, G. R. (later Sir George and finally Lord) Askwith.

Askwith was a barrister by profession who, for some time, had worked in the chambers of Sir Henry (later Lord) James, one time MP, Solicitor-General and Attorney-General. James acted as an arbitrator in a number of labour disputes and it was whilst working with him that Askwith learned the skills of conciliation and arbitration. In 1907 Lloyd George brought him into the Railway Department of the Board of Trade and in 1909 he was appointed Controller-General of the commercial, labour and statistical department of the Board of Trade. After severe industrial storms in 1911 a national joint board, the Industrial Council, was set up with a panel of thirteen employers and thirteen trade unionists. Askwith, by this time carrying the job title of Chief Industrial Commissioner and the rank of a permanent secretary, was appointed its chairman.

Although the task of the Council was to consider and enquire into trade disputes referred to it, there was no great willingness to accept its authority and it eventually died for lack of work. But the Chief

Industrial Commissioner remained in post and it was in that position that Askwith worked so tirelessly and became such a widely known public figure. Uniquely, he was not just a conciliator; he acted as arbitrator and chairman of committees of inquiry as well. (The post of Chief Industrial Commissioner continued to exist until after the second world war but by that time its influence had diminished; the office holder was substantially confined to acting as conciliator in major national disputes that were considered to require the attention of somebody more senior than the Ministry of Labour's Chief Conciliation Officer.

When Askwith arrived at the Board of Trade in 1907 the country was facing the threat of a national railway strike.

The Board of Trade drew up and virtually imposed upon the railway companies and trade unions the railway scheme of conciliation and arbitration. But the scheme fell far short of meeting the unions' objective of recognition for collective bargaining purposes. Full-time employees of the company concerned were permitted to represent railmen on the company conciliation boards, but full-time officials of the unions were only allowed to represent the men when, failing agreement in conciliation, a claim was referred to arbitration. Partial union recognition was eventually secured after another railway strike in 1911 but it was not until 1919 that an understanding on negotiating machinery was reached under which a committee of the two rail unions concerned was fully recognised for the purpose of dealing with all questions affecting rates of pay and conditions of service. The men covered by the agreement were described as conciliation grades, a description which is still used to this day by the older railwaymen.

In the engineering industry the famous 'York memorandum' was negotiated in 1914. This agreement set down the basic procedure which for nearly 60 years any trade union was obliged to follow if, on behalf of its members, it wished to pursue an unsettled claim or grievance arising in any factory of a member firm of the Engineering Employers' Federation.

The First World War itself saw further enormous changes in industrial relations. Union membership increased; trade unions were increasingly consulted by government; special measures were taken to outlaw strikes and lock-outs and to impose compulsory arbitration; pay was increasingly bargained on a national basis; and yet, despite this, the control of the national trade union leaders was under increasing pressure from the shop stewards' movement whose prime objective was devolution of authority to the place of work.

In 1916 the government decided to set up a Committee under the chairmanship of Mr J. H. Whitley, Deputy Speaker of the House of Commons, with terms of reference which required it:

- to make and consider suggestions for securing a permanent improvement in the relations between employers and workmen; and
- to recommend means for securing that industrial conditions affecting the relations between employers and workmen shall be systematically reviewed by those concerned with a view to improving conditions in future.[3]

The Committee's recommendations were far reaching and played 'an important part in the extension and formation of joint negotiating machinery, the extension of the Trade Boards system and the development of statutory machinery for the prevention and settlement of industrial disputes'.[4]

The recommendations of the Committee were:

- that joint industrial councils should be formed in well-organised industries;
- that works committees representative of the management and the workers should be appointed in individual establishments;
- that the system of statutory regulation of wages should be extended to badly-organised trades [Churchill's 1909 Act covered workers in 'sweated' trades, not those where they were poorly organised];
- that a permanent court of arbitration should be set up;
- that the Minister of Labour should be authorised to hold inquiries regarding disputes.

Whitleyism (as it came to be called) assumed that arrangements for negotiation and consultation would be on an industry-wide basis; that the voluntary approach to the negotiation of terms and conditions and the settlement of disputes would be preserved; and that adequate organisation on both sides was necessary.

The recommendations of the Whitley committee were favourably received by employers' organisations and trade unions. Those concerning a permanent court of arbitration and the Minister of Labour's powers to hold inquiries into disputes were subsequently embodied in the Industrial Courts Act of 1919. The Industrial Court was established as a permanent and independent tribunal to which unsettled disputes could be voluntarily referred for binding arbitration. Over the following 70 years the name of the Court would be changed from time to time (today it is known as the Central Arbitration Committee) and its scope would be varied. But in all its forms it has made – and continues to make – a considerable contribution to the resolution of industrial disputes. The work of the Industrial Court was supplemented by single arbitrators and *ad hoc* boards of arbitration, for which the parties sometimes expressed a preference.

During the inter-war years the conciliation branch of the Ministry of Labour quietly built up its reputation and expertise and the arbitrators went about their business. Wages Councils proliferated. During the Second World War strikes and lock-outs were again made unlawful (not that it made much difference to their number) and compulsory arbitration was reintroduced – to be followed in 1951 by a modified statutory form that lasted until February 1959.

After the Second World War the pace quickened as successive governments sought the solution to the country's deteriorating industrial relations. Much use was made of courts or committees of inquiry (another vital role for the independents) as a means of buying off or heading off industrial disputes which the government of the day had quietly decided that the country could not afford. A Royal Commission under the chairmanship of Lord Donovan was set up in 1965, and its recommendations (which were a disappointment to many) centred on the need to recognise and formalise by means of better agreements those parts of the industrial relations system that were operating on an informal basis.

In 1968 the Ministry of Labour had its name changed to the Department of Employment (for short), with a Secretary of State in place of a Minister. In 1969 a Labour government produced its famous white paper, *In Place of Strife*, and, in the teeth of bitter union opposition, subsequently withdrew some of its key proposals for reform. A Conservative government, borrowing heavily on US legislation and practice, enacted its Industrial Relations Act in 1971. The same government, which had been elected with a promise that there would be no statutory pay policies but had subsequently become convinced of their need, placed such a priority on their strict application that conciliation under state auspices became discredited. Trade unions and employers openly discussed the need for a conciliation and arbitration service that would be totally independent of the state.

But in a decade marked by more political disagreements than

agreements, one point of agreement that did emerge was the need for statutory protection against unfair dismissal. The process called individual conciliation did not start with the unfair dismissal legislation but it was this legislation that provided the impetus to such an extent that in the case of nearly all the statutory employment rights that came into force later, access to an industrial tribunal for relief had first to be preceded by an attempt at conciliation.

By 1975 the Industrial Relations Act had gone and a Labour government's Employment Protection Act was in place, noteworthy for the establishment on a statutory basis of the Advisory, Conciliation and Arbitration Service (ACAS). Under the Act, ACAS was charged with the general duty of promoting the improvement of industrial relations, and in particular of encouraging the extension of collective bargaining and the development and, where necessary, reform of collective bargaining machinery. To some observers it was a cause of surprise that when Mrs Thatcher's Government took office in 1979 it took no action either to repeal or amend the particular duty relating to the extension and development of collective bargaining – this despite the representation of bodies like the Institute of Directors. The 1975 Act was, after all, the invention of a Labour government and had been passed at a time not just when trade unions were strong and influential, but also when the collective relationship between employer and trade union seemed to some to be more important than individual relationships between management and employees. Sections 11 to 19 of the Act, which were designed to extract union recognition from a reluctant employer, remained in force until 1980 when, on the advice of ACAS, they were repealed.

The Conservative Government certainly carried no torch for collective bargaining. This was to be the age when the individual was to be encouraged – individual assessment, individual performance and individual reward. And yet ACAS is still charged with the statutory duty of encouraging and developing collective bargaining. Surprisingly perhaps, this conflict between the provisions of the law and the realities of the industrial relations world has not caused any great difficulty.

ACAS is empowered to undertake a range of activities – all provided free of charge. In the words of the Service itself:

> It may inquire into any industrial relations matter, provide advice on industrial relations and the development of effective personnel practices, and issue codes of practice containing practical guidance

> on the improvement of industrial relations. It may help to resolve industrial disputes through conciliation, or through providing facilities for arbitration, mediation or committees of investigation and offer conciliation in disputes over statutory employment rights between individual employees and their employers . . .[5]

The way in which codes of practice have developed is significant. They were first introduced into employment law by the Industrial Relations Act of 1971, but provision for them is to be found too in Section 6 of the 1975 Employment Protection Act and in Section 3 of the 1980 Employment Act. Under Section 6 of the 1975 Act ACAS was empowered to prepare codes of practical guidance for the purpose of promoting the improvement of industrial relations. The codes are not legally binding but are admissible as evidence in proceedings before an industrial tribunal or the Central Arbitration Committee, which must take into account any provision considered relevant.

The first code (the Industrial Relations Code of Practice) was issued under the 1971 Act by the Department of Employment. After it was set up in 1975 ACAS issued three codes:

- a code on the disclosure of information to trade unions for collective bargaining purposes;
- a code on time off for trade union duties and activities;
- a code on disciplinary practice and procedures in employment.

These three codes superseded parts of the Industrial Relations Code of Practice.

ACAS codes have the inestimable advantage that before being submitted to Parliament for approval, they have not only been the subject of wide consultation but they carry the approval of the tripartite ACAS council. They are essentially practical in approach. On the other hand, the need for tripartite agreement means inevitably that they are couched in general terms.

When the new industrial relations laws of Mrs Thatcher's Government were being discussed it became clear that the TUC wanted no part of them. They would certainly not be prepared to join with ACAS in drafting any codes of practice arising from the new legislation. And so, under Section 3 of the 1980 Employment Act, the Department of Employment was itself given powers to issue or revise its own codes (and to terminate any part of an ACAS code which the

Secretary of State regarded as being superseded by one of his own). These, too, might be taken into account by industrial tribunals and the CAC. But unlike the ACAS codes, they would also be admissible in both civil and criminal proceedings. So far the Department has issued two codes – one on the closed shop and the other on picketing. Early in 1989 a third – on pre-strike balloting – was in course of preparation. Inevitably they lack the objectivity of the ACAS codes. Instead, they reflect a Conservative government's industrial relations policies.

Statutory codes of practice have also been issued by the Commission for Racial Equality and the Equal Opportunities Commission dealing with discrimination in the field of employment.

Although some sections of the media persist in calling it the government's conciliation service ACAS is, in fact, totally independent of government and is strictly neutral as between employers and employees (and their organisations). Overall guidance on the running of the Service is provided by a tripartite council. As at September 1989 it comprised eleven members (a full-time chairman and ten part-time members), all appointed by the Secretary of State for Employment. Three of the members were appointed after consultation with the CBI and three after consultation with the TUC. One member was nominated by the Association of British Chambers of Commerce and one came from the ranks of trade unions not affiliated to the TUC. Two were independent members, with knowledge or experience of industrial relations. The council acts as a strong, visible reminder of the Service's independence of government.

ACAS is organised on the basis of a head office in London and offices in Scotland, Wales and seven English regions. When the Service was established the regional organisation was formed by taking over the regional conciliation and advisory staff of the Department of Employment. Thus the ACAS staff consisted and, apart from a small number of period appointees with specialised industrial relations experience, continues to consist of career civil servants from the Department of Employment group. Some make their career with ACAS; others are transferred on promotion or career development to and from other parts of the group.

The total number of staff employed by ACAS is determined by three factors – the changing nature of the responsibilities imposed by statute on the Service, an estimate of the numbers required to carry out the work, and the need for ACAS to bear its share of any general cuts in the Civil Service such as those imposed by Mrs Thatcher's

Government. Its annual report for 1988 showed a total complement of 618. This figure compared with a peak of over 800 in 1979.

Much of the recent labour legislation applies to Great Britain only. Separate but similar laws apply in Northern Ireland. This means that ACAS only covers Great Britain; a separate organisation, the Labour Relations Agency, discharges a similar range of duties and responsibilities in Northern Ireland.

These then are the independent roles in dispute resolution and avoidance which are investigated in the chapters that follow:

- conciliation in industrial disputes (collective conciliation);
- arbitration;
- mediation, inquiry and review;
- conciliation over alleged breaches of statutory employment rights (individual conciliation);
- setting national minimum wage rates:
- inter-union conflict.

It is all too easy to criticise the independents as men or women who are remote from the realities of the world of industrial relations and who use the precious advantage of hindsight to say exactly what went wrong and what in fact should have been done. When involved in industrial disputes they are accused of being compromisers, trimmers, or fudgers in an age in which a determination to stand fast, almost regardless of the circumstances, is regarded as a positive virtue. Conciliators are criticised for involving themselves in disputes in such an untimely way that the managerial 'dog' is prevented from seeing the trade union 'rabbit'. They are seen as being more interested in producing settlements for the benefit of their own reputations than in the merits of the settlements themselves. Arbitrators and the independent members of Wages Councils are accused of being irresponsibly generous with other people's money. And a worker who believes that one of his statutory employment rights has been broken sometimes complains that the conciliator's neutrality is a positive disadvantage when he seeks redress from the employer.

The chapters that follow try to give an objective account of the independent third party's work.

1 Collective Conciliation

Conciliation through Negotiation

Every year employers, employers' associations, employees, trade union officials and workplace representatives, engage in literally thousands of separate negotiations over pay, working conditions and other matters relating to employment. For the vast majority, negotiations end in amicable collective agreements without the slightest whiff or threat of a strike or any other form of industrial action. Inevitably, however, some of these negotiations end in deadlock.

If the employer is not a member of an employers' association the processes of negotiation terminate once the direct negotiations between management and union have come to an end. But in cases where the employer is a member of an employers' association there will almost certainly be a 'procedure' agreed with the trade unions in the industry concerned, which must be used if the union wishes to pursue its claim further.

These industry-wide procedure agreements differ both in principle and in detail, but it is a common feature of them all that they provide for an additional stage or stages of negotiation in which the representatives of the employers' association and full-time trade union officials will participate as well as the parties (management and employee representatives) directly concerned. These procedure agreements will also include the so-called 'peace clause' which, however it may be worded, rules out industrial action of all kinds until all stages of the procedure have been completed.

Employers' associations (and trade unions too) often regard their procedure agreements as providing an element of conciliation. While accepting a responsibility to defend and represent the interests of one of their members, an employers' association that considers a member against whom an employee's grievance has been laid has acted unreasonably may well try to persuade the management to make some concession. And if it suspects that a member firm is in the mood, however justifiably, to reject a claim in negotiation but is likely to give way immediately afterwards on the threat of a strike, it may well advise the management to settle with apparent good grace before a strike rather than be forced to give way once the employees have walked off the job.

Some years ago a leading academic in the field of industrial relations, commenting on the procedure agreement which existed in the engineering industry at the time, used the term 'employer conciliation'[1] to describe this approach. But the term was not altogether accurate; trade union officials, too, often accept that whilst their prime responsibility is to safeguard and where possible improve the living standards of their members, they have a responsibility in the course of procedural discussions to act as conciliators by seeking to persuade their constituents to moderate their more extreme or unrealistic demands.

The major difference in principle between industry-wide procedure agreements is that, under some, it is possible that the negotiators, despite all their efforts, may be unable to find an acceptable solution and end up by recording an inconclusive failure to agree. The procedure agreements in the engineering industry and agreements in other industries based on engineering are good examples. But under other procedures, both sides are required, whatever the difficulty, to reach an agreed decision which employer and trade union are obliged to honour. In other words, at the end of the procedural road there can be no such thing as a failure to agree. Examples of this kind are to be found in parts of the construction industry. The extent to which they may accurately be described as no-strike agreements provides endless scope for semantic discussion.

In deciding under which category a procedure agreement comes, we must not be misled by its title. In the civil engineering construction agreement, for example, provision is made for a conciliation board to which any claim that is not dropped or settled at an earlier stage is referred for settlement. In cases of urgency the issue is referred to a disputes sub-committee and then, for ratification, to the full board. But, by convention, there has to be a settlement at the final stage which the parties are required to implement. This is not therefore conciliation of the conventional kind but, in all but name, arbitration.

The chemical industry is another interesting example because the procedure agreement in that industry expressly provides at the final stage for either conciliation by a sub-committee of the industry's joint industrial council or binding arbitration by a disputes commitee. It is up to both sides jointly to agree which course they prefer. If they cannot, the procedure will only be deemed to be exhausted after a period of 21 days from the date of the last conference – an invaluable breathing space during which further attempts can be made to find a solution and so head off industrial action.

Indeed, now that national (multi-employer) bargaining on pay and conditions of employment is losing its historical significance in many industries, breathing space – the opportunity which industry-wide procedure agreements provide for fresh minds to be brought to bear on unresolved domestic issues – and the 'peace clause' are the major residual industrial relations advantages of belonging to an employers' association.

ACAS is under a statutory duty 'to have regard to the desirability of encouraging the parties to use appropriate agreed procedures'.[2] But even the subsequent involvement of ACAS in disputes affecting their members is not universally approved by employers' associations. Some of them take the view that their own procedures will lose credibility if a settlement is subsequently concluded elsewhere with ACAS assistance. The individual member firm may, however, see the matter in a different light. Provided a settlement of a damaging dispute can be reached on acceptable terms, the individual employer may not be so particular as to how this is achieved.

The principle of conciliation is also contained in agreements that operate within the nationalised industries, and may, in fact, have been enshrined within the original nationalisation statutes. In the coal-mining industry, for example, a national conciliation scheme was agreed after the nationalisation of the industry in 1946. But despite its title, the scheme also contained provisions for arbitration, and is therefore summarised in the next chapter.

So there are a number of ways in which the process of conciliation may be brought to bear on a dispute, but the only conciliation available to all employers and trade unions in Great Britain, which is both neutral and skilled, is that available from ACAS. It is provided for under Section 2 of the 1975 Employment Protection Act. Where a trade dispute exists or is apprehended, ACAS is empowered to provide assistance by way of conciliation or by other means. Conciliation can best be defined as an attempt, by a neutral third party, through discussion and negotiation, to help the parties in dispute to reach their own agreement.

Agreements Reached at ACAS

It is to be emphasised that ACAS is not a party (although it will be a witness) to agreements reached during the conciliation process. These agreements are no more legally enforceable than any other collective agreement. Except for the employer and trade union concerned, an agreement may be a thoroughly undesirable one, but it is no part of ACAS's responsibility to discourage an employer and a trade union from entering into an agreement which they both desire. Even in the days of statutory incomes policies ACAS, through its Council, decided in 1975 that conciliation should continue to be available to help parties in their negotiations, and that ACAS as an independent body should not act as an interpreter or an enforcement agency for the incomes policy. If an employer and a trade union decided to negotiate an agreement that was in breach of incomes policy, that was their affair:

> Nevertheless it was accepted that it would be realistic to inquire whether in any particular dispute the parties had taken account of the policy. If doubts arose it could be suggested to them that they should consult, where appropriate, the CBI or the TUC or seek an interpretation from the Department of Employment.[3]

While it is not a party to agreements resulting from conciliation, ACAS does have a responsibility to ensure that the wording of the agreements reached under its auspices are expressed with as much clarity and lack of ambiguity as possible. In 1981 a series of events led to the allegation that a major agreement reached under ACAS auspices had in fact been obscure. This was in the so-called variable rostering dispute between British Rail and the Associated Society of Locomotivemen, Engineers and Firemen (ASLEF). The dispute had its origins in the 1981 pay and conditions claim submitted by three rail unions, the ASLEF, the National Union of Railwaymen (NUR) and the Transport and Salaried Staffs Association (TSSA). The recommendations of the rail industry's own final reference body, the Railway Staff National Tribunal (RSNT) fell short of the unions' requirements and two of them, the ASLEF and the NUR, gave notice of national strike action as from 30 August 1981. But after a series of meetings at ACAS headquarters, agreed understandings on pay and productivity were reached, notice of strike action was withdrawn, and the understandings were subsequently ratified as formal agreements within the industry's own negotiating machinery.

A leader writer in one of the national newspapers enthusiastically described the agreement as a masterpiece of the conciliator's art. It may or may not have been. At all events it subsequently ran into difficulty because the interpretation placed on its terms by the ASLEF differed from that of the other two rail unions and British

Rail. In essence, British Rail was only prepared to pay the wage increase in full if the unions specifically agreed to deliver the productivity commitments. The ASLEF, for its part, contended that these commitments represented nothing more than commitments to discuss the changes in working practices, not to change them. British Rail withheld the pay increase and, in January 1982 the ASLEF called its members out on strike and intermittent stoppages lasted until July.

After many hours of discussion and negotiation the dispute was finally settled after an all-night session at ACAS headquarters involving the British Rail board and the TUC's Finance and General Purposes Committee. Under the settlement the ASLEF accepted the principle of variable rostering which, for the previous six months, had been regarded by the Board as the touchstone by which the productivity commitment of that union would be judged. But by this time the same leader writer who had previously been so complimentary about the original pay and productivity understandings reached at ACAS now condemned them as a monstrous ACAS fudge.

To Fudge or Not to Fudge

Mr Sidney Weighell, general secretary of the NUR at the time was quite clear. 'There was no fudge here'.[4] His union and TSSA were both prepared to meet their productivity commitments.

But there is a question to be asked. Are there ever any circumstances in which a deliberate fudge is justified in the course of the collective bargaining process or an ACAS conciliation? The answer is 'Yes' provided that the parties know what it is they are doing. There can come a moment in a protracted dispute when both employer and trade union have had enough but neither side, for reasons of its own, can be seen to give way. In such circumstances it can make sense deliberately to devise a form of words which will enable each side to declare that it has established its point while both sides have tacitly agreed that the issue is dead. The dangerous fudge is the one where an agreed form of wording is reached and yet in private each side retains its different interpretation and intends to act on it.

Perhaps the best example of this was the form of words (no agreement was ever reached) which the National Coal Board (NCB) and the National Union of Mineworkers (NUM) tried to draft to settle the coal-miners' strike of 1984–5. The strike had as its background the determination of the NUM to resist the closure of any pits on economic grounds. The parties were on common ground in agreeing that pits that were either exhausted or unsafe to work should be closed, but the NUM was resolutely opposed to closure on other grounds. In an attempt to reach agreement, the NCB and the NUM in their own direct negotiations after the dispute had started, sought unsuccessfully to find an acceptable form of words. Mr (now Sir) Ian MacGregor, the Board's Chairman has told us that the words over which the NCB and the NUM tussled in July 1984 were to the effect that if there were 'no further mineable reserves that are workable and which can be beneficially developed, such a colliery should be deemed exhausted'.[5] P. Wilsher, D. Macintyre and N. Jones wrote that 'beneficially' was not the first word to be considered, 'It was the latest and far from final product of a wide-ranging semantic debate which prompted McGahey [at that time, the NUM's Vice-President] at one stage, to call for Roget's Thesaurus . . .'.[6] By September 1984 Mr MacGregor was apparently telling the NUM that there had to be a form of words which meant 'that there was, as there always had been – a third category of closure which was neither safety nor complete exhaustion of the coal reserves'.[7] He told them:

> Gentleman, it comes as a total package. You don't get the first two things unless we get the third. If we can agree it – then I will give you something you can use to go off and claim a great victory, provided we can still genuinely say that we have retained, at the end of the day, the right to manage the business.[8]

By this time the word 'beneficially' had disappeared from the draft. It had been reworded, according to Mr MacGregor, to read that 'closures would take place where . . . there were no further reserves which can be developed to provide an acceptable basis to the Board for continuing operation.'[9] The NUM choked on the word 'acceptable'.

When, with great reluctance, both sides agreed to further talks under ACAS auspices the search for this elusive formula continued. Luckily it could not be found. Luckily, because the commitment of each side to its own point of view was so strong, and the willingness of the main protagonists to talk at length to the media so great, that an agreed formula of the kind contemplated would never have successfully withstood examination by journalists present in the ACAS building, let alone subsequent application in the industry.

Getting ACAS Involved

Conciliation through ACAS carries no legal compulsion. It can come about because the employer and the trade union (or both) request the involvement of the Service. It can also happen in other ways.

In the first place ACAS is so organised that its officials who discharge the Service's important advisory responsibilities are each entrusted with a geographical 'patch'; collectively they cover the whole of Great Britain. These officials maintain regular contacts with as many employers and local trade union officials as possible. Through such contacts, they try to keep themselves widely informed about potential disputes that may in due course require the involvement of the Service's conciliation staff. There are certainly very few strikes indeed, big or small, of which ACAS officials are unaware through their own contacts.

A second and supplementary channel of information is, of course, the media. The appetite of the British public for knowledge of the country's industrial relations problems means that these receive extensive media coverage. A regular examination of local newspapers can occasionally bring to light news of an industrial dispute that has not percolated through the normal ACAS contacts.

The third way in which the conciliation services of ACAS are called into play is less widely known. In recent years some employers and trade unions have jointly perceived the value of incorporating the conciliation process into their own procedure agreements. In other words, provision is made for the involvement of ACAS as a final stage in the procedure in cases where earlier negotiations involving the two sides directly have failed to reach a settlement.

This procedure provision can take two forms. It can be a compulsory stage which means in effect that neither side is free to embark upon any form of direct action until and unless the conciliation staff of ACAS have been involved in the issue; or it can be a voluntary stage, the procedure agreement containing a provision which merely acts as a reminder to both sides of the availability in the last resort of conciliation by ACAS. If, in these circumstances, one side does not want to involve ACAS, it can obstruct the desire of the other side to involve it; reference to ACAS requires the agreement of both sides.

There are two views as to whether it is wise for procedure agreements to make provision for the automatic involvement of ACAS. Those who support the provision do so on the grounds that it is right to take every reasonable step to settle a problem through negotiation, and that it is therefore preferable as a last resort to involve an ACAS official in the procedural process itself rather than seek the assistance of that same official after the procedural processes have been exhausted and a strike has actually started. The contrary view holds that to provide automatically for the involvement of ACAS as a final procedural stage will weaken the will and determination to reach an agreement during the earlier stages of direct negotiation. The involvement of ACAS should therefore be confined to those cases where negotiations have finally broken down and where a timely ACAS intervention could help to break a deadlock.

In so far as any general principles can be laid down, the use of ACAS conciliation as a mandatory stage in procedure agreements should best be left to cases where:

- the two sides are relatively inexperienced, for example, in the period immediately following recognition of the trade union for collective bargaining purposes;
- the consequences of industrial action would be both immediate and severe;
- so-called no-strike agreements are in operation which require a conciliation stage as a preliminary to final and binding arbitration.

Increasing provision for conciliation in procedure agreements, the wide range of ACAS contacts, and the increasing reputation of the Service itself are major contributory factors to two other features of the conciliation work of ACAS:

- in over 80 per cent of the cases handled by ACAS each year no strike is actually in progress. This can simplify the task of the conciliator;
- a steadily increasing proportion of the cases in which ACAS conciliates are the result of a joint reference by employer and trade union.

It is unusual for a joint request for conciliation – or indeed a unilateral request from an employer or trade union – to arrive out of the blue. This is what happens. As soon as ACAS knows that a dispute has started, or is threatened, a process of 'running alongside' (to use the ACAS jargon) commences. An ACAS official is charged with making informal contact with both sides in order to brief himself about the background and to make sure that both sides are aware of the services that ACAS has to offer. It is as a result of these contacts that a joint request for conciliation may eventually emerge. Alternatively, one side may indicate a willingness to become involved in an ACAS conciliation, which then provides the Service with a basis for making a separate approach to the other side. By the time that ACAS officials formally issue an invitation either to exploratory talks or, indeed, to a conciliation meeting, they nearly always know, as a result of the preceding process of 'running alongside', that the invitation will be accepted.

The timing of the invitation is a vital part of the peace-making process. A conciliation meeting called too soon, particularly when a strike has already commenced and feelings are running high, may prove abortive and lead only to an escalation of the dispute and an increase in bitterness and recrimination. On the other hand a meeting too late may mean that an opportunity to work towards a settlement has been lost and will not immediately present itself again.

Timing cannot be automatically read off a fixed scale. It depends both on the will of the two sides and on the judgement of ACAS. Where there is a high risk of rapid escalation or where the employer's product is a perishable one (for example, news) conciliation may take place within hours of a dispute starting. In other situations ACAS may only issue an invitation to conciliation after months of 'running alongside'. The coal-mining strike of 1984–5 started in Yorkshire in March 1984, but the first conciliation meeting at the London headquarters of ACAS was not held until 11 October, over 31 weeks later. Industrial action over a pay claim covering teachers in primary and secondary schools in England and Wales started in February 1985. ACAS did not issue its first formal invitation to a conciliation meeting until January 1986, almost a year later.

Because the process is essentially voluntary the question is sometimes asked whether there is any pressure that can be put on a hesitant or unwilling party to accept an invitation to a conciliation meeting. The answer is 'very little'. Perhaps the most potent weapon is a reminder that a successful outcome to a dispute depends among other things, on winning the public relations battle. The party that is known to have rejected the possibility of a peace initiative may be in danger of losing a round in that battle, if not the battle itself. But only rarely does ACAS issue an invitation to a conciliation meeting without first having received some indication from behind the scenes that both sides will accept it.

Another question that is sometimes asked is whether there is any case for making conciliation compulsory, for example, in disputes affecting essential industries or services. The answer is 'No', if only for the old reason about the horse and the water; you can compel both sides in a dispute to attend a meeting but there is nothing that can compel either side, once they get there, to bargain seriously or to make concessions.

The Success Rate

By whatever route the parties may eventually arrive, the record of success through conciliation by ACAS is a remarkable one. Remember that it is only the more intractable disputes that are handled, where an earlier solution has eluded the two parties concerned despite, perhaps, many hours of direct negotiation. Year in, year out, about two-thirds of the cases that come to ACAS for conciliation are settled by agreement; if to this figure is added the number of cases in which some progress is made towards a settlement (admittedly a matter of subjective judgement) successful conciliations regularly amount to about 80 per cent of the total number of cases handled each year.

There are a number of reasons for this success rate.

Sometimes a union will accept an invitation to a conciliation meeting, not because it is expecting the employer to improve upon his last offer, but because such a meeting provides confirmation that the last offer has in fact been made. Union officials can then assure their members that they have been 'right to the top' and that they must now settle on terms already on the table or, if they wish to continue pressing their claim, face up to the need for industrial action. Similarly, where conciliation is a mandatory provision of the procedure agreement, as soon as it is apparent that the employer has no improvement to propose, the last offer made in direct negotiation will often be accepted.

But even in disputes where employer and trade union come to a conciliation meeting in a less predetermined way, the success rate is still high. There are probably four reasons for this:

- the perspective has changed and the employer is now face to face with reality. A strike he believed would never happen now looks like a reality; or a strike he believed would happen and could be withstood now looks like a serious disruption of the business;

- the perspective has changed for the work-force; they are showing less enthusiasm about the prospect or reality of strike action than earlier indications (including perhaps those obtained through secret ballot) might have suggested;
- there has been some other significant change, for example, a settlement of a similar claim elsewhere, or fresh facts have emerged since the breakdown of direct negotiations;
- there is still a deep-seated determination on the part of many employers and union officials to settle their differences peacefully and thereby avoid strike action. A last-minute compromise, devised with the help of ACAS, can provide the solution.

Another reason why ACAS sometimes becomes involved in a conciliation is because the essential requirement of mutual trust between employer and trade union has at least temporarily disappeared. This was the publicly-declared reason why the National Association of Colliery Overmen, Deputies and Shotfirers (NACODS) came to ACAS at the height of the dispute between the NCB and the NUM. In September 1984 (in the words of the ACAS annual report for that year) the union:

> which had expressed disquiet about the closure issue and the treatment of members not crossing NUM picket lines, ballotted its members on three issues; the proposed reduction in capacity; the Board's attitude to the use of the industry's own Conciliation Procedure (a jointly agreed procedure for the resolution of differences); and an NCB decision, following guidelines issued on 15 August, not to pay NACODS members who failed to cross NUM picket lines.[10]

Although the Board subsequently offered to discuss the operation of the Conciliation Procedure, to withdraw the August statement and to repay payments deducted as a consequence, the membership ballot resulted in 82.5 per cent voting in favour of a strike.

The union, 'anxious to resolve their own dispute'[11] and 'also keen to see whether the solution to their dispute might help resolve the wider issue'[12] sought talks with the NCB at ACAS. This approach opened up the way for the involvement of ACAS in the NUM dispute. Those talks failed but, eventually, an agreement was reached at ACAS between the Board and NACODS:

> The agreement included commitment to introduce an independent review body into the Colliery Review Procedure and that full

> weight would be given to its findings. The Board also agreed to reconsider the 6 March proposals [which had sparked off the NUM strike] in the light of the loss of output because of the dispute. The Board's 15 August statement on payment for attendance was withdrawn and agreement reached on retrospective payments.[13]

NACODS called off its threatened strike. If it had taken place, it would have involved the Nottinghamshire pits (which had not ceased work with the rest of the NUM) – with results for the NUM that might have been different from the eventual outcome. To be fair to Ian MacGregor, he was always confident that, despite the result of the ballot, a national strike by NACODS members would not take place.

The significant point about the involvement of ACAS in the NACODS problem was not that ACAS developed the proposals that settled the dispute, but that by its presence when they were agreed, the union had greater confidence that they would be observed.

The Conciliation Process

A successful outcome depends to a significant extent on ACAS's capacity to judge the timing of its intervention correctly. It also depends to a great extent on the nature of the conciliation process itself – a process in many ways quite different from that of direct negotiation. It is infinitely variable; there is no fixed procedure; the only powers available to conciliators are reason and persuasion; the only assumption they can make is that both parties come to conciliation because they desire agreement or understanding, and that either one or perhaps both of them is prepared to modify its previous position in order to bring that about.

A conciliation meeting is sometimes prefaced by a preliminary briefing (indeed this may be part of the 'running alongside' process described earlier) which has enabled the conciliator to gain an understanding of the broad issues in dispute and the attitudes of the parties. At some point in these preliminary briefings, the conciliator may decide that it is timely to start the conciliation process. He may decide to call a joint meeting under ACAS chairmanship or he may prefer to begin with side meetings involving each party separately. In this case the conciliator will assume a dual role – acting as a member of a group seeking to find a solution to the problem, and as the channel of communication and consultation between the two parties, described by Sir Michael Edwardes as the 'ACAS shuttle'.[14]

The advantages of separate side meetings are:

- their relative informality;
- the opportunity to 'think aloud' about possible solutions without the other party being privy to them;
- the opportunity for the conciliator to ask questions, offer comments and make suggestions;
- the ability to discuss in private with one party the proposals that have been received from the other and to help in formulating counter-proposals which stand a reasonable chance of acceptance.

Joint meetings serve somewhat different purposes:

- they provide the forum in which each side can set out its formal position to the other;
- they enable the issues in dispute to be clarified beyond all reasonable doubt;
- they enable the conciliator to observe both sides together and take a view on the degree of priority which each party attaches to the various issues (if there is more than one) and indeed on the personalities themselves.

In either setting it is a major task of the conciliator to identify 'signals', to pick up hints and develop ideas, however tentatively and vaguely they may be floated. By listening, communicating, asking intelligent questions and injecting ideas of his own, a conciliator can often manage to identify or suggest a possibly new approach by one side or the other. This can initially be discussed in separate meetings without an obligation on either side to adjust its formal position. But if and when the conciliator judges that a revised position on one side will now receive a favourable response he can arrange for this to be formally put forward, either at a further joint meeting or through his role as an intermediary.

The conciliation process can involve periods of seemingly endless waiting by one side or the other, or by the ACAS conciliator. This may be a tactical ploy, for example, the union that has decided quickly that a new proposal is not acceptable may wish to give the impression that it is giving it serious consideration; the employer who has a new proposal to make after an earlier one has been rejected may wish to give the impression that he is only making the new proposal after agonising deliberation; the ACAS conciliator, faced with a seemingly intractable dispute, may himself decide that it would be helpful if both parties were allowed to stew for a time.

Reading of the number of hours that a conciliation has been taking place an outsider may think 'What on earth can they find to talk about for hours and days on end?' The answer is that they aren't necessarily together all the time. On occasions, one side or the other, apart from indulging in tactical delay, may find it necessary to engage in a lengthy process of consultation before it either rejects a proposal or makes a new one. Indeed on occasions one side or the other may be quietly smuggled out of the ACAS backdoor so that a union executive or a board of directors can be consulted. So far as the public eye can discern, however, the conciliation is still in progress. The important point to realise is that an ACAS conciliation is a deadly serious affair and that for one side or both the stakes are so high that each move has to be carefully and painfully thought through.

In summary, the conciliation process comprises a judicious mix of long periods of waiting, separate side meetings, joint meetings and, sometimes, private meetings involving no more than the ACAS conciliator and the heads of the two negotiating teams. Many of the exchanges are verbal; occasionally proposals and counter-proposals are set down in writing, any final undertakings invariably so. All of this activity has a single purpose – to help the employer and trade union to a position in which they can conclude an agreement which enables them at the worst temporarily to patch up their differences and at best, enter into arrangements that offer the prospect of enduring peace.

The setting in which the final agreement is concluded is therefore of some significance as an indication that more stable relationships are being re-established. An agreement signed by both sides in the same room is more desirable than an agreement signed by each side in a separate room. On the occasion of three major disputes settled at ACAS (the 1981 rail dispute, the national dock strike of July 1984 and a threatened national electricity supply strike in May 1985) the head of the ACAS conciliation team took the chair whilst the agreements that had been reached were actually 'written into' the proceedings of special meetings of the joint negotiating bodies of the three industries.

Conciliation and the Media

The success of the conciliation process depends substantially on the knowledge that each side can talk to the ACAS conciliator on the basis that, unless duly authorised, no account of what has taken place will be transmitted to the other. In other words an essential feature of all conciliation meetings is their confidentiality. It is for this reason that in its briefing of the media ACAS normally takes refuge in 'safe' and relatively uninformative statements which conceal much more than they ever reveal.

An exception to this rule occurred in the coal-mining dispute of 1984–5. In the words of the ACAS annual report for 1984:

> Talks between the NCB and NUM at ACAS concentrated on the main issue on which the parties' own discussions ... had broken down – the criteria which might determine the future closure of pits. A series of documents were exchanged during these ACAS discussions. Normally any notes or papers produced during conciliation are kept private to the parties – unless they wish otherwise. On this occasion extracts from the various documents appeared daily in the newspapers which speculated about their status as well as their meaning. To clarify the public debate which ensued, the Service – quite exceptionally – agreed to lodge the documents in the House of Commons Library ... The different formulations in the documents reveal differences of only a few words but these differences reflected substantial differences in the parties' positions ...[15]

The brevity of ACAS press handouts is not always matched by the same discretion on the part of the protagonists themselves. The ACAS conciliator may issue solemn warnings that ill-timed comments to the media may undo any progress that has been made to date. Even if there is a commitment to say nothing (and this is not invariably the case), the sight of a microphone, a camera or a reporter's notebook often proves irresistible to the extent that on occasions the very success of an ACAS initiative has been put at risk. That most admirable of labour correspondents, Nicholas Jones (now BBC Radio's political correspondent), identified three occasions during the variable rostering dispute in British Rail when 'the confrontation that resulted from radio and television interviews influenced the pace of events'.[16]

A total news blackout whilst an ACAS conciliation is in progress is clearly impracticable. It is as well to acknowledge that, each for their own different reasons, an employer and a trade union involved in a dispute may see advantage in ready access to the media. For the employer the ability immediately to brief (albeit indirectly) such important audiences as politicians, bankers, customers and suppliers is sometimes vital as a means of retaining their confidence. For the union official the media may offer the quickest channel of communication to the membership – quicker than is normally available through the union itself.

Both sides are all too aware of how important a sympathetic public is to the successful outcome of a dispute. Where the settlement is complex, as it frequently is, there is an advantage to at least one side in trying to time the end of negotiations, and thus the release of details to the media, so that an imminent deadline does not preclude an accurate analysis of the terms. For it is almost impossible to eradicate the impact of the first headline; it conveys an impression about a settlement that no subsequent disclaimers or corrections will ever remove.

A case which illustrates the point occurred at the end of the national strike in the water service in 1983. Weeks of ACAS involvement eventually led to an understanding that the issue (manual workers' pay) should be referred to an ACAS-appointed committee of inquiry for final resolution (namely, arbitration in all but name). The award provided for an increase of over £11 in rates of pay compared with a mediator's earlier recommendation of around £6. The news was released to the media shortly before evening deadlines. Evening news bulletins on radio and television and banner headlines in the next day's newspapers duly reported the increase. The significant fact that only about £6 of the increase was 'new money' and that the balance of £5 consisted of a transfer of 'old money' from bonus to rates of pay was either ignored or played down. A charismatic and articulate union leader did his job well, the employers much less so.

The issue was of more than academic interest because the government of the day had already shown by its earlier actions in the dispute that it regarded a reasonable settlement in the water service as an important plank in its overall policies on pay. An inaccurately reported settlement could well have led to an escalation of pay expectations and settlements elsewhere. Certainly the government was less than enchanted with its terms.

The Views of the 'Customers'

ACAS conciliators are a dedicated and professional group of men and women who take considerable pride in their performance. But how are they regarded by the users of collective conciliation?

It has to be remembered that conciliation takes place at times of stress. The process takes a great deal of time and may not be fully understood by the participants. It requires the attention of both parties to the exclusion of other pressing tasks. The meetings can be very protracted. One side or the other may feel a sense of resentment that they are even involved in an ACAS conciliation; participation may be felt to be a slur on their own professional competence. The ACAS conciliator may be regarded as too assertive (for example, he advances his own views and advice too strongly), or not assertive enough (for example, he advances no views at all but merely acts as a channel of communication). Even though by definition the conciliation process allows the parties to decide what concessions (if any) to make, the reasons for having made any concession may subsequently be laid at the door of ACAS, particularly if the resultant settlement is criticised for its generosity.

So it is not, perhaps, surprising that the most common form of farewell to an ACAS conciliator, even after a successful conciliation, is an expression of thanks combined with the hope that any future contacts will be entirely social. Nor is it odd that there is little on the public record about the role played in various disputes by ACAS conciliators. But Sir Michael Edwardes in his account of his 'apocalyptic experience' at British Leyland did write in relation to the Company's 1987 pay crisis that 'ACAS conciliators played an important and highly professional role during the 36-hour crisis'.[17] In his diaries Mr (now Sir) Peter Hall described ACAS as 'a curious institution. One party is in one room, the other in another, and a mediator runs between them trying to get each to a point when they are prepared to face each other across a table'. Perhaps as the then director of Britain's National Theatre he was entitled to describe the setting in unusually dramatic terms – 'A Kafkaesque building with the usual run down tattiness of government offices and seemingly infinite. Only the smell of borsch and cooked greens is needed to complete the Kafka picture'.[18] The building in which the National Theatre dispute was handled was not the one in St James's Square which ACAS occupied from 1982 to 1988. But even that very elegant building allegedly provoked Mr Ian MacGregor on entering it for the first time, to remark that 'this place stinks'. Mr Sidney Weighell, general secretary of the NUR at the time of the 1981 conciliation meetings with British Rail, believed that:

> ACAS officials like to keep everybody in their building to speed-up the resolving of disputes, but I became so fed up with eating

sandwiches and fish and chips round the clock that I insisted on going off for a hot meal in a restaurant with my NUR colleagues.[19]

It is, incidentally, not part of the ACAS approach to conciliation either to exhaust the protagonists by the sheer continuity of the meetings, or deliberately to serve them with an inadequate diet with a view to starving them into making some concession! But experience has proved that once a conciliation has started, the momentum must be maintained. Untimely adjournments either for food or rest can retard any progress that might already have been made.

The list of 'customers' since ACAS was established is a very long one. At some time or another there have walked through the doors of ACAS buildings, Kafkaesque or stinking, in London or the provinces, representatives of probably every trade union (large or small) that is affiliated to the TUC as, too, have representatives of non-affiliated unions. Employers have included the National Health Service; the nationalised industries like electricity supply, British Rail, British Shipbuilders and the National Coal Board; local authorities; the newspaper industry, the BBC and the independent television and radio companies; banks, insurance companies, motor manufacturers; and many others too numerous to mention.

If there seems anywhere to have been a principled resistance to the involvement of ACAS it has been within government itself so far as its own employees are concerned. In 1981 there was a long national strike in the Civil Service, but the readiness of ACAS to assist was not picked up. In the national strike in the Health Service, which took place in 1982, ACAS was not initially involved in an official capacity – although Mr Norman Fowler, the then Secretary of State for Social Services, invited the then chairman of ACAS to act 'an an intermediary and go between in a personal and private capacity as a channel of communication acceptable to both sides'.[20] Subsequent meetings gradually assumed the conventions of a normal ACAS conciliation to the extent that ACAS was eventually 'able to assist the parties to reach a basis of understanding . . .'.[21]

But despite the apparent misgivings of central government, ACAS has been officially involved in conciliations involving the National Health Service at district level; and even in the Civil Service, protracted local disputes have eventually involved ACAS, for example, 1984 disputes involving the Crown Agents and the DHSS computer centre at Newcastle upon Tyne.

So what, other than anecdotal views and comments, is there to indicate how its 'customers' regard the collective conciliation work of ACAS?

The most comprehensive survey (the Bradford Survey) was carried out by Jean Hiltrop, formerly of Bradford University and now Professor of Personnel Management and Organisation at the Catholic University of Leuven in Belgium, and David Burrill, a research student at Bradford University Management Centre.

The data for this survey were derived from the 1985 workload of ACAS. Returns were received from 161 employer representatives and 174 union officials. They were asked to comment on four main topics:

- The role of ACAS conciliators.
- The quality of ACAS conciliators.
- The quality of agreements reached in conciliation.
- The parties' enthusiasm for third-party involvement.

As regards the role of ACAS conciliators it was felt, not surprisingly, by 74 per cent of managements and 81 per cent of union respondents, that 'the conciliator should wait before entering a dispute until all agreed procedures for negotiation or the settlement of disputes have been exhausted, or a deadlock in the negotiations had been reached'. Once involved, however, ACAS conciliators should in the view of the vast majority of the respondents (94 per cent of managements and 89 per cent of union officials) 'not hestiate to make suggestions for compromise'. A substantial majority (73 per cent of managements and 83 per cent of union officials) felt that 'the conciliator should not hesitate to emphasize the need to make concessions on one or both sides'; only 26 per cent and 15 per cent, respectively, thought it 'appropriate for the conciliator to vigorously support the position of the other party on an important issue in side meetings'. Thus, the researchers concluded, there was a clear preference for the conciliator, while being positive, to avoid taking the side of any one party and preserving his neutral role. There was majority support amongst both parties 'for the view that the number of stoppages in industry would increase significantly in the absence of ACAS conciliation'.

The correspondents were asked what qualities they regarded as important for effective conciliators to possess; and to what extent those particular qualities had been displayed by their conciliator. Highest on the list of essential conciliation qualities were trustworthiness, impartiality/independence, knowledge of industrial relations and collective bargaining, and an ability to understand complex problems quickly. As to the qualities actually demonstrated, both management representatives and trade union officials placed these in the same order, namely, the conciliator:

- had acted impartially;
- had sufficiently understood the issues involved; had sufficient experience/knowledge about industrial relations;
- had demonstrated confidence;
- had the trust of both parties.

Of particular significance was the indication that 98 per cent of managements and 89 per cent of trade union officials considered that their conciliators had acted impartially: only 4 per cent believed that the conciliator did not enjoy the trust of both parties.

Where the respondents were able positively to identify the behaviour of the conciliator, the analysis showed that the conciliators most frequently:

> used their position to clarify and communicate issues between the parties, helping them to understand each other's position, identifying their 'bottom line' or 'final' positions and clarifying points of agreement and disagreement. In addition, the conciliator is able to control this flow of information by controlling the nature of the form in which the parties meet – most frequently meeting the parties both separately and together throughout the conciliation. Gentle pressure is also brought to bear on the parties by the conciliator through pointing out the implications of continued disagreement. It is striking that set with these behaviours the conciliators are reported to have frequently made suggestions for resolving issues, arguably the strongest form of intervention open to a conciliator.

As to the nature of the settlements reached in conciliation, respondents who had reached an agreement were asked to rate its quality and also to assess the conciliator's contribution. Only 6 per cent of respondents regarded their agreement as poor in either the short or long term. Ninety per cent regarded the conciliator's contribution to the settlement as good, very good or excellent. The researchers concluded that despite:

> the difficulties associated with the measurement of the effectiveness of conciliation the evidence accumulated here does indicate a high level of favourable response to the conciliator's ability to induce a settlement between the parties. The figures support the view that the ACAS service performs a valuable function.

Who are the ACAS Conciliators?

The chief executive of ACAS is its chairman, but he rarely becomes directly involved in a conciliation himself (the ACAS Council never so). Unless the dispute is of great national significance or has major political implications, he leaves the control of the collective conciliation activities to the Chief Conciliation Officer. Conciliation staff are located both at ACAS head office and in its provincial offices. Head office generally conciliates in industry-wide disputes or those involving issues of national significance and public concern. It is because these disputes are the ones that tend to attract the attention of the media that the impression may be gained that all the conciliation work is done at head office. In fact the great majority of the disputes (963 out of a total of 1059 cases completed in 1988) were handled by conciliators located at ACAS offices in Scotland, Wales and in seven English regions.

All the ACAS conciliators are career civil servants. They are part of the Department of Employment group. Virtually all of them have had previous experience in other areas of ACAS activity (individual conciliation or advisory work) before they move to collective conciliation. Like all ACAS operational staff they are trained both on and off the job. But very few of them have had direct experience in personnel/industrial relations management or as trade union officers. If this is a disadvantage, it is outweighed by two advantages. First, career civil servants do not carry the 'stigma' of having at one time worked for either management or trade union. They are thus credible in a role of absolute neutrality. Secondly, the qualities of a good civil servant are vital in a good conciliator; analytical skills; the ability to summarise and communicate objectively the views and attitudes of others; and a sense of modesty and subtlety of mind which allow a strongly-held view or firm suggestion to be advanced in a way which allows others to pick it up and present it as if it was their own proposal.

In addition, the good conciliator must have a feel for industrial relations. He must be possessed of infinite patience, an ear for 'signals', an intelligence which can produce the brick of an idea from the most unlikely looking straw, and an ability to capture in clear outline the vague ideas and suggestions that emerge during the process of conciliation. He will never lose his temper (unless he does so deliberately). He will possess the stamina of an ox and the resolution never to be the one that calls it a day first. Above all he must gain and keep the trust and confidence of both sides. A conciliator who is believed (however unjustly) to be partial to management or trade union can never perform an effective job.

Of the 'consummate conciliator'[22] of the day, G. R. Askwith, Ben Tillett, the dockers' leader, wrote in 1912:

> the patient plodding man, with pigeon holes in his brains; who listened without sign of being bored or absorbed, who concealed his mind like a Chinaman. Emotionless, except that he would peer through his glasses at someone making a statement of moment, never raising his diplomatic voice, or appearing to hurry over anything; guiding without falter or apparent effort the disputants however heated they may be, himself the inscrutable, patient listener. And such patience! It was more than dour in its persistence and calmness; it compelled by its coldness, and saved us from the bickering on occasions when the wisest become puny and spiteful.[23]

The Workload

There has been a steady decline in the number of cases handled by ACAS each year from a peak of the 2891 cases that were completed in 1977 (see Table 1.1).

Table 1.1 Completed collective conciliation cases 1975–88

Year	*No. of cases*	*Year*	*No. of cases*
1975	2017	1982	1634
1976	2851	1983	1621
1977	2891	1984	1448
1978	2706	1985	1337
1979	2284	1986	1323
1980	1910	1987	1147
1981	1716	1988	1059

Source: ACAS, *Annual Reports*, 1975 to 1988.

If this decline were due to a growth of mistrust of ACAS itself, a lack of confidence in the ability of its staff, a belief that it was lacking in neutrality, or a suspicion that it was under political control, there would indeed be cause for concern. In fact, the annual volume of conciliation requests to ACAS has regularly been of a higher order than was previously experienced by the conciliation service when conciliation was provided by a government department. Moreover, despite the decrease over the past decade in the number of reported stoppages of work, ACAS has consistently been involved in more disputes than there were stoppages. In other words many settlements are secured before industrial action begins.

There are a number of reasons for the decline in the conciliation workload, most of them encouraging:

- in the early days of ACAS, which coincided with the existence of statutory pay policies, there may have been a tendency to resort to conciliation precisely because it was, for the first time, free of state surveillance or influence;
- for over two-thirds of ACAS's life a Conservative government has been in power which has commended the virtues of employers standing on their own feet;
- given a change in the economic and political climate since 1977 many employers probably think twice before putting themselves in the hands of an outside agency which was created by a Labour government;
- in the years following the establishment of ACAS, statutory provisions relating to trade union recognition (Sections 11 to 16 of the 1975 Employment Protection Act) imposed special tasks on ACAS; there were undoubtedly some employers who denied themselves the use of the Service because of its suspected bias. This was a state of affairs that ACAS found intolerable and on the strong representations of the ACAS Council these statutory recognition provisions were subsequently repealed by Section 19 of the Employment Act, 1980;
- the decline in union membership and the consequences of recession in the early 1980s so changed the balance of bargaining power that employers who in different circumstances might have seen the need for an ACAS conciliator now decided they could do without him;
- there is a correlation between the conciliation workload of ACAS and the total number of strikes. A fall in the number of strikes inevitably means that there will be some fall in the demands on ACAS.

Perhaps of even greater significance (it is far too soon to make a firm judgement), Great Britain may at last be getting its industrial relations right. A decline in the conciliation workload of ACAS, so long as it takes place in an improving climate of industrial relations, is a healthy symptom. The unremitting hard word of many managements, positively assisted by changes in employee and (some) trade union attitudes, may at last be beginning to pay off.

2 Arbitration

Within the British industrial relations system there is probably nothing that causes more heated argument and differences of opinion than arbitration – the process whereby a claim or grievance is handed over for final determination to an independent third party.

Those who favour arbitration as a means of settling industrial disputes quote with approval the words spoken by Lord Salisbury in 1883, that the 'broad distinction between a civilised and an uncivilised community is this – that in a civilised community individuals or parties of men who quarrel submit their differences to an arbitrator, while in savage states they fight it out'.

Yet despite these lofty sentiments, arbitration as an acceptable alternative to war has never been universally attractive to the politicians; and to unions and employers, the same is true of industrial disputes. Despite its cost to their members and to the economy, trade unions, with few exceptions, cling by choice to the use of the strike weapon as the well-tried means of bringing the employer either to his senses or his knees. Employers cling with equal conviction to the view that once everything that can be said over an issue has been said, it is their decision that must prevail. And so far as the public sector is concerned, Her Majesty's Treasury is very reluctant to hand over to an arbitrator the right to decide how much and in what way some of the taxpayer's money should be spent.

Some Definitions

Compulsory arbitration takes place when both sides have agreed as a final stage in their procedure agreement that an unresolved issue must be referred to arbitration for settlement.

Voluntary arbitration takes place when both sides, either because of a clause in their procedure agreement or because of an *ad hoc* arrangement, jointly agree that a dispute should be settled by arbitration.

Unilateral arbitration takes place because, as the final stage, the procedure agreement gives either side the right to refer an issue to arbitration.

The Trade Union View

The trade union attitude towards arbitration has largely depended on their perception of the strength of their bargaining position – a weak union will agree to arbitration more readily than a strong union. According to Professor Henry Phelps Brown, when:

> Ben Tillett was trying to hold the dockers together in a period of reaction after the fervour of 1889, year after year he put to the Trades Union Congress a resolution for it. Richard Bell of the Society of Railway Servants faced companies that would not recognise his union: he brought in a bill to provide that the wages of railwaymen should be fixed by a court of three, and either side could take the other to it . . . But the stronger unions agreed with the chairman of the Royal Commission [the Royal Commission on Labour, 1891–4] that lock-outs and strikes were 'the assertion of . . . essential liberties on the part of employers and workmen: they were not prepared to give up their right and power to reject terms of employment they did not like . . . [they] would intensely dislike the prospect of being committed to accept terms before they knew what they were. So in the Trades Union Congress of 1906 the stronger unions defeated a resolution in favour of compulsory arbitration for the eighth year running'.[1]

If a resolution were to be submitted to the TUC today in favour of compulsory arbitration, it would be defeated, this despite the fact that some unions in weak bargaining positions (for example, in parts of the public sector) would like it. But, as we shall see later, one of the features in some of the so-called new style or no-strike agreements is unilateral access to arbitration as an alternative to strike action.

Clive Jenkins and Barrie Sherman probably reflected the typical trade union view when they wrote that there:

> is a place for arbitration in collective bargaining but that is not the centre of the table. It has its uses when all else fails or when nothing else will do. It can resolve a dispute or leave both sides unsatisfied, thus creating trouble for the future. It takes time, consumes expertise and should be used sparingly.[2]

The Employers' View

Arbitration, according to many employers, is the process whereby key business decisions are handed over to well-meaning but

ill-informed outsiders. Thus when the post office workers threatened strike action in 1987, Sir Bryan Nicholson, Chairman of the Post Office, resisted the suggestion of arbitration as a means of settling the dispute on the grounds that 'Arbitrators don't run businesses'. But despite this typical employer view it is timely to recall the point made in Chapter 1 that under the provisions of certain procedure agreements between employer associations and trade unions, a decision other than failure to agree must be reached at the final stage if it cannot be agreed earlier. And either party has the unilateral right of access. Nobody calls it arbitration – and certainly not a no-strike agreement – but that's what in effect it is.

The State and Arbitration

Except in times of war, governments have turned their face against the provision of compulsory arbitration as a basis for resolving industrial conflict. Perhaps the lesson was learnt as far back as 1896 when the government of the day was legislating on the recommendations of the report of the Royal Commission of 1891–4. There was no parliamentary support for compulsory arbitration provisions of any kind and in the Conciliation Act of 1896 three existing but unused arbitration acts were actually repealed. The furthest the Act went in the field of arbitration was to make statutory provision for the appointment of an arbitrator on the application of both parties.

Another government took another bite at the arbitral cherry in 1919 following the publication of the reports by the Whitley Committee on relations between employers and employed. The Committee stated as follows:

> We desire to emphasise the advisability of a continuance, as far as possible, of the present system whereby industries make their own agreements and settle their differences themselves . . .
>
> We are opposed to any system of Compulsory Arbitration: there is no reason to believe that such a system is generally desired by employers and employed, and in the absence of such general acceptance, it is obvious that its imposition would lead to unrest . . . For the same reason we do not recommend any scheme relating to conciliation which compulsorily prevents strikes or lock-outs pending inquiry . . . We further recommend that there should be established a Standing Arbitration Council for cases where the

parties wish to refer any dispute to arbitration, though it is desirable that suitable single arbitrators should be available, where the parties so desire . . . .[3]

Under the Industrial Courts Act of 1919 passed in the wake of the Whitley report, the Minister of Labour could, if he thought fit and the parties agreed, refer an existing or an apprehended dispute for settlement by arbitration. The forms of arbitration would be:

- the Industrial Court set up under the Act;
- one or more persons appointed by the Minister;
- a board of arbitration comprising an equal number of employers and worker nominees plus an independent chairman.

It is this 1919 bedrock on which all the subsequent statutory provisions (save in times of war) have been based, namely, arbitration should be voluntary and only take place with the agreement of the parties. Another requirement of the 1919 Act was that before there was resort to arbitration the issue should first have been discussed under any procedures that existed in the industry concerned for the settlement of disputes. A similar requirement has been a feature of subsequent legislation.

It was also under the 1919 Act that power was given to the Minister of Labour to set up courts of inquiry to inquire into the causes and circumstances of industrial disputes (see Chapter 3).

The War-time Experience

During both the First and Second World Wars, powers were taken to provide for compulsory binding arbitration. In 1915 the Munitions of War Act prohibited strikes and lock-outs in a wide range of industries and occupations. Disputes had to be reported to the Board of Trade which could then refer them to arbitration. The awards were legally binding.

In 1940 a joint committee of union leaders and employers (the Consultative Committee of the National Joint Advisory Council) unanimously recommended to the Minister of Labour and National Service that matters that could not be settled through normal negotiating machinery should be referred to arbitration. Settlements, whether by direct negotiation or by arbitration, should be binding and strikes and lock-outs should not take place. Mr Ernest Bevin, the

Minister, accepted the recommendations and he introduced the famous Order 1305 (the Conditions of Employment and National Arbitration Order). This enabled him to refer unsettled disputes to compulsory arbitration by the National Arbitration Tribunal (NAT). Strikes and lock-outs were prohibited unless the dispute had been referred to the Minister and he had not referred it to the NAT within 21 days. Employers were also obliged to observe terms and conditions which had been determined by collective agreements or by arbitration for their trade or branch of industry in their particular district (a similar provision had been introduced in the First World War). Order 1305 operated from 1940 to 1951 during which time the National Arbitration Tribunal issued 1723 awards. During the same period the Industrial Court continued to operate in cases which employer and trade union had voluntarily agreed should be decided by arbitration.

Sadly, however, for the sake of the country's war effort, the advent of Order 1305 did not put an end to strikes. In a paper which he presented to the Royal Society of Arts on 23 April 1986, Correlli Barnett pointed out that:

> the days lost through strikes in Britain were higher every year from 1941 to 1945 than in 1938, the last full year of peacetime. Coal was far and away the worst offender, with no fewer than 1.2 million man-days and two million tons of coal lost in the first quarter of 1944 alone.[4]

Despite this appalling strike record the government was strangely reluctant to take any kind of action against strikers or their unions. It was perhaps this ability to choose whether to take the lawful course of referring an unsettled dispute to arbitration or, with impunity, to embark upon strike action unlawfully that reinforced employer opposition to arbitration after the war. There was, however, one famous war-time dispute in which action was taken against strikers and their union.

In December 1941 an independent arbitrator found against a claim of mineworkers employed in Betteshanger Colliery in Kent for improved allowances for working in a difficult seam. The miners rejected the award and about 4000 of them, backed by local union officials, ceased work.

The Secretary for Mines decided to prosecute and charges were laid against 1000 underground workers. A number of test cases were chosen and all the accused, apparently with union connivance, pleaded guilty. As a result the three union officials were sent to prison (one for two months and two for one month, all with hard labour), 35 men were fined £3 or given one month's imprisonment, and nearly one thousand were fined £1, or 14 days.

In the words of the written evidence presented to the Donovan Commission by Sir Harold Emmerson (a former Permanent Secretary of the Ministry of Labour and its Chief Industrial Commissioner from 1942 to 1944):

> Protests came against the severity of the sentences, particularly against the imprisonment of three union officals . . . There was talk of sympathetic strikes. But the real trouble was that the only men who could call off the strike were now in gaol. The Secretary for Mines went down to Kent to see them accompanied by Mr Ebby Edwards, then the National President of the Miners' Union. Negotiations were re-opened and five days after the hearing an agreement was signed, in prison, between the colliery management and the Kent Miners' Union. Apart from some face-saving words, it gave the men what they wanted. Then the Secretary for Mines took a deputation to the Home Secretary asking for the immediate release of the three local officials. The men would not start work until their leaders were free. After eleven days in prison they were released. The mine re-opened and in the first week the normal output of coal was nearly trebled.[5]

Only nine of the miners ever paid their fines.

The Betteshanger dispute of 1941 became famous because, exceptionally, court action was taken against men for unlawfully going on strike in time of war. But for almost another 40 years, whenever consideration was being given to the practicality of sanctions against workers for striking in breach of contract, the call to 'remember Betteshanger' was such a forceful argument that the idea was dropped.

The ghost of Betteshanger was not finally laid until the introduction of the Thatcher government's employment legislation under which unlawful industrial action is tackled, not by action against workpeople, but against the funds of their unions. Five other ghosts were laid by the same legislation – those of the 'Pentonville Five'. These were the five docker shop stewards who were imprisoned in 1972 for contempt of court after deliberately flouting court orders. A major industrial and constitutional crisis was only averted when a hitherto unknown figure – the Official Solicitor – sprang them from gaol. Contempt of court is now tackled through fines on the union and if adjudged necessary (as both the National Graphical Association and National Union of Seamen found to their cost), by sequestration of union assets.

Post-war Developments

By 1951 both trade unions and employers had had enough of Order 1305. Even if they were so minded, union leaders were finding it difficult to exercise any control over a membership that was increasingly prepared to use its muscle power at shop-floor level, and they disliked the obloquy they were incurring for frequent breaches of the no-strike requirements of the Order. Employers disliked the way in which the Order was, in practice, providing trade unions with both the belt of arbitration if their members didn't want to strike, and the braces of strike action if they did. However unjustifiably, union leaders and employers alike were becoming increasingly cynical about their experiences before the National Arbitration Tribunal. They felt that almost regardless of the merits of the particular case before it, the Tribunal was so concerned to preserve the credibility of the arbitration process as a whole that it found in favour of employers and trade unions on a numerically balanced basis.

Be that as it may, during 1950 and 1951, 'it became clear that the provisions of the Order which prohibited strikes and lock-outs no longer commanded general assent . . .'.[6] In August 1951 it was replaced by the Industrial Disputes Order, generally known as Order 1376. This Order provided for unilateral arbitration but unlike its predecessor, it did not contain any prohibition on strikes and lock-outs. There were a number of other differences as well:

- certain types of dispute were excluded from the scope of the new Order;
- the National Arbitration Tribunal was replaced by a new body, the Industrial Disputes Tribunal;
- The obligation imposed by Order 1305 that employers generally should observe at least the recognised terms and conditions of employment was discontinued. Instead, provision was made that issues concerning the observance of minimum conditions by an individual employer could be raised.

Under Order 1376 disputes no longer had to be reported to the Minister of Labour but if either party did decide to exercise that option (normally, of course, it would be the trade union) the other nearly always felt obliged, however reluctantly, to appear before the Industrial Disputes Tribunal as well. The party that deliberately failed to show up (and there were a few) ran the risk that the Tribunal would automatically award against it.

Order 1376 was renewed annually, but as the Defence Regulations on which the Order was based were progressively dismantled, the question arose in 1957 as to whether any provision should be made in permanent legislation for compulsory arbitration. The employers were not prepared to support any compulsory system and so in 1959 the Order was revoked. By that time the Industrial Disputes Tribunal had made 1270 awards of which 1070 were concerned with the settlement of disputes and 200 with the settlement of issues involving the observance of recognised terms and conditions of employment.

But this was not to be the end of unilateral arbitration. Section 8 of an Act passed in 1959 (the Terms and Conditions of Employment Act) established machinery which gave to representative organisations of employers or of workers the right, through the Minister of Labour, to seek adjudication by the Industrial Court in cases where it appeared that an employer was not observing the recognised terms and conditions of employment. Such cases could be reported to the Minister without the agreement of the employer against whom the claim was made.

These provisions lasted until 1975 when Harold Wilson's government presented the trade unions with yet another belt and pair of braces. Section 8 of the 1959 Act was replaced by the notorious Schedule 11 of the Employment Protection Act. Under this Schedule claims could be raised by an employers' association or a trade union (in practice it was invariably the latter), that the terms and conditions of workers were less favourable than the recognised terms and conditions or, where there were none, the general level observed by employers for comparable workers in the trade, industry or section and in the same district in which the employer was engaged and whose circumstances were similar.

As Brian Doyle pointed out, the 'recent pedigree of Schedule 11'[7] could be traced back to Orders 1305 and 1376 and to the Terms and Conditions of Employment Act of 1959. But such a pedigree did not save the infant Schedule 11 from the wrath of employers who saw the second leg in particular as both an engine for wage inflation and as a sure guarantee for instability in their pay structures. The more respectable of the trade union arguments was that the reduced significance of collective bargaining over pay at both national and local level justified the introduction of the 'general level' leg into the Schedule. But Jenkins and Sherman were honest enough to point out that a Schedule which was designed primarily to assist low-paid employees could 'be used on behalf of those better off'.[8] This pointer was most timely because claims brought either under Schedule 11 or, indeed, under the Fair Wages Resolution (described later in this chapter) were exempted from the limitations of the statutory pay policies that were in operation in the mid-1970s.

Schedule 11 cases could be referred unilaterally and were channelled to the Central Arbitration Committee (CAC) for determination. There were two other situations covered by the Employment Protection Act in which there could also be unilateral access to the CAC:

- complaints by a recognised trade union that it was not receiving information from an employer that was necessary for collective bargaining purposes;
- cases where an employer refused to comply with an ACAS recommendation that a trade union should be recognised. The union could refer to arbitration a claim relating to terms and conditions of employment (but not for recognition *per se*).

When the Equal Pay Act of 1970 came into force in 1976 there could also be unilateral access to arbitration (via the CAC) over equal pay claims that involved collective issues. The CAC also inherited arbitral responsibility for cases arising out of other statutes, for example, the Road Haulage Act of 1938 and the Fair Wages Resolution.

The first Resolution had been passed by the House of Commons in 1891 and was amended in 1909 and again in 1946. It required government departments to insist that contractors and sub-contractors observed fair labour standards. The employees of a contractor enjoyed no direct rights under the Resolution, but a complaint on their behalf could be unilaterally referred to an arbitral body, latterly the CAC, acting as a non-statutory independent tribunal.

The Resolution laid down two criteria. The contractor was required either to pay wages and to observe working conditions not less favourable than those established by collective bargaining in the trade or industry in question or, where there were no established conditions, to apply the general level observed by comparable

Table 2.1 Analysis of CAC awards, 1976–81

	Number of awards					
Type of case	*1976*	*1977*	*1978*	*1979*	*1980*	*1981*
Terms and Conditions of Employment Act, 1959	30	18	2	–	–	–
Employment Protection Act, 1975						
Schedule 11	–	149	519	307	139	9
Union Recognition	–	2	7	5	10	–
Disclosure of Information	–	–	10	14	15	2
Fair Wages Resolution	13	115	271	243	25	16
Voluntary Arbitration	5	8	3	9	10	8
Others	22	16	24	16	10	–
Totals	70	308	836	594	209	35

Source: CAC, *Annual Reports*, 1976–81.

employers in similar circumstances (the similarity between the Resolution and Schedule 11 of the 1975 Act will be noted).

The caseload of the CAC in relation to both voluntary arbitration and to these unilateral arbitration provisions is shown in Table 2.1. The number of Schedule 11 and Fair Wages Resolution cases handled during the peak period of statutory pay policy (1977–9) is to be particularly noted.

The Central Arbitration Committee

We have noted already that the Industrial Courts Act of 1919 provided for the establishment of the Industrial Court. It is from that Court that the Central Arbitration Committee (CAC) can trace its ancestry.

The Industrial Court lasted until 1971 when it was replaced by (or perhaps, more accurately, its name was changed to) the Industrial Arbitration Board established under Edward Heath's short-lived Industrial Relations Act. In February 1976 the Board was itself replaced by the CAC, provision for which was made in the Employment Protection Act of 1975.

The Committee comprises a chairman, deputy chairmen, persons experienced as representatives of employers and persons experienced as representatives of workers – all appointed by the Secretary of State for Employment. The first and, so far, only chairman of the CAC is Sir John Wood, CBE, Edward Bramley Professor of Law at Sheffield University, a highly-skilled and respected arbitrator of many years' standing and, prior to his appointment, one of the independent members on the ACAS Council.

Despite the CAC's ancestry, Sir John has not allowed it to be just a pale shadow or carbon copy of the Industrial Court and Industrial Arbitration Board. From time to time the Committee has been prepared to take a chance and, as a result, has occasionally had its wings clipped by the divisional court when cases have been referred for judicial review. Perhaps more than anything else the CAC, although required to operate within a legal framework, tries always to be sensitive to the practical industrial relations consequences of its decisions, for example, the need to watch carefully the impact on wage strucures of occupational claims raised under Schedule 11. To quote from its 1977 report: 'the Committee's chief aim is to approach its various tasks in an informal way. The legal framework covering a particular type of case is acknowledged and respected but the work of the Committee, within that framework, is industrial arbitration.'[9] The CAC does not try to build up a system of binding precedents but common sense dictates that from time to time members of the Committee meet to discuss the wider issues involved in the cases that are referred. But it is always the merits of the particular case that are paramount.

During the period 1976–81 the CAC issued 2052 awards, but of those only 43 were voluntary arbitration cases. Over the same period ACAS arranged 1826 voluntary arbitrations (cases by single arbitrators and by boards of arbitration). In its evidence to the Donovan Commission, the Ministry of Labour showed that, over a five-and-a-half-year period from 1960 to mid-1965, the Industrial Court issued 310 awards of which 212 were voluntary arbitration cases.

In view of these figures it is hardly surprising that in an important formative period, the CAC came to be known largely in connection with its statutory jurisdictions. When Schedule II of the Employment Protection Act was repealed in 1980 and the Fair Wages Resolution was rescinded in 1983, the CAC was set free to concentrate on the speedy resolution of disputes referred to it voluntarily. But for its work in this field the CAC depends substantially on ACAS. This is because most employers and trade unions, when they agree to refer an issue to a board of arbitration, instinctively think first of ACAS. In any discussion with the parties the Service always indicates that a reference to the CAC is one option but, as an alternative, also mentions the possibility of an *ad hoc* board appointed by ACAS itself.

In its 1980 report ACAS set out what it perceived to be the difference between the procedure for arbitration provided directly by ACAS and by the CAC:

> When arbitration is arranged directly by ACAS, acceptance of arbitration is often secured by allowing the parties to nominate or select their side-members and to be consulted about the choice of a chairman. This can make the parties more ready to accept arbitration and can sometimes provide a chance of communication with the arbitrator through side-members. It can also be a consideration that the award from an ACAS arbitration board is private to the parties. In contrast, the CAC draws its side-members from a list of 56 appointees, 28 for each side, and is required to publish its awards. Often these procedural differences may not matter: the CAC side-members offer wide experience: and in any event nearly all the deputy chairmen of the CAC are on the ACAS list of arbitrators. The Service encourages use of the CAC whenever appropriate, but in some cases the parties regard the procedural differences as significant because they do not expect the same privacy, flexibility, or informality from the CAC. These differences in procedure may seem to be of little practical significance, but they may be influential especially for parties considering the possibility of arbitration for the first time.[10]

Sir John Wood and his CAC collegues would no doubt challenge any assumption about their lack of flexibility or informality. So far as privacy is concerned, the Committee announced in its 1981 report that in voluntary arbitration cases its awards, too, would in future be private to the parties. Perhaps of greater significance is the emphasis that the CAC places on its collegiate approach and on its view that boards of arbitration drawn from the Committee's standing membership are more likely to share a common sense of purpose, unity and philosophical approach than *ad hoc* boards appointed by ACAS for specific tasks and then disbanded. Certainly the CAC has been able to avoid the situation that has once or twice confronted an ACAS-appointed board in which the side-members could not agree on what had to be done, leaving the chairman with no alternative but to assume the role of umpire and make his own award.

Table 2.2 Number of Boards of Arbitration 1978–88

	Number of cases
ACAS-arranged boards	250
Central Arbitration Committee	64

Sources: ACAS and CAC, *Annual Reports*, 1978–88.

The comparative figures for the period 1978 to 1988 are shown in Table 2.2.

The statutory relationship between ACAS and the CAC is not readily comprehensible. Linda Dickens and David Cockburn stated that the CAC is technically 'part of ACAS which has a consultative role regarding the appointments made by the Secretary of State. In practice this means little more than the CAC making its annual report to the Secretary of State via ACAS'.[11] With somewhat less accuracy, Mr (now Professor) Roy Lewis stated that ACAS was given a statutory constitution and powers and 'was provided with a Central Arbitration Committee'.[12]

Certainly ACAS has a statutory responsibility under the Employment Protection Act to provide premises, staff and facilities, but the Act did not deal specifically with the relationship beween the two bodies. In the past the CAC has shown some sensitivity over this matter. In its 1978 report, having drawn attention to its statutory basis; to the fact that the chairman, deputy chairmen and members of the Committee are all appointed by the Secretary of State for Employment (in the case of the chairman and deputy chairmen, after consultation with ACAS); to the requirement upon ACAS to report to the Secretary of State each year on the activities of the CAC (hence its annual report); and to its all-important independence, the Committee stated as follows:

> it [the CAC] is a standing arbitral body, composed of those with industrial relations experience, concerned with performing arbitration and like functions in the field of industrial relations. It has certain statutory powers but it is available, as were its direct predecessors, to those who seek resolution of their problem by way of arbitration. It has complete independence, both in substance and in spirit. Its only constraints and those are welcome, is that it is subject to review by the High Court so that should it make an error of law, or transgress the accepted canons of fair procedure, the

> parties are not without redress. The Industrial Court has, since its inception, been recognised as a valuable component of the judicial structure of the country performing its function in the specialised area of industrial relations and providing a regular and constitutional forum for resolving disputes. This Committee intends to continue in that way.[13]

If there ever were any doubt in the minds of 'some commentators' (the CACs own words) about its role these observations may be forgiven. Perhaps the CAC is a little resentful of the fact, particularly at times when the caseload is thin, that so much of its voluntary arbitration depends on the goodwill of ACAS officers. Perhaps it would prefer a situation in which ACAS stuck to the last of conciliation and left all the arbitration or, at least, boards of arbitration, to the CAC (but that's not what the law provides). Happily at the personal level the relationships between the two organisations are good – a fact which the CAC has regularly acknowledged in its annual reports.

When Schedule II of the Employment Protection Act and the trade union recognition part of the Act itself were repealed, the workloads of both the CAC and ACAS were affected. Dickens and Cockburn commented that while:

> ACAS can point to its continuing role in conciliating industrial tribunal claims, which engages the majority of the Service's operational staff and can emphasise its advisory services, the CAC lacks the ability to compensate for its declining dispute settlement activity. This must raise a question mark over the future of the CAC.[14]

This is examined later in this chapter when the advantages and disadvantages of establishing a single arbitration body for industrial relations questions are explored.

Standing Arbitral Bodies

The Civil Service

When arbitration was regarded as a much more acceptable means of settling industrial disputes a number of standing arbitration bodies were set up to deal specifically with the unsolved problems of particular industries and services. In 1916, for example, the Civil Service Arbitration Board was established, only to be abolished in 1922. But in 1923 the government of the day once more accepted the principle of arbitration in the Civil Service, and from then until 1936 arbitrations covering the Service were heard by the Industrial Court. In 1936 the Civil Service Arbitration Tribunal (CSAT) was re-established and exists to this day – albeit with very little to do.

Since 1925 the government's acceptance of any awards covering the Civil Service has been in accordance with the Treasury pledge given at that time, namely that 'subject to the overriding authority of Parliament, the Government will give effect to the awards of the Court Tribunal'.[15]

Certain kinds of claim were not eligible for reference to arbitration, but the wording of the agreement regarding access to arbitration was clear: 'where there is a failure to agree . . . the case shall be reported by or on behalf of either of the parties to the dispute to the Minister of Labour for reference to arbitration . . .'.[16] In other words, a right of unilateral access to arbitration. But according to an article that appeared in 1961 in *The Bulletin* (the journal of the Council of Civil Service Unions), Professor Frankel, a Canadian academic, found four occasions (out of 611 cases) between 1925 and 1959 when the government refused arbitration on the ground of 'major policy'. And according to *The Bulletin*, there were at least four further occasions when there was a dispute over claims going to arbitration. And in February 1979 the Secretary of State for Employment stated in a letter to the CCSU that, although the government recognised the obligations imposed on it by the 1925 agreement, it had 'always reserved to itself the right to refuse arbitration "on ground of policy"'[17] – a point which, he stated, had been spelt out in a booklet ('Staff Relations in the Civil Service') first published in 1949.

Present-day government attitudes towards arbitration in the Civil Service were, perhaps, shaped in 1961 at the time of the Conservative Government's 'pay pause'. Arbitration on that year's salary claim was refused unless it was accepted that the terms of reference provided discretion as to the operative date of any pay increase that might be awarded. The claim was for an increase of 5.5 per cent, the official side (namely, the employers) had offered 2 per cent, the CSAT awarded 4 per cent, 1.5 per cent above the Government's maximum figure in its 'guiding light'. It was no wonder that John Cole, then Labour correspondent of the *Guardian*, wrote at the time that the government's incomes policy was 'in tatters'.

Another significant policy change occurred in 1981. Up to that time, apart from a period during the preceding Labour Government's term of office, negotiations on Civil Service pay had been based on reports on the pay and conditions in comparable jobs outside the Civil Service, prepared by the Civil Service Pay Research Unit. But in 1981, at a very early stage in the discussion of that year's national salary claim, the Lord President of the Council (then Minister responsible for the Civil Service) ruled out any comparability exercise and stated that because arbitration could not apply where it would be contrary to the requirements of national policy, it followed that 'there could be no arbitration on the Government's cash limits'.[18] The result was a 20-week national strike the financial cost of which to the taxpayer will never be known. But it has been alleged that the eventual settlement:

> which included a government undertaking to consult with the unions before deciding on cash limits for the next pay round, a willingness to accept arbitration and the establishment of the Megaw inquiry into Civil Service pay, could undoubtedly have been reached ten weeks earlier, saving the government an estimated £500 million in interest payments on borrowing and lost revenue.[19]

The Lord President of the Council lost his job.

Government willingness to accept arbitration in the Civil Service was, in fact, confined to the 1982 claim. Since then, although both sides have solemnly continued to put forward their nominations to the CSAT, the Tribunal has not been called upon or allowed to function. Perhaps with the new kind of agreements that are now being negotiated in the Civil Service (see p. 60), in which provision is made for mutually agreed access to arbitration, the position will change.

The Police

For the police force there is an independent panel of three arbitrators – the Police Arbitration Tribunal – appointed by the Prime Minister. Pay, and most of the terms and conditions of employment for the police, are negotiated at national level by a body called the Police Negotiating Board, which was set up in 1979 following recommendations made by a committee of inquiry chaired by Lord Edmund-Davies. By law, membership of ordinary trade unions and the right to take industrial action are denied the police. The establishment of this inquiry was the government's reaction to grass-roots pressure on the

Police Federation (the policemen's 'trade union') to support a call for the right to strike. The work of the Board (which itself replaced the Police Council for Great Britain) is conducted by five autonomous standing committees which consider matters affecting:

- chief officers
- superintendents
- inspectors
- sergeants
- constables and cadets
- issues common to all ranks
- pensions

Any disagreements may be referred to the Police Arbitration Tribunal.

Perhaps for the sake of its longevity it is just as well that the principle for determining movements in police pay was laid down in a formula recommended by the Edmund-Davies Committee and subsequently accepted by the government of the day. Broadly speaking, the formula provides for annual improvements in police pay to be linked to the monthly index of average earnings. So far there has been no attempt to break that link.

The Post Office

The present-day arbitration arrangements in the Post Office flow from the requirements of the Post Office Act of 1969. Paragraph 11(1)(a) of Schedule 1 of the Act imposed a duty on the Post Office, through consultation, to conclude agreements 'with respect to the establishment and maintenance . . . of machinery' for settlement by negotiation of terms and conditions of employment 'with provision for reference to arbitration in default of such settlement in such cases as may be determined by or under the agreements.'

An agreement of August 1970 between the Post Office and its six trade unions laid down that disputes not settled by negotiation could be referred to arbitration by the Post Office Arbitration Tribunal (POAT) at the request of any of the parties, that is, unilateral arbitration. Cases had to fall within the scope of eight broad areas covering terms and conditions of employment:

- rates of pay
- allowances in the nature of pay (other than the introduction of allowances for responsibility)

- overtime rates
- subsistence rates
- travelling and lodging allowances
- conditioned hours
- annual leave allowances
- starting pay on promotion

Although there was a unilateral right to decide whether to refer a disagreement to arbitration, both sides were required to accept any award of the Tribunal.

Normally, if any initiative is taken to change from a unilateral right of access to arbitration to a jointly-agreed requirement, it comes from the employer. But in the case of the Post Office it was one of its unions (and numerically the strongest), the Union of Communication Workers (UCW) that made this request. As a result, it was agreed in 1971 by the Post Office and the UCW that the 1970 agreement should be amended, so far as that union was concerned, so that, in future, arbitration would only take place with the consent of the PO management and the UCW.

Perhaps this change is indicative of how strong the trade union movement was in 1971. Far from wishing to be dragged by the employer to an arbitration and then committed to accept the POAT's award, the UCW apparently preferred the freedom to take industrial action in the expectation that better terms could be extracted from the management by this method.

In September 1981, the Post Office, reflecting both the mood of the moment and the attitude of the government regarding unilateral right of access to arbitration, gave six months' notice of termination of the 1970 agreement. At the same time it stated its wish to negotiate a new agreement which would:

- require referral by agreement of both parties before the POAT could make an award binding on both parties;
- allow one party to refer an issue but only on the basis that the POAT would make, not a binding award, but a recommendation to help both sides reach a settlement.

A new agreement containing these two proposals (the Post Office Arbitration and Mediation Agreement) was concluded in 1983. The independent chairman of what is now the Post Office Arbitration and Mediation Tribunal (POAMT) is nominated by ACAS and side-members (one representing the Post Office and one representing the trade unions) are drawn from lists kept by the Service for this purpose.

By September 1989 there had been only one reference to POAMT under the 1983 agreement.

British Telecom

British Telecom was once part of the Post Office. An agreement between BT and the UCW dated May 1986, after the separation, provided for arbitration not through a standing body but, by joint agreement, through reference to ACAS. This agreement provides that in the event of an agreed reference to arbitration, 'it is the intention that there should be no industrial action' – presumably another no-strike agreement of a kind. BT has a similar agreement with the Communication Managers' Association.

The Railways

The railways provide an interesting example of a standing board whose decisions are either binding or not binding according to the prior determination of both sides. Thus in British Rail the Railway Staff National Tribunal (RSNT), which consists of three members not associated with the railways or the rail trade unions (one selected by the British Rail Board, one by the unions and a chairman appointed by agreement between the Board and the unions), only issues a binding award if there is an agreed reference requiring the Board so to do. Although the chairman of the RSNT is empowered to make a binding award on interpretative and certain other issues, they are the exception rather than the rule. Non-binding awards are akin to the formal recommendations of a mediator: they may be accepted, rejected or used as a basis for further negotiation.

The RSNT deals with issues over salaries, wages, hours of duty and other conditions of service affecting salaried and the quaintly named conciliation grades. The latter comprise a wide range of manual workers engaged in the day-to-day operation of the railways at stations, marshalling yards and signal boxes. Train crews, permanent way employees and those employed in signal and telecommunication installations are amongst other occupations that are also covered.

Sydney Weighell, one time general secretary of the National Union of Railwaymen, has recounted[20] how in 1975 the RSNT recommended a rise of 27.5 per cent on railwaymen's basic pay, which was accepted by the two other rail unions but rejected by his own. The NUR executive voted decisively for strike action. In accordance with the practice of the day beer and sandwiches with Harold Wilson duly followed at Downing Street and a few days later the British Rail Board settled for 29.8 per cent. In 1981 it was the turn of the Board to turn down an award of the RSNT. During preceding negotiations the Board had offered 7 per cent in response to a claim for a substantial increase in pay. On appeal, the RSNT awarded a two-stage increase of 8 per cent as from 20 April 1981 and 3 per cent as from 1 August 1981. The Board stated that it would not implement the RSNT's award unless the rail unions committed themselves to specific productivity improvements. The talks collapsed and it was against this sorry background that ACAS became involved in the major conciliation already summarised in Chapter 1.

The RSNT was again in the news in July 1989 when its recommendations for setting the 1989 salary claim of TSSA helped to break the deadlock in a serious dispute between British Rail and the NUR over pay and bargaining arrangements.

London Regional Transport (LRT) has its own standing body – the London Regional Transport Wages Board. Like the RSNT this Board comprises three members, and like the RSNT its decisions are binding or non-binding according to the predetermination of the parties. The Board acts on references from the Railway Negotiating Committee concerning the rates of pay, hours of duty and other conditions of service of underground staff – but only after direct negotiations within the Committee have failed to produce an agreement. Interestingly, LRT also negotiates with the TGWU over the pay and conditions of 'bus crews but this part of its business is not covered by provisions for arbitration of any kind.

Coal-mining

To an outsider the collective bargaining arrangements in operation within the coal-mining industry are complex – even more so following the arrival of the Union of Democratic Mineworkers (UDM) in the wake of the coal-miners' strike of 1984–5. The essential foundation is the Coal Industry Nationalisation Act of 1946. Under Section 46 of the Act the National Coal Board (now British Coal Corporation) was under a duty to enter into consultation with the mining trade unions with a view to concluding agreements which would provide joint machinery for the settlement by negotiation or arbitration of terms and conditions of employment, and for consultation on various matters.

The 1946 national conciliation scheme entered into between the NCB and the NUM following the Act laid down machinery for dealing with questions raised at national and district level and not surprisingly, it was agreed that arrangements previously established in 1943 would continue in being with only such changes as were necessary following the creation of the NUM in 1945 and the NCB in 1946. These arrangements comprised:

- A joint national negotiating committee
- A national reference tribunal

The tribunal was, in fact, an arbitral body to which it was originally intended that any question that could not be settled by the negotiating committee would be referred, namely, compulsory arbitration. District questions would be dealt with by a district conciliation board and, failing settlement, would be referred to arbitration by a district referee. But any question that was found to have national implications could be 'kicked upstairs' into the national machinery. For questions that were unique to a single pit or a group of pits a separate agreement (the pit conciliation scheme) was signed in January 1947. As its name suggests, this scheme provided additional machinery for the settlement of questions arising in individual pits. There was a six-stage procedure, the final stage of which involved a reference of the question to an umpire for final decision. It was again provided that pit questions which were found to involve district or national issues could be passed upwards for reference to the district conciliation board or, if appropriate, to the joint national negotiating committee. The national conciliation scheme covered industrial grade mineworkers but it acted as a model for similar schemes covering other negotiating groups in the industry.

In the brave new socialist world of the post-war years, the National Coal Board was able to say in its annual report for 1947 (and presumably meant what it said), that 'if . . . everyone keeps to the rules laid down, there should never be any need for a strike'. The reality proved to be very different – not that the coal-mining industry should be singled out for special criticism. The ship-building and automotive industries, to name but two others, were also proving that if there was no will to conform with procedure agreements, they were hardly worth the paper they were written on.

The national conciliation scheme, with its in-built provision for compulsory arbitration, continued unchanged until July 1961 when a major amendment was made at the request of the NUM. It was agreed that, in future, unsettled national questions could no longer be sent to the national reference tribunal if either party objected. In other words, what had previously been compulsory arbitration now became voluntary arbitration by joint agreement. In the words of the coal industry's historian, Professor William Ashworth: 'At most times this made little practical difference, but it was eventually found that, in the case of very serious disagreements, this change closed one avenue that might have helped to secure a settlement'.[21] In fact, between 1961 and 1985 there were only three occasions on which national questions were referred to the tribunal for arbitration.

After the coal-mining dispute of 1984–5, the Coal Board concluded that the scheme agreed in 1946 had been undermined by the emergence of the UDM and in accordance with Section 46 of the 1946 Act, invited the NUM to enter into consultations over a new agreement involving both unions. The Board gave six months' notice to the NUM of termination of the old scheme. But the NUM took the view that the 1946 agreement and conciliation scheme were legally enforceable and thus binding on the Coal Board. It argued that any modifications of the scheme should be as directed by the national reference tribunal.

In the High Court (National Coal Board v. National Union of Mineworkers) to which the issue was referred by the NCB, Mr Justice Scott made three declarations:

- that the 1946 agreement was not legally enforceable;
- that the NCB was under a duty to enter into consultations with the UDM and the NUM;
- that the national reference tribunal had been dissolved for all purposes.

After the case, British Coal entered into consultation with both unions with a view to establishing joint machinery. This did not prove possible. But an agreement was eventually negotiated with the UDM under which that union was given negotiating rights for mineworkers in any unit at which a majority of mineworkers employed were UDM members. The agreement provided that, subject to the concurrence of both sides, unsettled unit questions might be referred for arbitration by a unit umpire; likewise, unsettled area questions might be referred to an area referee and national questions to a national arbitration panel. Provision for passing upwards those questions with wider implications than the unit or area level at which they were first raised, was maintained. Failing settlement, what are termed industry questions, may be referred either by joint agreement or, by British Coal's unilateral decision, to the national arbitration panel.

To date, the NUM continues to reject British Coal's preferred option of joint conciliation arrangements with the UDM, nor will they accept separate arrangements based on the 'majority unit' principle to which the UDM has agreed.

The Thatcher Years

It is hardly surprising that a government committed to the deregulation of the employment market thought nothing of either Schedule II of the Employment Protection Act or (despite its longevity and survival under earlier Conservative administrations) of the Fair Wages Resolution. Schedule II was repealed by the Employment Act of 1980 and the Fair Wages Resolution was rescinded with effect from September 1983. By this time ACAS had already advised Mr Jim Prior, the then Secretary of State for Employment, to repeal the statutory (trade union) recognition procedures laid down in the Employment Protection Act of 1975. This was done by Section 19 of the Employment Act of 1980.

There thus disappeared from the statute book three of the grounds for unilateral access to arbitration, with effects on the arbitration caseload that have been noted earlier in this chapter, And under the Sex Discrimination Act of 1986 the provisions of the 1970 Equal Pay Act which allowed unilateral right of access to the CAC over issues involving the terms of collective agreements, employers' pay structures and statutory wage orders which applied specifically to men only or to women only were also repealed.

But the antagonism of Mrs Thatcher's Government to unilateral arbitration went much deeper. Philip Bassett, one-time Labour editor of *The Financial Times* and a much respected journalist has written that in 1981:

> the Cabinet's secret economic committee reviewed arbitration across the entire public sector, and, according to a Cabinet paper, concluded that 'the only sure way for employers to avoid the risk of awards they cannot afford is to refuse to go to arbitration. It follows that arbitration should not take place without their consent, but only on mutual agreement'.[22]

The Thatcher government is thus not totally opposed to the principle of arbitration but it must only take place on a jointly-agreed basis (in effect, each side has the right of veto). This attitude is reflected in an agreement negotiated in 1988 between the Treasury and the Civil Service unions on behalf of Grades 5–7; in further agreements negotiated with the Institution of Professional Civil Servants (now the Institution of Professionals, Managers and Specialists) and the Inland Revenue Staff Federation, there is an identical provision for arbitration:

> The parties attach high importance to the orderly settlement of disagreements and to the avoidance of industrial disputes. When negotiations fail to produce an agreement the parties will therefore explore avenues to seek a resolution of the difference; these avenues may, if so agreed, include reference to the Civil Service Arbitration Tribunal . . .

Similar wording now appears in agreements covering members of the Civil and Public Services Association and the National Union of Civil and Public Servants.

Arbitration in Practice

Arbitration is the process under which employer and trade union agree to hand over to an independent person (or group of persons) the responsibility for telling them how a dispute or difference should be settled. ACAS will not set up an arbitration (either directly or through the CAC) unless the parties have given an undertaking in advance that, whatever its terms, they will accept the award as binding. Some arbitrations are arranged privately but the number is not known. Awards under arbitrations arranged by ACAS and those carried out by the CAC are not covered by arbitration legislation and are not, therefore, legally binding. They are binding only in honour but they are invariably observed. Private arbitrations come under the arbitration legislation (unless the parties expressly agree to the contrary) and the awards of private arbitrators can thus be legally binding and enforceable.

Arbitration can be conducted by:

- a single arbitrator drawn in the case of ACAS-arranged arbitrations from a list maintained by the Service;

- an *ad hoc* board of arbitration which normally consists of three people – an independent chairman and two others, one of whom is nominated by the trade union and the other by the employer. In the case of ACAS-arranged arbitrations, lists are maintained by the Service for this purpose;
- the Central Arbitration Committee (CAC);
- exceptionally these days, a standing arbitral body for a specific industry or service.

About 90 per cent of arbitrations arranged by ACAS are handled by single arbitrators.

ACAS much prefers to reserve *ad hoc* boards of arbitration for the more serious, complex or important disputes. Earlier in this chapter we noted that when it is agreed that a dispute should be referred to a board, it is a matter for the parties themselves to decide whether the issue should go to an *ad hoc* board or to the CAC.

Any arbitration, whether carried out by a single arbitrator or a board, can take one of two forms:

- conventional arbitration in which the arbitrator is given complete discretion, within the agreed terms of reference, to determine the nature of his award;
- so called pendulum arbitration under which the arbitrator, again on the basis of agreed terms of reference, is confined to awarding either the union's final claim or the employer's final offer. Under pendulum arbitration the arbitrator is thus expressly denied occupation of the middle ground.

ACAS will normally arrange an arbitration only after it has satisfied itself that direct negotiations between the two sides have failed to produce an agreement and that there is no possibility of a conciliated settlement. But the processes of conciliation and arbitration are not mutually exclusive. They, and indeed the process of mediation, can all be used in the context of a single dispute. (A mediator does not make a binding award. He makes formal recommendations to help the parties resolve a dispute. His recommendations may be accepted, rejected or used as a basis for further direct negotiations.)

The 1982–3 national strike of water workers was a case in point. It was an open secret, widely reported in the press at the time, that the employers were minded to reply to the unions' pay claim with an offer of 6 per cent but were 'leaned upon' by the government to reduce this to 4 per cent. With no serious attempt to negotiate, the employers thereupon offered this figure and, when it was rejected, they proposed that in keeping with the arrangements then operative in the industry, the dispute should be referred to arbitration. The unions refused on the basis that there had been no attempt by the employers to negotiate with them first.

Before the national strike commenced, ACAS attempted to conciliate between the parties and it was agreed (virtually on the eve of the strike) that negotiations should be resumed under an ACAS-appointed mediator. The mediator duly made his formal recommendations to both sides. They were accepted in full by the employers who made a revised offer but this was rejected by the unions. By this time the national strike had commenced.

Further attempts at conciliation were again made by ACAS in the course of which the employers made minor improvements to their earlier offer. When this was rejected by the unions the employers again requested that the issue should be put to arbitration. On the grounds that the employers had still not bargained in good faith the unions refused, but ten days later they agreed that the issue should be referred to an ACAS-appointed committee of inquiry. Given the terms of reference agreed by the parties this was arbitration in all but name.

Sadly, the members of the committee of inquiry were unable to come to a unanimous decision and so the chairman had to exercise his powers of umpire to formulate an award. The terms were accepted by both sides and the dispute was settled.

The terms on which the unions' pay claim would have been settled if the government had not marked the employers' card so openly will, of course, never be known. It was no routine claim – the unions' members were restive about the widening gap between their pay and that of workers employed in gas and electricity supply. The unions had certainly prepared themselves for a battle.

All employers can learn one lesson from the national water dispute. If there is the remotest prospect of arbitration at the end of the road they should beware of the danger of inching up their offer either during any preceding conciliation stage or as a result of mediation. The reason is obvious. Even though improved offers made through ACAS either in conciliation or mediation may be withdrawn when rejected, their existence will almost certainly become known to the arbitrator during the arbitration. He would be less than human if he did not judge the case on the basis of the difference between the union claim and the employer's last proposal, withdrawn or not.

It is important to note that between its conciliation staff, and the arbitrator it appoints to any case, ACAS operates a system of 'Chinese walls'. This means that as far as ACAS is concerned, what goes on in conciliation remains private to the conciliator (what either party may say later to an arbitrator is their affair).

Choosing the Arbitrators

But who are the arbitrators? Where do they come from? What kind of experience can they offer? And what element of choice are the users allowed?

Because arbitrators are independent and neutral it follows that however much they might be capable of doing the job, practising managers and active trade union officials rarely appear on either the ACAS list of single arbitrators or on the CAC list of its deputy chairmen. To one side or the other, however unjustly, there must always be a question mark hanging over their impartiality. In many ways this is an ironical disqualification because these are just the men and women who could bring the right kind of practical experience to bear in so many disputes.

Based on research carried out for ACAS in 1986 by Alice Brown of Edinburgh University, the typical arbitrator in so far as there is one, will:

- be over 45 years of age;
- have been educated in a grammar school (or its Welsh or Scottish equivalent);
- be a graduate;
- if still in employment, work in a university as professor, head of department, lecturer or tutor;
- have had some managerial experience in industry, commerce, the Civil Service or university;
- already have handled ten or more arbitrations.

The present Chairman of the CAC is a professor of law. According to the CAC *Annual Report* for 1987, seven of his deputy chairmen filled or had filled academic posts in universities; one was a barrister and two were retired officials of the Department of Employment.

ACAS-appointed boards of arbitration are normally chaired by one of its more experienced arbitrators. Much of the practical industrial and commercial experience is provided by the side-members. Two are allocated to each arbitration – one experienced employer representative and one experienced worker representative drawn from lists maintained by the CAC or ACAS.

Although ACAS issues a guide to its arbitrators there is no training manual which can be provided by either ACAS or the CAC, but whenever ACAS adds an arbitrator to its list, he is given a thorough induction. Since 1981 ACAS has organised an annual series of seminars for its arbitrators, in which the CAC participates. Experiences are exchanged and major topics and problems of the day are discussed. In an acknowledgement of this development in its 1981 report, the CAC stated that 'any move to strengthen the coherence or professionalism of all engaged in industrial relations arbitration is a real gain'.[23]

As for case allocation, the general principle is to try and maximise user-acceptability. In the case of arbitration by a single arbitrator, the parties are often prepared to leave the decision to ACAS, but if they insist on an element of choice, a short list of suitable arbitrators, together with biographical details, is sent to both sides. Each side is asked to place the names in order of preference and ACAS selects the person who is shown as having a high preference on each list. In the case of ACAS-arranged boards of arbitration, the Service, so far as is practicable, allows the two parties to nominate or select their respective side-members and to be consulted over the choice of chairman. This approach has two advantages:

- it ensures the greatest possible amount of user acceptability;
- it is sufficiently flexible to enable the right 'horse' to be selected for the 'course', for example a legally-qualified chairman if the case is likely to turn on points of law or side-members with practical job-evaluation experience if it is a pay structure issue.

The Nature of the Arbitration Process

Arbitration is not a legal or adversarial process, nor is it highly formalised with the parties bound to adhere to strict rules of evidence. Normally the two parties are represented by those who were responsible for conducting the preceding direct negotiations, for example, trade union official and personnel/industrial relations manager, perhaps flanked, in the one case, by workplace representatives and, in the other, by management colleagues. Legal representation is very much the exception to the rule.

It is, of course, vital that every arbitrator is perceived by both sides to be impartial, independent, understanding and possessed of those qualities that enable him to gain and retain their confidence.

The procedure for hearings is now well established. Once the formalities of drawing up agreed terms of reference, of deciding upon the arbitrator and of fixing dates for a hearing have been completed, each party is encouraged to prepare a written statement of case and prior to the hearing, to send a copy to the arbitrator and to exchange statements with the other side.

At the hearing itself it is normally a matter of personal choice by the leader on each side as to whether he should read his statement of case in full or summarise its contents. The claimant party usually puts its case first and then the other side responds. Once this has been done either side is free to comment on the case or to ask questions of the other. Almost inevitably, the arbitrator, too, will wish to ask questions in order to establish facts that may still be obscure or, of equal importance, to try and gauge the underlying disposition and attitude of each side. Despite formal adherence to the claim, or to any offer, is there, for example, an underlying flexibility that can be detected which gives some indication as to the nature of an acceptable compromise?

The wise words of the CAC reflect the view of all good arbitrators:

> The Committee hopes to prevent the parties or witnesses from feeling that they are taking leading parts in a murder trial. They are encouraged to assist the Committee by evidence as to facts and opinions with, as far as possible, participation in the task of problem solving which, in the ultimate, lies with the Committee.[24]

Other than for reasons of urgency the wise arbitrator refrains from immediately announcing his decision even if his mind is already made up. Either he or the board (if board it be), is well advised to sleep on the evidence before advising the parties of the decision.

To Reason or Not to Reason

'Give you a reason on compulsion! If reasons were as plenty as blackberries, I would give no man a reason upon compulsion'.[25]

Falstaff was no arbitrator but his principle is one to which all arbitrators involved in industrial relations disputes should adhere. The arbitrator's typical award will comprise seven main elements:

- the terms of reference;
- a summary of the background to the dispute;
- a summary of the union's arguments in support of the claim;
- a summary of the employer's arguments in reply;
- general considerations;
- the decision.

Commentators on the arbitration system or, occasionally, the party that has lost the actual case, bemoan the fact that the arbitrator never gives reasons for his decision but takes refuge in that part of his award entitled 'General considerations'. The unwillingness of arbitrators to give detailed reasons for their awards is not new. For many years it was:

> the practice of the Industrial Court to express its awards in the form of decisions, with a full statement of the rival arguments but without discussion of the merit of those arguments or of the factors on which the awards are based, though brief references are occasionally made to exceptional features which have been taken into account by the Court.[26]

At a time when national incomes policies were seen as a continuing part of the British economic scene, it was perhaps not surprising that the Donovan Commission took a different view. It not only recommended legislation which would place on all arbitrators an obligation to take incomes policy into account when making their awards. It went on to say that:

> arbitrators should be encouraged to give reasons whenever they can, especially in major decisions on pay which are likely to be significant for the development of incomes policy, and in those cases where they do not feel able to give reasons to state so plainly.[27]

But the legislation recommended by the Commission was never passed and both ACAS-appointed arbitrators and the CAC have decided as a matter of policy to confine themselves to a summary of the general considerations and not to give reasons for their awards. The CAC has articulated very clearly the reasons for this policy:

> Arbitration cases usually come at the end of a long period of dispute and often follow conciliation. The parties are well aware of all the issues. What they want above all is settlement. To give

reasons is to invite yet another reconsideration of the various issues – with a good chance of renewed strife. The nuances of the words chosen to express the reasons may rekindle old disputes. It was for this sort of consideration that the Industrial Court and the Industrial Arbitration Board rarely gave reasons.

Against this view there are several strong arguments. Modern practice is tending to look to all decision makers to give reasons. Only if reasons are given can a consistent pattern be seen to emerge from the various decisions in the same or related areas. Reasons enable other disputes to be voluntarily settled or parties to disputes which are submitted to prepare their cases more effectively. These factors weighed heavily with the Committee and it decided that the parties should be given an indication of the considerations which led to the award.[28]

In making their decisions arbitrators should always confine themselves to their terms of reference. From their lofty and detached position they may see with a blinding clarity that will convince nobody but themselves what needs to be done to solve a whole set of apparently connected but, in fact, quite different industrial relations issues. Recommendations should not therefore be attached to an award unless requested by both sides. It is far better to draw to the attention of ACAS (so that ACAS can raise them privately later on), any matters that would benefit from further advice or assistance than to make uninvited recommendations which may do no more than cause further controversy and detract from the acceptability of the award.

The need to stick to the terms of reference is important in every case, but particularly vital in cases involving pendulum arbitration. If trade union and employer have agreed that the arbitrator's decision should either be the union's final claim or the employer's final offer, they don't want to be told that if he had been given a free hand the arbitrator would have awarded neither but somewhere in between.

Splitting the Difference

Writing in 1960 George Cyriax and Robert Oakeshott quoted a 'prominent' arbitrator's description of his system of arbitration as follows:

Find out the amount that the union is really aiming to get (this is usually a lower figure than its published claim) and the amount that

> the employer is really resigned to have to pay. Often there is hardly any difference between the figures and then the arbitrator's task is easy. When there is a difference, you usually have to split it, but preferably you should never split if fifty-fifty or you will create an awkward precedent for next time.[29]

There are probably many people who still regard this description of the arbitrator's approach as accurate. 'Everybody knows that arbitrators always split the difference' is still the typical reaction of every employer resisting a suggestion that his particular dispute should be settled through arbitration.

In response to the charge, the first and most obvious point to make is that over a dispute of right, namely, an issue involving the application of the terms of existing agreements or rules, it is impossible for an arbitrator to split the difference. Such questions as 'Was Mr X dismissed fairly or unfairly?' or 'Should this job be placed in Grade 1 or Grade 2 of the company's pay structure?' only allow for one answer, for example, the dismissal was fair or the proper grade for the job is Grade 2.

As part of the research referred to previously in this chapter, Alice Brown carried out a survey of arbitration procedures in the course of which she examined a sample of one out of every ten voluntary arbitration cases over the years 1942–85 (a total sample of 467 cases). She found that no fewer than 329 cases, or over 70 per cent of the total, were disputes of right. Information about disputes of interest, namely cases involving the establishment of new terms and conditions of employment or new rules, was just as illuminating. Out of a total of 134 such cases, the arbitrator was required to make a straight choice (in today's parlance, pendulum arbitration) in no fewer than 41 cases. So in only 93 cases of the total of 467 cases (or one in every five) examined was the arbitrator free to introduce an element of compromise. In fact it was in only 74 cases (or 16 per cent of the total) that he did so. And that suggests that in the remaining 4 per cent of cases the arbitrator was free to issue a compromise award but, in fact, awarded fully in favour of either the employer or the trade union.

A compromise award in only 74 out of 467 cases hardly justifies the cry that arbitrators always split the difference. And what evidence there is (not part of Alice Brown's research) suggests that where an arbitrator does make a compromise award the terms are very much nearer to the employer's last offer than to the union's final claim. This is hardly surprising given the way in which union claims are often formulated, for example, at union conferences or shop stewards' meetings. The pay claim of a union represents 'aspirational' money, namely, money which the union doesn't expect to negotiate and receive in full. On the other hand, any money which the employer offers is real money which sooner or later will have to be paid over to the employees.

There are three main reasons why an arbitrator in a conventional arbitration improves on the final offer made by the employer in direct negotiation:

- the merits of the case deserve it;
- by having agreed to refer the case to arbitration both sides have signalled they don't want a strike – and that may only be avoidable by varying the last offer;
- during the arbitration hearing, there have been indications or the arbitrator has deduced that the figure the employer is prepared to pay is in fact greater than his last offer.

Alice Brown's figures go a long way to destroy the myth that arbitrators always split the difference. But to those trade unions or employers who fear that in their particular case the arbitrator will make an unjustified compromise award, pendulum arbitration is an alternative to refusing arbitration altogether – and it is to pendulum arbitration, its origins and its pros and cons, that we turn now.

Pendulum Arbitration

Pendulum arbitration (the process whereby the arbitrator is confined to awarding the union's final claim or the employer's final offer, but nothing else), has recently come to the fore in the context of the so-called 'new-style' or no-strike agreements. Many give the credit for this development to Roy Sanderson, one of the national officers of the Electrical, Electronic, Telecommunication and Plumbing Union (EETPU), who was responsible for negotiating a number of new-style agreements with Japanese companies that were setting up shop in Great Britain. But Roy Sanderson himself, according to Philip Bassett 'came across the theory and practice in the USA . . .'[30] But, as Bassett went on to point out, pendulum arbitration seems in fact to have first been developed in the UK. Writing in 1986 in the journal *Industrial Relations* (University of California), John G. Treble stated that the technique had 'been used intermittently in several British industries from 1860 on'. According to Treble the 'arrangement seems to have originated with the conciliation board set up by A. J. Mundella in the Nottingham hosiery industry in 1860'. It subsequently spread to other industries, notably coal-mining. But shortly after the First World War pendulum arbitration disappeared as a specific concept from the British scene, even though Alice Brown's research has shown us how, in fact, many arbitration cases continued to involve the pendulum principle. Pendulum arbitration as a specific concept eventually re-surfaced in the USA, first in a number of arbitrations affecting public sector employees and then, much more importantly, in an influential paper by Professor Carl Stevens ('Is compulsory arbitration compatible with collective bargaining?') which appeared in the *Industrial and Labor Relations Review* in February 1966.

But for all the recent attention pendulum arbitration has received from commentators and journalists in the UK, the number of new agreements which in some way or another provide for it is still very small. In the first report of its Special Review Body, published in 1988, the TUC identified only 18 such agreements: the number of employees covered by them is not known and estimates vary widely. It seems unlikely that the number exceeds 20 000 and may well be less than 10 000. IRS Employment Trends of 27 June 1989 was able to identify 52 single union agreements covering less than 20 000 workers; 24 of these agreements provided for pendulum arbitration. But these agreements and the circumstances in which they were negotiated have caused more controversy within the TUC than any other issue for a very long time.

The controversy about these agreements is not that they provide for pendulum arbitration *per se*, but that they were negotiated within the context of a bitter inter-union struggle for new members, in the course of which the EETPU was accused of being prepared to give up that most treasured and sacrosanct of workers' rights – the right to strike as a means of redressing grievances or advancing claims. Some of these agreements undoubtedly do just that. The earliest of the new-style agreements was the one signed in April 1981 by Toshiba Consumer Products (UK) Limited and the EETPU. The negotiating procedure contains two in-house or domestic stages. The agreement then goes on to state as follows:

> Stage Three: If the matter is not resolved a joint reference shall be made to an independent arbitrator.

> Arbitration: Both the Company and the trade union shall represent their case to an agreed independent arbitrator. The terms of reference of the arbitrator will be to find in favour of either the Company or the trade union. A compromise solution shall not be recommended. Both parties agree to abide by the decision of the arbitrator.[31]

In this agreement there is no peace clause (namely, a prohibition on industrial action until the procedure has been fully used). The reason is obvious. If the procedure has to be used right through to the final stage (compulsory arbitration), and both sides are committed to abide by the arbitrator's decision, provision for strikes can be ruled out. They have become unnecessary.

But two points must be remembered:

1. An agreement doesn't have to provide for pendulum arbitration in order to merit the title of a no-strike agreement.
2. An agreement can provide for pendulum arbitration but the possibility of strikes is not ruled out.

As to the first point, the overwhelming majority of procedure agreements contain a peace clause. In some agreements, a failure to agree at the final stage releases both sides from this peace obligation. The procedure therefore postpones the possibility of a strike but doesn't rule it out altogether. But other procedure agreements don't allow for a 'failure to agree' at the final stage. Decisions have to be reached. In other words, they provide in all but name for arbitration. And although this kind of agreement has operated for decades, nobody has ever called it a no-strike agreement, although under the definition used by the critics of these agreements that's what in effect it is. And there are other agreements (admittedly not as numerous as they were) which provide, not for pendulum arbitration, but for conventional arbitration as a final compulsory stage in the event of earlier disagreement. In the report of its Special Review Body the TUC identified three such agreements in a list of 25. If it be the case that these agreements and any others like them rule out any form of direct action when an issue is in procedure and then, as a final stage, require the issue to be put to conventional arbitration, they are as much no-strike agreements under the current definition as those that provide for pendulum arbitration.

As to the second point, there are some agreements which provide for pendulum arbitration but this is only triggered when both sides agree. On the TUC's list of 25 agreements, eight provided for arbitration on this basis. If the employer does not agree to arbitration as a final and binding way of settling a dispute, the implication must be that in agreements of this kind the union is at liberty to try and concentrate his mind by the traditional means, namely strike action: in other words, agreements which provide for pendulum arbitration only when both sides agree are not no-strike agreements.

Thus in the case of the agreements between Nissan Motor Manufacturing (UK) Ltd and the Amalgamated Engineering Union, the key provisions are as follows:

> 4(e) The Company and the Union are totally committed to resolving . . . negotiations within the Company Council. However, in exceptional circumstances if this is not possible the outstanding matters will be referred to the Advisory, Conciliation and Arbitration Service for resolution. In the event of conciliation not producing a solution both parties may agree to arbitration. The arbitrator will be requested to determine positively in favour of one side or the other. The arbitrator will be asked to take account of those aspects which are already agreed. Both parties agree to accept the decision of the arbitrator.
>
> 4(f) During the course of such negotiations, conciliation or arbitration there will be no industrial action.[32]

Peter Wickens, Nissan's Director of Personnel and Information Systems, has stressed the importance attached to resolving matters in-house, that reference to ACAS at any time is regarded as undesirable but that, in the exceptional circumstance of non-resolution in-house reference to ACAS for conciliation would be automatic. Having gone through the in-house negotiations and subsequent conciliation without finding a solution:

> there would be considerable pressure on both parties to take the final step to arbitration . . . there is no compulsion in the Agreement for them to do so. It needs the agreement of both the company and the union to take that step to pendulum arbitration with prior commitment to accept the decision. It follows then that the Nissan-AEU procedure agreement can end after the conciliation phase. If this is the case, and it is the union that does not wish to proceed, industrial action taken at this time would be constitutional. It is in this specific as well as the general sense that the Nissan-AEU Agreement cannot be described as a no-strike deal.[33]

And yet, the TUC has pointed out that 'the [Nissan] agreement too has been a controversial one'.[34]

One interesting agreement provides for the possibility of either pendulum or conventional arbitration. This is the agreement signed in August 1987 by IBC Vehicles Ltd (a joint venture company formed by General Motors of the USA and Isuzu of Japan) and five trade unions to cover the Company's van operations at Luton. Under this agreement all collective issues are processed through an in-house procedure the final stage of which is the company joint council. If 'in exceptional circumstances' the issue is not settled, it goes to ACAS for resolution. In the event of conciliation having failed, the parties concerned may agree to arbitration on the following basis:

(10.3) Whenever arbitration is agreed, the following provisions will apply:

(i) the arbitrator will be appointed by ACAS.
(ii) the terms of reference and the form of arbitration (conventional or pendulum) will be agreed for each case.
(iii) the parties to the arbitration agree to accept and to abide by the award of the arbitrator.
(iv) the award of the arbitrator will be legally binding on the Company and the Unions and will be incorporated (as appropriate) into the respective contracts of employment of the Employees of the Company.

(10.4) The Company and the Unions agree that until all negotiation, conciliation and, where agreed, arbitration have been completed neither party will engage in or participate in industrial action of any kind.[35]

Conciliation through ACAS is thus obligatory if agreement is not reached in-house. But this agreement is more noteworthy for the alternatives of conventional and pendulum arbitration that are then available on a voluntary basis, and for the fact that if it is agreed that the issue should go to arbitration, the award is not just binding in honour but legally binding as well (a most unusual provision in British collective agreements). The IBC agreement lays down similar conciliation and arbitration procedures for dealing with individual grievances.

It was not pendulum arbitration (or indeed arbitration generally) that stirred up so much controversy within the ranks of the TUC, nor was it the issue of pendulum arbitration that led to the expulsion of the

EETPU. Voluntary arbitration has, for long, been a principle acceptable to trade unions even though it doesn't feature in many agreements. During the Wapping dispute the print unions actually put forward an offer of compulsory arbitration as an alternative to the management's demand for a legally binding agreement. Moreover, with the move of most national newspapers from Fleet Street and the introduction of new technology, the print unions (perhaps as a result of the bruising they had received at the hands of Eddie Shah and Rupert Murdoch) were prepared to accept compulsory arbitration in the new house agreements that accompanied the move. The *Daily Telegraph*, for example, entered into agreements with the unions which, amongst other things, provided for a 'no disputes' agreement involving binding arbitration. The Mirror Group, although maintaining an operation in central London, entered into a number of new house agreements which included the right of unilateral access to arbitration through ACAS. And in 1987 News International entered into an agreement with the National Union of Journalists which contains an elaborate arbitration procedure that can be initiated unilaterally by either side. Finally, as we have already noted, the new generation of agreements being negotiated in the Civil Service provide for jointly-agreed access to arbitration through the CSAT.

The root cause of so much inter-union controversy was not arbitration *per se* or even pendulum arbitration, but the allegation that under these agreements the right to strike had been foresworn. The germane points to bear in mind in examining these agreements are these:

- the typical British collective agreement is not legally binding and, call it what you will, no agreement can ever guarantee there will never be a strike;
- any question that cannot be raised under a procedure agreement (even an agreement which has arbitration as a final and mandatory stage for questions that can be raised) is at least by implication, a strikeable issue. A good example is the typical US labour agreement which provides arbitration as a final stage for issues that can be raised but does not rule out the possibility of strikes over other issues like work standards and health and safety matters;
- any term agreement, for example, a pay settlement to last 12 months, is a no-strike agreement over pay for 12 months;
- the objective of the peace clause in all procedure agreements is

to defer strikes until the procedure has been fully utilised. But any procedure agreement which at the final stage (whatever it is called) requires a clear decision, as distinct from permitting a failure to agree, is tantamount to a no-strike agreement. There are probably few major trade unions in the land that are not parties to at least one agreement in this category;

- any agreement with a procedure which specifies that arbitration (conventional or pendulum) can only be exercised with the agreement of both parties can in no sense be called a no-strike agreement;
- it is only those procedures which, in the event of disagreement at the earlier stages, specify conventional or pendulum arbitration as a compulsory final stage that justify the no-strike label – and these agreements are very rare.

On the arbitration issue the somewhat ambiguous decision of the TUC's Special Review Body was as follows:

> Unions, when making recognition agreements, must not make agreements which specifically remove, or are designed to remove, the basic democratic lawful rights of a trade union to take industrial action. This is not meant to deter unions using arbitration, pendulum or otherwise, at the request of one or both parties.[36]

Perhaps the most bizarre feature of the whole debate over pendulum arbitration is the impression it has given that employers are queuing up to persuade unions to agree to this form of arbitration. The fact is that for all the arguments that have been deployed in its favour, employers generally are as much opposed to pendulum arbitration as they ever were to arbitration of the conventional kind. Even the considerable influence of the Institute of Directors has so far counted for nothing. After the national water strike in 1982–3, the Institute suggested pendulum arbitration as the way to avoid future strikes in the essential services – but apparently nobody was interested.

The advantage claimed for pendulum arbitration can be simply stated. Two negotiating parties, faced with the possibility of arbitration of the conventional kind, will probably keep a little 'in reserve' during the course of their direct negotiations. But if it is known that any arbitration would be of the pendulum kind, they will realise that extremism, whether in the form of an extravagant claim or an unreasonably low offer, is likely to be penalised by the arbitrator.

Thus in their negotiations both sides are forced to abandon extreme positions and are inexorably driven closer together so that eventually the gap in their negotiating positions is so narrow that with a little more give and take, it can be bridged and agreement reached.

In the case of those new-style agreements which expressly provide for pendulum arbitration at the end of the procedural road, the number of claims that have actually been referred to an arbitrator has so far been extremely small – indication perhaps that the theory is actually working in practice. There was, however, one well-publicised difficulty in a case involving Sanyo Industries and the EETPU. A difference of opinion emerged in 1985 as to how the arbitration procedure should operate. The Company argued that pendulum arbitration should operate on the basis of the position of each party at the last formal negotiating session: the union argued that before resorting to arbitration, the arbitrator should first try and conciliate between the two sides. In the event, thanks to the arbitrator's efforts, a mediated settlement was achieved and it was also agreed that procedural guidelines should be drawn up for the future. Talks through ACAS to settle the procedural problem did not lead to a change of position by either side, but in a subsequent ballot the work-force decided by a 2 to 1 majority in favour of the Company's position. A code of practice to reflect this was thereupon added to the procedure agreement.

As to the merits of pendulum arbitration, ACAS pointed out in its 1986 Report that particularly:

> in a complex bargaining situation, where several issues are under discussion at the same time, it may be unhelpful for an arbitrator to be compelled to endorse the full position of one side or the other if long term stability and equity are the aim. Important questions therefore remain about the way in which the successful party takes all can best fit with the more participative, consensus seeking objectives of new style agreements.[37]

In its 1984 report[38] the CAC emphasised that arbitrators did not 'crudely split the difference' and that where awards did 'fall between offer and claim' this was likely to be 'the result of an evaluation of a complex of different arguments'. Perhaps at times there was some merit in each side's case:

> In dealing with a complex claim and offer, too, with each side offering convincing arguments in some areas, the right answer may

be to award differentially; i.e. for the employer on some aspects and the union on others. Simple 'pendulum' arbitration would appear to rule this out.

The CAC concluded that 'a professional arbitrator needs the opportunity of avoiding the dilemma in which neither of the proffered solutions is without serious flaw'. A degree of flexibility must be retained except in the most straightforward cases. John G. Treble, whose paper has already been quoted, was of the view that opposition to pendulum arbitration in the coalfields came not from the negotiators but from the arbitrators. History seems to be repeating itself.

The success of no-strike agreements is not to be measured just by the use that is made of arbitration, conventional or pendulum. Most of the agreements cover greenfield sites that are unencumbered with out-dated attitudes and restrictive customs and practices. More importantly, they are of a consensual kind containing much sought after provisions like single status and advanced systems of employee involvement. In such circumstances maintaining good industrial relations ought to be just that little bit easier.

Arbitrators and the National Interest

In July 1966 Sir Roy Wilson, at that time president of the Industrial Court, told the Donovan Commission: 'I feel strongly that no arrangement whatsoever should be made to ensure that the national interest and the interests of consumers are taken into account by arbitrators'.[39] In its issue of 30 July 1966, *The Economist* wryly wrote of Sir Roy: 'There is no evidence that he was trying to be funny'.

In his earlier testimony Sir Roy had asserted that:

> arbitration as a method of settling wage issues arising out of collective bargaining became unpopular in 1961 when the government was encouraging a 'pay pause' and asking arbitrators to respect such policies. As a result, the number of disputes referred to arbitration fell to a very low level and the popularity [sic] of this method of dispute resolution never recovered.[40]

In its evidence to the Commission the Ministry of Labour pointed out that, in the past, the interests which had determined the awards of arbitrators had been primarily, though not solely, those of the parties even though arbitrators were supplied by the Ministry with wages and earnings statistics and such statements of government policy as the white papers on prices and incomes. But, it was emphasised, no attempt had been made 'to prescribe the limits within which arbitrators should work or to suggest to them any particular way in which their awards should reflect current national policy'.[41]

The Ministry went on to ask whether, in 'circumstances where the Government and industry are committed to a prices and incomes policy as part of a long term economic plan and in which there has been laid down by agreement a "norm" for increases in incomes', these arrangements were 'fully adequate'.[42] In essence, the Ministry stated, the problem was 'how to ensure that the normal processes of arbitration can be reconciled with the national interest'.[43]

Lord Donovan and his colleagues were in no doubt:

> It is desirable . . . that effect should be given to incomes policy in the making of the arbitration awards. To this end we recommend legislation placing on all arbitrators an obligation to take incomes policy into account when making their awards.[44]

In the late 1960s the Ministry of Labour and the Donovan Commission were not alone in believing that government pay policies of one kind or another would be a permanent feature of the British economic landscape. The fact that pay policies have gone and are unlikely to reappear only goes to show how a recommendation which might, at the time, have seemed reasonable, or at least worthy of debate, could so quickly be invalidated by subsequent events. But even in the short term, that is to say, while statutory pay policies continued to exist, no indication was ever given of any government intention to introduce permanent legislation on the basis of the Donovan recommendation. Even so, arbitrators did not completely escape the attention of successive governments.

Even prior to the publication of the Donovan report the Labour Government's 1966 white paper, *Prices and Incomes Standstill*, had stated that arbitration awards, like settlements negotiated voluntarily 'will be subject to the requirements of the periods of standstill and severe restraint'. The same Government's white paper of June 1967, *Prices and Incomes Policy After 30th June 1967*, was addressed to a wider audience:

> These considerations and the criteria . . . are intended to be applied by all concerned with the determination of employment incomes in

the private and public sectors whether at industry, company or plant level and including arbitrators, independent review bodies and statutory wage fixing bodies.

A similar provision appeared in 1968 in the next white paper, *Productivity, Prices and Incomes Policy in 1968 and 1969*.

In 1970 (by which time the Donovan report had appeared) a Conservative government completely opposed to a formal prices and incomes policy was elected. In the background, however, there was an undeclared policy of reducing the level of pay settlements in the public sector. But by November 1972 the government felt obliged to think differently. And perhaps one dispute which had a major impact on its thinking was the strike of 60–70 000 local authority manual workers which took place in September and October 1970.

In April 1970 the trade unions had submitted a multi-part claim of which the major element was a pay increase of 55s. per week. The employers' final offer was made in October, that is, after the strike had started – its main constituents were a two-stage increase in basic rates (37s. or 38s. per week according to grade payable in September 1970 and a further 10s. to all grades in April 1971) plus certain pay guarantees.

The government's position was that:

- inflation was the country's most crucial and immediate problem;
- no progress could be made with the expansion of the economy and with a reduction of taxation until cost inflation was brought under control;
- there was no intention of assuming detailed control by means of a pay and productivity policy, backed by statutory powers;
- the responsibility for dealing with the problem lay squarely with employers and the first step was for the local authority employers to stand firm on a reasonable offer;
- there was no intention of imposing a norm – the government was relying on its appeal to employers in both the public and private sector to bear in mind the national interest.

As important as these statements of policy were, far more significant was the government's announced intention not to provide the services of the Department of Employment's conciliation department (save for the purpose of helping the parties towards a settlement within the total cost of the package already on offer) nor to appoint an arbitrator or a court of inquiry.

The employers were on their own. Although divided politically they were united in their concern for the inconvenience and distress the strike was causing the general public. They therefore took the highly unusual step of canvassing the unions on the possibility of both sides agreeing to set up their own committee of inquiry which would be quite independent of the state machinery. Eventually the unions agreed, and a committee under the chairmanship of Sir Jack Scamp was duly appointed.

The committee's main recommendation was for a single increase in basic rates of 50s. per week payable in November 1970. Other recommendations covered shift pay, holidays and the rapid extension of productivity schemes. The recommendations were accepted by both sides although, so far as the unions were concerned, by no means unanimously.

The committee's reasons for its recommendations were set out very clearly in its report. The average earnings of local authority manual workers were low:

- The most hopeful means of improving their position in relation to the earnings of other workers is to raise pay and productivity in step, although progress has so far been slow and further progress will necessarily take time. The only alternative is an incomes policy which can succeed in restraining increases for high paid workers while the lower paid improve their relative position. We should welcome such a policy but at the moment it does not exist and there does not appear to be any early prospect of it.
- even without a policy we do not accept that the earnings of local authority employees should fall further behind those of other workers.
- Given the pace of inflation in the country as a whole there is no chance that it can be arrested by a somewhat smaller pay increase for local authority employees.
- In absolute terms our proposals are expensive – very expensive. We can only repeat that this is also true of the employers' offers and most pay settlements made in Britain this year. In our opinion any less expensive settlement might mean a worsening of the position of workers who already earn well below the national average; and it would not bring any diminution in the pressure of inflation.[45]

The employers put as brave a face on the situation as they could. But on the members of the committee of inquiry the roof fell in. They were heavily criticised and subjected to much personal abuse at the hands of the government and media for what was regarded as the irresponsible nature of their recommendations.

A few months later there was another serious pay dispute – this time in the electricity supply industry – and on this occasion the government did set up a court of inquiry (the Wilberforce inquiry).

A leading article in *The Times* of 12 February 1971 stated that as a percentage increase in actual workers' pay 'Wilberforce and Scamp are virtually identical'. This made it odd that the two reports should be so differently regarded particularly by the government:

> Certainly the myth that Sir Jack Scamp was responsible for an irresponsible infraction of the Government's policy can be laid aside. In that case the Government refused either to conciliate, to arbitrate or to set up a court of inquiry; they privately accepted Sir Jack Scamp's inquiry but decided not to submit any evidence to it, or offer it any advice, and the dispute was settled on terms which, though too high, had in effect already been offered.
>
> In the electrical dispute the government did conciliate, did set up a court of inquiry, did offer not only its own evidence but its own terms of reference and the dispute was settled on terms which, for most of the men, were more than fifty per cent higher than had ever been offered them. As against that the productivity situation made this an inexpensive settlement in terms of labour costs.
>
> It is probably true that the Scamp report was more reasonable, and Wilberforce less satisfactory than most initial reactions suggested . . .

The Times concluded with a stern warning regarding the role of arbitration – 'very important as a way of mitigating the rigour of industrial bargaining', but if the government 'wants to have an incomes policy, or to make its incomes policy work, it will have to find means other than a sequence of arbitrations to achieve its objective'. (Technically speaking, of course, the Scamp and Wilberforce inquiries were not arbitrations.)

By 1972, despite its earlier protestations, the Conservative Government felt obliged to introduce a statutory pay and prices policy. In its white paper that year entitled *A Programme for Controlling Inflation: The First Stage*, it was firmly stated 'Arbitrators, independent review bodies and statutory wage fixing bodies are expected to take account of the Standstill'. When in January 1973 it published its next white paper, *The Programme for Controlling*

Inflation: The Second Stage, the words were different, the sentiment stronger:

> *Arbitration, etc.*
> The policy applies to all settlements whether reached by direct negotiations, conciliation, arbitration or by other methods of pay determination whether statutory or otherwise . . .

Edward Heath's Conservative Government disappeared in February 1974 to be succeeded by Harold Wilson's Labour administration. In September 1974 a social contract was endorsed by the TUC and in July 1975 a white paper entitled *The Attack on Inflation* was published. This provided for a pay limit of £6 per week over the following 12 months, with nothing for those earning over £8500 per year. The following warning which appeared in the white paper contained no reference to arbitrators or conciliators:

> The Government will be asking the review bodies for the armed forces, for doctors' and dentists' remuneration and for top salaries in the public sector, to comply in their recommendations with the pay limit. It will also be necessary to suspend the operation of pay research in the Civil Service for the period of the policy.

By this time of course, ACAS had been established, its arrival accelerated by the increasing control exercised by the previous government over the supposedly independent processes of conciliation carried out in the Department of Employment. Under the 1975 Employment Protection Act express provision for the independence of the new agency was guaranteed in Schedule 1, Paragraph 11 (i):

> The functions of the Service and of its officers and servants shall be performed on behalf of the Crown, but . . . the Service shall not be subject to directions of any kind from any Minister of the Crown as to the manner in which it is to exercise any of its functions under any enactment.

Paragraph 27 of the same schedule provided for the independence of the Central Arbitration Committee in words that were virtually identical.

In the light of these declarations of independence the Labour Government, even if it were so minded, could hardly have instructed or even reminded arbitrators to do their duty in relation to pay policy.

And if there were any doubts about the determination of ACAS to act and to be seen to be acting independently, these must have been allayed when, as we have already noted in Chapter 1, ACAS steadfastly maintained that it would not act as interpreter or agent of government in relation to the relevance of pay policy in any particular dispute. But, with the arrival of Mrs Thatcher's administration in 1979, formal pay policies were abandoned even though informal policies of the 'arm twisting' kind seem to have continued. There have, however, been no white papers or other forms of adjuration to remind arbitrators of their duty or of any implicit need to be mindful of the national interest *as perceived by the government of the day*.

And that surely is the nub of the matter. Any arbitrator who is asked to be mindful of the national interest is in truth being asked to comply with a political requirement. But arbitrators have a somewhat different perspective. Their task is:

- to conform with the laws of the land;
- to listen to and weigh up all the evidence submitted to them, including any put forward by whomsoever claims to represent the national interest;
- to reach a decision based on all the evidence submitted.

In the light of all he has heard, an arbitrator may take a different view from the politicians as to the national interest but he ought not, for that reason, be branded as unpatriotic, irresponsible or deaf. In fact the evidence that arbitrators made a habit of ignoring the national interest is pretty thin if only for the reason that, during the years of pay policy, arbitrators (as distinct from courts of inquiry) were not called upon to determine many pay claims of national significance. A 4 per cent award by the CSAT to civil servants in 1962 against the background of a pay 'norm' of 2 per cent may on the face of it have seemed excessive, but faced with evidence of other occupations like dockers who had been allowed to break through the 'norm' (perhaps that was what the national interest required in their case), who could blame an arbitrator for having some regard to the principles of fairness and equity? And who was to say in 1970 that the national interest would have been better served if the Scamp committee had recommended continued adherence to a pay limit which had not even been publicly declared when the consequence was not just the prospect but the reality of garbage piled in the streets?

Perhaps with the demise of statutory pay policies the demand that arbitrators should have regard to the national interest at the expense of equity and other considerations will not be repeated. But Sir Roy Wilson was wrong when he inferred that arbitrators should ignore the national interest. What he should have said is that the need to have regard to the national interest (however it be defined) is but one of the factors that must be taken into account by an arbitrator whenever evidence to that effect is submitted to him.

The Future of Arbitration

Despite Sir Roy Wilson's assertion regarding its one-time popularity, arbitration, as a method of dispute resolution, even over disputes of right, has never been widely used in the United Kingdom. In this chapter a number of possible reasons have been advanced for this state of affairs:

- traditional trade union preference for strike action if and when direct negotiation with the employers has failed to produce an agreement;
- the unwillingness of employers, particularly in disputes of interest, to hand over what they consider to be key business decisions to an independent outsider;
- disenchantment with the war-time experience of compulsory arbitration;
- employer suspicion that regardless of the merits of the case, an arbitrator will invariably 'split the difference'.

Figures, included in the Ministry of Labour's written evidence to the Donovan Commission, showed that over the period 1960 to mid-1965 the total number of voluntary arbitrations of all kinds was 373, an average of 68 cases per year. The number of conciliations was reported as varying between 300 and 400 each year. Over the period 1978–88 the total numbers increased considerably to 2460 voluntary arbitrations, and 8185 conciliations, including claims raised unilaterally under Schedule 11 of the Employment Protection Act and the Fair Wages Resolution (yearly averages of 224 and 1653 respectively.)

The reason why the conciliation process is preferred lies in the single word, control. The trade union and the employer who agree to conciliation remain very much in control of events. Either can pull out at any time – the union can decline to vary its claim and the employer can decline to improve his offer. Continued disagreement may be preferred to an agreed settlement on unsatisfactory terms.

But when both sides agree to arbitration and to be bound by the outcome, they effectively lose control of events. Win, lose or draw, they are stuck with the award.

The high profile that ACAS enjoys and, as a result, the wider understanding of the availability of conciliation, makes it unlikely that we shall see a dramatic increase in the number of voluntary arbitrations, particularly as the right of unilateral access to arbitration has now diminished. The arrival of a small number of so-called new-style agreements which provide for arbitration in some form or another will in no way compensate for this diminution. But should collective agreements ever become legally enforceable, the use of arbitration would certainly increase.

Sadly, at the present time a proposal by one side to refer a labour dispute to arbitration is likely to be construed by the other side as a sign of weakness. If the trade union makes the proposal it will be seen to be uncertain of its members' support for the alternative of strike action, and when the employer makes the proposal he will be believed to be fearful of the possibility of a strike he doesn't want. In our industrial relations we are thus still a long way from accepting arbitration in the way so idealistically but unrealistically described by Lord Salisbury. There is no early prospect of employers and trade unions, regardless of their relative bargaining strengths, agreeing to refer their unsettled disputes to arbitration just because it is the civilised thing to do.

But there is surely a case for actively encouraging the wider use of arbitration in disputes affecting one large and important group of employees, namely those covered in the non-trading part of the public sector, for example, civil servants, school teachers and National Health Service workers. In their approach to the determination of pay for this group, successive governments have resorted to an *ad hoc* approach of a kind which would have made an old-time industrial relations manager turn green with envy.

In 1978, following threats by the police to have to resort to the strike weapon, a committee of inquiry recommended a formula for annually uprating pay on the basis of a link to the monthly index of average earnings. The Labour Government of the day accepted the recommendation. In 1977–8 the nation's firemen, unlike the police, actually went on strike and, as part of the eventual settlement, they too secured indexation in the form of an undertaking to bring their pay up to the upper quartile of manual workers' earnings by November 1979 and to maintain it at that level thereafter. (In 1980, in an attempt to comply with the Conservative Government's pay guidelines for the public sector, the employers offered a 6 per cent increase, but in the face of threatened strike action they eventually conceded the 18.8 per cent increase required by the formula.) In 1981 there was a national pay dispute affecting the Civil Service out of which there came a Conservative Government decision to set up an inquiry into Civil Service pay (the Megaw inquiry). In 1982 the same government made clear its opposition to the extension of indexation to any other groups. This attitude was maintained during the 1989 ambulance drivers' dispute.

During the national pay dispute of 1983 in the NHS, the nurses or, to be accurate, those of them in membership of the Royal College of Nursing, did not go on strike, and in return for their 'angelic' behaviour, they and some other categories of NHS employees were rewarded with a review body which removed them from collective bargaining and subjected future movements in their pay to the process of recommendation by the review body and subsequent prime ministerial decision. Unfortunately for the sake of principled consistency there are other unions (for example, the Confederation of Health Service Employees (COHSE) and the National Union of Public Employees (NUPE)) which also have nurses in membership who did go on strike. Even so, they, too, receive the salary increases determined under the review body system. Finally, in 1986 the Secretary of State for Education abandoned the Burnham Committee as the forum for the negotiation of teachers' pay in primary and secondary schools in England and Wales and replaced it by an interim advisory committee on school teachers' pay and conditions.

Indexation and the process of pay determination by a review body do not rule out strikes but probably make them less likely. But for other groups of employees in the non-trading part of the public sector where collective bargaining continues to exist, strikes are still a possibility when negotiations break down.

Perhaps in the past too low a priority was given to the need to deal equitably with these groups. Perhaps it was all too easy to dismiss their grievances as those of a privileged but unproductive work-force that enjoyed the advantages of job security and index-linked pensions. Perhaps, too, the assumption was made that their traditional loyalty to the public, patients and pupils made industrial action unthinkable. The relative ease with which many groups in the private sector could avoid the worst consequences of statutory pay policies contrasted strongly with public sector employees who were stuck with adherence to their strict letter. Thus was the problem aggravated, and when the disparity of treatment eventually became so great that special catch-up exercises were unavoidable (perhaps during the run-up to a general election), parts of the media could then indulge in short-term comparisons of pay movements which purported to show how well the public sector was doing compared with those employed elsewhere. And then the cycle started all over again.

But the nature of employment in the public sector has now changed. Job security, for example, in the Civil Service, is much less assured; index-linked pensions are increasingly being made available to employees in the private sector; and employees in the public sector have been obliged to step up their efficiency either because of the employment of fewer numbers or the introduction of improved management systems. And, finally, there have been enough indications over the past two decades to show that however much we may regret it, public sector employees, sometimes chivvied by a hard core of militants, are no longer prepared to subordinate their own grievances to an overriding sense of duty to the public.

Any government concerned with the morale of its employees, or with the future of the country's industrial relations, cannot afford to ignore these developments. The theory and practice of good personnel management require pay to be fixed at levels which are not just sufficient to recruit and retain but to motivate as well. All too often in recent years the importance of the motivation factor seems to have been ignored or under-estimated.

Collective bargaining in the public sector is obviously very politicised. What also makes it different is not that the bargaining is constrained by a cash limit or a pay factor (this is the case in the private sector too), but that these constraints may be known ahead of the commencement of bargaining itself. The process is also differentiated by two other factors – first, the absence of ordinary commercial criteria by which management (in this case, the government) can take a view as to the length of time a strike can be withstood without economic damage, and secondly, the enormous but largely hidden consequences of industrial action when it does occur, for example, lost revenue, interest payments on borrowing and longer hospital waiting lists.

Strikes in these parts of the public sector are inconvenient and perhaps the public feels uncomfortable that its public servants should have to pursue grievances against their employer in this way. Probably too, many public employees are much less militant and committed to full-blooded industrial action than some of their leaders and, in the absence of indexation or a review body, would infinitely prefer the option of peaceful resolution by arbitration if it were made available to them.

Despite the long history of unilateral arbitration in the determination of Civil Service pay, the Megaw committee did not favour it. But it did agree that jointly-agreed arbitration could have an important role, and we have already noted that in the new generation of agreements to which most of the civil service unions are now committed provision is made for this kind of arbitration. It will be interesting to see how the Treasury, in these circumstances, reacts to a union request for arbitration. Certainly such an arbitral provision should never have been agreed if it is the Treasury's undeclared intention never to agree to its use.

The ancillary workers in the NHS are not covered by a pay review body, and it seems to be the Conservative Government's policy that until their unions renounce industrial action and enter into a no-strike commitment there is no prospect of their being so covered in future. But perhaps both sides prefer the present freedom of action they enjoy. The unions could hardly be blamed if they declined to give up the right to strike until experience showed that a pay review body would work to their advantage. And however much the Government might like a no-strike commitment, it can draw comfort in its absence from the fact that many ancillary workers are drawn from an underprivileged section of the population. This, coupled with the ability to put some services out to private contract, will blunt the militant edge to trade union claims.

At the district level managers and trade unions are not averse to making use of ACAS conciliation and arbitration but the extension of arbitration to the resolution of national disputes in the National Health Service seems unlikely.

The difference in the government's treatment of school teachers is to be noted. Apart from one union (the Professional Association of Teachers), the teaching unions are not averse to industrial action to back their demands but, despite this, they have had a review body of a kind imposed (perhaps temporarily) upon them. Whatever may emerge in future, a return to collective bargaining of any kind under a Conservative government, coupled with access to arbitration in the event of disagreement, seems unlikely.

A Comprehensive Arbitration Service?

The responsibility for providing and administering arbitration in Great Britain is diffuse. ACAS carries the general responsibility for arbitration and provides the administrative back-up to the CAC; the CAC is constitutionally separate from ACAS and in addition to providing voluntary arbitration when requested to do so, it still has the responsibility for deciding any issues unilaterally referred to it under Sections 17 to 21 of the Employment Protection Act (disclosure of information provisions). The Office of Manpower Economics provides the secretariat for the Civil Service Arbitration Tribunal, but ACAS provides the secretariat for the Railway Staff National Tribunal, the Police Arbitration Tribunal and the Post Office Arbitration and Mediation Tribunal.

The question is sometimes asked whether the cause of arbitration in labour disputes in the UK would be better served if a single body were established with total responsibility for all arbitrations other than those set up privately.

The advantages are seen to be these:

- arbitrators could be appointed and would be seen to be appointed against a defined specification;
- the professionalism of arbitration would be enhanced;
- the collegiate approach would be strengthened;
- the confidence of potential users would be increased;

As a result more disputes would be referred to arbitration for settlement.

One way of giving effect to the idea would be to consolidate the provision and administration of all conciliation and arbitration under ACAS, including the CAC. Another would be to separate the conciliation from the arbitral (judicial) function by establishing two separate agencies – a conciliation service and an arbitration service.

But either approach would require changes to the law and a necessary prerequisite to that would be greater government commitment to arbitration as a means of dispute settlement – an unlikely development at the present time. For all its imperfections, therefore, the present system seems unlikely to change. Nevertheless, should a situation, for whatever reason, arise in which arbitration begins to play a more significant role, the case for a single, comprehensive arbitration service (either under ACAS control or not) would certainly be worthy of detailed consideration.

3 Mediation, Inquiry, Investigation and Review

Conciliation and arbitration are by far the most widely used processes of dispute resolution involving a third party. But there are others of which mediation, inquiry, investigation and review are the most significant.

ACAS, in its 1981 report, stated:

> Mediation is carried out by an independent person or on rare occasions by an *ad hoc* board. The mediator proceeds by way of conciliation but is given terms of reference agreed by the parties and is expected to make his own formal recommendations for resolution of a dispute; these may either be accepted as they stand or provide the basis for further negotiation between the parties. Mediation differs from arbitration in that it produces recommendations of a non-binding nature whereas a joint agreement to go to arbitration traditionally commits both sides to acceptance of the award.[1]

Mediation is thus a half-way house between conciliation and arbitration. As a process it has two special advantages. It provides:

- a basis for third-party involvement where it would be difficult to put the issues to arbitration in clear-cut or precise terms, for example, where the employer's attitude towards the size of a pay increase is heavily conditioned by the concessions on manning or flexibility which the union might be prepared to trade in return;
- a means of resolving a particularly difficult dispute in circumstances where one or both of the parties is unwilling to accept arbitration but public opinion is expecting an early solution.

Sometimes the technique is adopted of combining, by prior agreement, mediation and arbitration into a single process. Two such cases were summarised in ACAS's annual report for 1987. One case concerned the introduction of revised working patterns as a consequence of reorganising the BBC's film and videotape library. There were two crucial areas of disagreement – the proposed reduction in shift working, and the method of recruiting additional supervisors. In the words of the ACAS report, 'the person appointed . . . was able to secure agreement on nearly half the specific issues in dispute. An arbitration award resolved the residual differences'.[2]

The second dispute involved the National Theatre where again there were two distinct issues – one concerning the management's cost reduction proposals in three departments (cleaning services, production workshops and stage), and the other over touring activities. Again in the words of the ACAS report:

> the parties decided upon an all-embracing reference to mediation/arbitration which subsequently involved 18 meetings and three site visits. The mediator found that there were many unresolved points of detail, some of which were settled by agreement with his assistance and some which he determined by arbitration. The end product of this lengthy process was a series of revised agreements on working practices, re-written job specifications and amended pay structures and terms and conditions arrangements.[3]

The complex nature of these two problems will be noted.

Through the eye of an employer a procedure under which it is agreed that the mediator should, as a last resort, also become the arbitrator is preferable to an arrangement under which the processes of mediation and arbitration are separate. A mediator could hardly make formal recommendations for settling a dispute one day and then, assuming the role of an arbitrator a few days later, issue an award that was fundamentally different. A different arbitrator is under no such obligation.

Like conciliation, mediation is a flexible process. The mediator can, if he sees fit, assume a conciliator's role, working patiently with the parties separately or together; alternatively, he can act like an arbitrator by receiving the formal submissions and counter-arguments of the two sides. Whatever procedure is adopted, however, he ends up, in the continued absence of agreement, by making formal recommendations as a possible basis of settlement. ACAS officials do not themselves act as mediators. A mediator or a board of mediation is appointed by ACAS from lists of names held for this purpose.

Compared with conciliation or, indeed, arbitration, mediation is very sparingly used as Table 3.1 shows.

The mediation figure does not include one particular dispute which, in terms of duration and complexity, presented ACAS with one of its greatest challenges since the Service was established in 1974. This was the dispute involving primary and secondary school teachers

Table 3.1 Numbers of collective conciliations, arbitrations and mediations, 1978–88

	Number
Conciliations completed	18 185
Arbitration awards	2 469
Mediations completed	197

Sources: ACAS, *Annual Reports*, 1978–88.

in England and Wales which took place in 1985 and 1986. The cause of the dispute was a salary claim. The participants were the local authorities who employ the teachers, the six unions representing the teachers, who were at times the uneasiest of bedfellows, and the Department of Education and Science, whose interest in the outcome centred as much on finding solutions to a number of long-term problems, as the fact that it would be expected to pick up a substantial part of the tab for whatever salary increase might eventually be agreed. Added complexities were the fact that in the middle of the dispute the political balance of the employers' side switched from Conservative to Labour and that the Secretary of State exercised his statutory powers to change the numerical representation of some of the teaching unions on the negotiating body.

Although the dispute commenced in early 1985 it was to be another year before ACAS, despite repeated contacts with the parties, was able to set up a conciliation. This took place in January 1986, and it was clear that there were more fundamental issues involved than a straightforward salary claim. And so after four days of conciliation an agreement was reached between the employers and five teaching unions (by this time the National Union of Teachers had walked out of the talks) which disposed of the 1985 salary claim but under which the two sides committed themselves 'to negotiate "constructively and expeditiously" on the outstanding problems'. An independent and impartial panel would be appointed to:

> guide, advise and assist as a matter of urgency, the management and teachers to provisional agreements on the pay structure and career progression and any other related matters, e.g. conditions of service and procedures for negotiation, which either party may wish to bring forward for discussion and negotiation.[4]

The panel (a very experienced one) was not a board of mediation as such but its task involved elements of both conciliation and mediation. It commenced its work in March 1986 but sadly, some nine months later, despite the dedicated efforts of all concerned, including the National Union of Teachers which decided to return to the negotiations, the results were inconclusive. An agreement was certainly reached – but only with four of the six unions (two of which subsequently decided not to ratify it). Of equal significance was the decision of the Secretary of State not to provide the funding that would be necessary to meet the cost of the agreement. He took this decision because the agreement did not provide for the pay structure which he had proposed while the negotiations were in progress under the panel's auspices. He thereupon introduced legislation which gave effect to his own solution.

Inquiry and Investigation

Under the Conciliation Act of 1896 the Ministry of Labour was empowered to publish reports of inquiries into disputes. These powers were re-enforced by Part II of the Industrial Courts Act of 1919 which empowered the Minister 'to inquire into the causes and circumstances of any trade dispute whether reported to him or not, and, if he thinks fit, to appoint a court of inquiry to inquire into the matter and report to him'.[5] A court of inquiry is neither a conciliation nor an arbitration (any attempt to settle the dispute by conciliation will normally have been made before a court is set up).

> Courts of inquiry are primarily a means of informing Parliament and the public of the facts and underlying causes of a dispute. A court is appointed only as a last resort when no agreed settlement of a dispute seems possible, and when an unbiased and independent examination of the facts is considered to be in the public interest. It is obvious, therefore, that the power to set up a court of inquiry can only be used sparingly and it is reserved for matters of major importance affecting the public interest.[6]

A court of inquiry usually comprises a chairman and two side members. The process of inquiry consists of listening to the arguments and counter-arguments of all the interested parties and then submitting a report to the Secretary of State for Employment (previously the Minister of Labour). This normally includes non-binding recommendations as to how the dispute could be settled.

In other words, a court of inquiry discharges a highly visible mediation role.

Since the establishment of ACAS, and the consequential distancing of government from labour disputes, the number of government-appointed courts of inquiry has declined dramatically. Between 1946 and 1974 inclusive there were 64 such courts: since 1975 there have been only two, the most important of which was the inquiry headed by Lord Justice Scarman into the Grunwick dispute. The post-war hey-day of the court of inquiry was during the Labour Government's term of office between 1964 and 1970 when no fewer than 25 courts were set up – over a third of the post-war total.

It was during this period that government-appointed courts of inquiry became devalued as a means of settling disputes over pay and conditions of employment. They were not really set up to inform and enlighten public opinion about the causes and circumstances of particular disputes because by the time they were appointed the media had so crawled over the dispute that to anybody interested all the issues were widely known. They were set up by governments in the expectation that, however arbitrators might interpret the national or public interest, courts of inquiry would recognise that it required them to make whatever recommendations were necessary to settle the dispute. Indeed, in its evidence to the Donovan Commission, the Ministry of Labour freely admitted that the underlying purpose of appointing a court of inquiry 'has been generally to bring about a resumption of normal working (if this has been interrupted) and to enable a settlement to be reached'.[7] More often than not this required the employer to improve on any offer made during the preceding negotiations.

The post-war court of inquiry was a far cry from the 1920 court of inquiry at which Ernest Bevin, then assistant general secretary of the Dockers' Union, first burst upon the public stage. Bevin persuaded the dockers to refrain from striking over a pay claim for 16s. per day and, instead, to submit the issue to a court of inquiry set up under the new Industrial Courts Act. As the 'Dockers KC', Bevin won the case by the power of his advocacy. At one stage he actually produced for the court's examination several plates on which were set out the miserable scraps of food on which each docker would have to shift 71 tons of wheat a day if the court accepted as adequate the family budgets outlined by the employers and supported by the statistician, A. L. Bowley.

Perhaps in its evidence to the Donovan Commission in 1965 the

Engineering Employers' Federation was reflecting a wider disenchantment than just its own when it stated:

> The Federation's experience ... has not been altogether a happy one. There have been three occasions on which, failing a settlement on a national wages claim, the Minister of Labour ... intervened and set up a court of inquiry. In each case, a wage increase greater than that previously offered by the Federation was suggested ... These increases were recommended not so much because of the merits of the particular claim but because of a decision that an inflationary wage settlement, whatever its long-term disadvantages, was preferable to any other course of action ...[8]

In cases where the public interest was not regarded as involved to any important extent, the Minister of Labour was empowered by legislative authority derived from the Conciliation Act of 1896 and the Industrial Courts Act of 1919 to appoint a less formal inquiry such as a committee of investigation. These powers continue to exist to this day, but even before the arrival of ACAS they were relatively rarely used. The report of a committee, unlike that of a court of inquiry, was not laid before Parliament. Its recommendations, like those of a court, frequently led to a settlement of the dispute.

An interesting but relatively short-lived experiment in the court of inquiry field was introduced by Harold Wilson's Labour Government in 1965. In that year there were a number of major stoppages in the motor industry and, clearly concerned and irritated on both industrial and political grounds, Mr Wilson summoned the principal manufacturers and national officers of the trade unions concerned to a meeting at Downing Street. As a result, in November the Motor Industry Joint Labour Council was set up under the chairmanship of Mr (later Sir) Jack Scamp with the following terms of reference:

(a) to inquire into particular disputes leading to serious unofficial strikes or lockouts in breach of procedure;
(b) to review the state of industrial relations in individual firms;
(c) to keep the general state of relations in the industry under review and to examine matters of general significance for relations in the industry.[9]

To have obtained agreement to the establishment of the Council was no mean feat. The companies from which the employers' side of the council was drawn were in intense competition with each other;

two of them (Ford and Vauxhall) had US parents to whom the slightest whiff of openly-concerted policy-making was anathema; unlike the other six companies they were not members of the Engineering Employers' Federation; and all eight companies were concerned that the very act of introducing a procedure to deal quickly with unofficial strikes, far from reducing their number, would give them a new status and hence encourage other workers to similar action. This had certainly been the view of the TUC and the British Employers' Confederation (one of the founding employer organisations of the Confederation of British Industry) when the Ministry of Labour had earlier suggested a special procedure for dealing with unofficial strikes generally. It would give recognition to unofficial strike leaders who were sometimes in conflict with their own union officials, and it might actually encourage employees to strike so that their grievance would be handled more quickly under an inquiry procedure than through the normal machinery.

But, by all accounts, when Mr Wilson and his colleagues met the motor industry employers and the trade unions, they took a pretty hard line. Unless they took action to put their own house in order, they would have a system of compulsory arbitration imposed upon them. This was the background against which the industry's Joint Labour Council was formed.

Despite its terms of reference the Council found little time to deal with anything else but immediate disputes, even though three long-term problems were identified for examination (indiscipline and unofficial strikes, wage structure and training).

In a number of intractable disputes the Council was given the powers of a court inquiry appointed under the Industrial Courts Act of 1919. Thus the bizarre situation arose under which, if a dispute arose between, say, Ford and the TGWU, Jack Scamp's colleagues on the inquiry would be a management representative from a company in competition with Ford and a representative from a trade union that might or might not be an ally of the TGWU elsewhere in the motor industry. That the Council was able to chalk up any successes at all owed much to the qualities of Jack Scamp.

By 1969 the Council had been superseded by a voluntary body called the Motor Vehicle Industry Joint Council. Despite a few attempts to assist in finding solutions to the continuing problem of unofficial strikes, this Council gradually drifted into obscurity.

It was not until the 1970s that employers in the industry finally appreciated that each had to find the solutions to its own problems through its own determined efforts, by which time it was too late to save the Rootes Group, and almost too late to save British Leyland.

The statutory power to appoint courts of inquiry still exists but with the establishment of ACAS the responsibility to institute inquiries and investigations was substantially assumed by the Service. But between 1978 and 1987 inclusive, only four committees of inquiry were appointed by ACAS. One of these, although called a committee of inquiry, was, by its terms of reference, required to act as a board of arbitration in order to settle the national dispute in the water service in 1983.

But there is another form of inquiry that must be mentioned. Contained within Barbara Castle's ill-fated 1969 white paper, *In Place of Strife*, provision was made for the creation of the Commission on Industrial Relations (CIR). Amongst its tasks the CIR, acting on questions referred by the Secretary of State for Employment, was required to help 'bring about a general move towards reform and re-structuring of collective bargaining arrangements . . .'.[10] But the CIR could also be required, 'by reporting on references by the Secretary of State, to tackle other problems that are not now the direct responsibility of any public agency, so that its work will represent a novel extension of public involvement in industrial relations in this country.'[11] Once a reference had been received it would be up to the CIR to make its inquiries, but its report would be submitted to the Secretary of State, and any recommendations would be pursued by the Department of Employment's newly-created manpower and productivity service. (In 1974 this service was transferred to ACAS and formed the nucleus of its advisory service.)

In anticipation of legislation the Labour Government in 1969 used a royal warrant to establish the CIR on a voluntary basis. In its Industrial Relations Act of 1971 the Conservative Government placed the Commission on to a statutory footing with terms of reference under which the Secretary of State could refer 'any question relating to industrial relations generally or to industrial relations in any particular industry, or in any particular undertaking or part of an undertaking'.[12] But sadly for the CIR the trade unions' objections to other parts of the Act were so vehement that at a special meeting held in March 1971 the TUC and its affiliated unions withdrew their co-operation. The CIR continued its twilight existence until 1974 when it was abolished by the incoming Labour Government and some of its functions were transferred to the newly-created ACAS.

The Commission thus had a short life and it has to be said that while it lasted it made no lasting contribution to solving the country's industrial relations problems. Up to the time that the trade unions withdrew their co-operation, nine company references had been investigated and reported upon. In a valuable appraisal of the extent to which this type of third-party intervention could bring about a reform of industrial relations John Purcell[13] drew a pretty negative conclusion.

Perhaps the most useful lessons are that successful industrial relations reform requires the full-blooded but voluntary commitment of both sides, and that it is difficult to achieve if company and trade union shortcomings are publicly reported as a forerunner to actually tackling reform itself. ACAS undoubtedly learned some valuable lessons from the CIR's approach.

The advisory work which ACAS undertakes (they are not labelled inquiries) is only done with the full co-operation of both sides. Reports are private to the parties and, most important of all, the ACAS adviser who undertakes the investigative work (and thereby can build up the essential element of trust) is available subsequently to act as the catalyst to help drive through the changes that have been identified as necessary.

Review

On 2 November 1970 Mr Robert Carr (now Lord Carr of Hadley), Secretary of State for Employment in Mr Heath's Government, told the House of Commons that in the public sector 'there is a clear need for co-ordinated machinery for advising the government on the remuneration of certain groups for whom no negotiating machinery is, for one reason or another, appropriate'.[14] The government therefore intended:

> to establish at an early date three Review Bodies with a degree of interlocking membership. One will advise on the remuneration of the boards of nationalised industries, the judiciary, senior civil servants, senior officers of the Armed Forces and such other groups as might be appropriately considered with them. Another will advise on the pay of the Armed Forces generally. A third will advise on the remuneration of doctors and dentists in the National Health Service. These three Review Bodies will have at their disposal and working to their directions a secretariat provided by a new Office of Manpower Economics.[15]

Mr Carr added that the government also intended to use the new OME 'to service any *ad hoc* inquiries which are necessary from time to time to examine in depth particular pay structures and related problems'.[16]

Looking at the wording of Mr Carr's statement one would be entitled to assume that in setting up these three review bodies the government was breaking new ground. Far from it. Since 1962 the Kindersley committee had been advising previous governments on doctors' and dentists' salaries until it resigned in 1970 because the government of the day had declined to accept its recommendations in full; and the National Board for Prices and Incomes had been advising the government on the pay of the armed forces.

To a certain amount of cynicism Mr Carr assured the House of Commons that 'the recommendations of the bodies will be accepted by the Government unless there are clear and compelling reasons for not doing so'.[17]

In 1980 another Conservative government decided to remove the chairmen and members of the boards of nationalised industries from the scope of the Review Body on Top Salaries (TSRB) and in 1983 the same government decided in the wake of the 1981–2 national pay dispute in the NHS to establish a Review Body for Nursing Staff, Midwives, Health Visitors and Professions Allied to Medicine (NAPRB). Unlike those covered by the other three review bodies, staff within the scope of this new review body had previously been covered by collective bargaining arrangements.

Table 3.2 shows the review bodies in operation at September 1987, their scope, and the approximate numbers covered.

There is a degree of interlocking membership between the review bodies, and the fact that the Office of Manpower Economics (OME) provides the secretariat for them also ensures some consistency of approach. At Mrs Thatcher's request the reports of the review bodies are now submitted each year in time for decisions on them to be made and announced by mid-February at the latest. This arrangement has the advantage that the government's decisions are known well ahead of the commencement of the financial year to which they relate.

The procedures adopted by each review body are broadly similar. Each receives written evidence from the government and, where they exist, from representative bodies covering the groups within scope. Other interested bodies may also submit evidence, and it is the usual practice of each review body to hear oral evidence from some, if not all, of the parties who make written submissions. Additionally the

Table 3.2 Review bodies, scope and numbers covered (approx.), as at September 1987

Review Body on Top Salaries (TSRB)	
Higher judiciary and certain other judicial appointments; Senior civil servants; Senior officers in the armed forces	2 000
The TSRB also carries out regular reviews of the pay, allowances, expenses and pensions of Ministers and MPs and of the allowances for peers. A special sub-committee advises the full review body on matters concerning the judicial salary structure.	
Review Body on Armed Forces Pay (AFPRB)	
Personnel up to brigadier and equivalent rank	315 000
Review Body on Doctors' and Dentists' Remuneration (DDRB)	
Hospital doctors and dentists; General medical practitioners; General dental practitioners; Community doctors and dentists	115 000
Review Body for Nursing Staff, Midwives, Health Visitors and Professions Allied to Medicine (NAPRB)	
Nursing staff, midwives and health visitors	489 000
Physiotherapists, radiographers, remedial gymnasts, occupational therapists, orthoptists, chiropodists, dieticians and related grades	31 800
The NAPRB deals only with pay. The main conditions of service of those within scope are negotiated by new bodies which were set up after their Whitley Councils were abolished in 1983. Some conditions of service, for example, London weighting, are still negotiated in the General Whitley Council for Health Services.	

Sources: 1989 Reports of TSRB, DDRB and NAPRB: 1989 Statement of Defence Estimates.

review bodies may meet at first hand some of the groups within their scope, for example, the TSRB visits government departments and military establishments, the AFPRB discusses points of concern about pay and conditions of service with servicemen and servicewomen of all ranks, and the NAPRB undertakes a programme of visits each year to a few health districts. This enables members of the NAPRB to increase their understanding of the work of the staff within their scope, and gives staff a chance to raise informally matters relating to their pay.

Given the antagonism of Mrs Thatcher's government to the concept of pay comparability, it is interesting to note that among its tasks the OME undertakes certain comparability studies. For the TSRB, for example, surveys of remuneration in the private sector at levels of responsibility broadly corresponding to those within the scope of the review body are carried out. And in connection with the new pay agreements in the Civil Service, the Treasury and certain unions, from time to time, require information from the OME on pay movements and levels in the private sector.

Whatever the wish of any government, the plain fact of the matter is that comparability between the pay and conditions of one group and those of other groups will never cease to be made. Such comparisons are the very 'bread and butter' of collective bargaining and pay review bodies will never be able to avoid them either. What has to be accepted is that pay comparison is but one argument and not as was once the case in the Civil Service the only argument worthy of consideration in judging the case for increases in pay.

In addition to the four review bodies whose work has already been summarised, there exists the Pharmacists' Review Panel (PRP). This is an independent body set up in 1981 with a remit to consider matters affecting retail pharmacists' remuneration and to help resolve disputes. The members of the panel, unlike the other review bodies, represent particular professional specialisms (the law, accountancy, industrial relations, retail commerce and economics). Between 1981 and the end of 1988 there had been only five references. The PRP sends its recommendations to the Department of Health and to the pharmaceutical profession but, unlike the other four review bodies, its reports are not published.

We have already noted earlier in this chapter the decision taken in 1986 by the Secretary of State for Education and Science to abolish the Burnham committee as the forum for negotiating the pay of teachers in English and Welsh primary and secondary schools, and to replace it by the interim advisory committee on school teachers' pay and conditions. Under the Teachers' Pay and Conditions Act of 1987 the Education Secretary is empowered to impose constraints within which this committee is obliged to work. On the occasion of its first remit the committee was told that the government did not intend to make major changes to the pay structure or to provisions relating to teachers' duties and working time. The committee was also told that its recommendations must not cost more than an additional £300m in the 1988–9 financial year or in later years. Thus, it seems that the teachers' committee, for as long as it remains in existence, will be much more constrained than the conventional review bodies as to the recommendations it makes, in this instance not to the Prime Minister but to the Education Secretary.

Public opinion will expect any trade union whose members come within the scope of a review body to use the strike weapon sparingly even if they are not prepared to renounce it altogether. Particularly this would be the case if a recommendation of the review body were approved by the government of the day without amendment. But as the 1988 fracas over the grading of nursing staff in the NHS showed, industrial action is not necessarily a thing of the past even if a review body, in this case the NAPRB, does exist, and even if its recommendations are approved by the government. In fairness, however, it has to be added that the cause of the action in this instance was not the levels of pay recommended by the NAPRB but the way in which the regrading of staff was carried out on the basis of a new structure that had already been negotiated directly by the NHS and the nursing unions.

For those covered by review bodies the crux of the matter is whether they have fared better in recent years than those covered by the process of collective bargaining. The answer is probably 'yes', if only for the reason that those covered by the review bodies are highly-skilled professionals whose differentials, particularly in the years of statutory pay policies, had become compressed and were seen to be in need of expansion. This is a factor that the school teachers would be advised to consider in considering whether a pay review body would serve them better than a return to collective bargaining. Certainly during the Thatcher years most of the recommendations of the four review bodies have been accepted by the government, although on a number of occasions their staged implementation was required.

But review bodies operate under two disadvantages:

- their members are likely to be seen as placemen (and women) of the government of the day whose independence, for this reason, and however unfairly, is likely to be suspect;
- their recommendations can be subject to political veto or adjustment, not by parliament, but by prime ministerial dictat.

It was interesting to note that, while the NAPRB was still carrying out its 1988 review to determine what recommended pay levels should be attached to the new pay structure for nurses, there were political demands that the government should commit itself in advance to meeting the cost of whatever was recommended. If the government had agreed this would have meant that the review procedure would have become, in all but name, arbitration. Not surprisingly, Mrs Thatcher's government refused.

If the world were a more rational place there would be much to be said for having a single system of pay determination which covered all employees in the non-trading part of the public sector in a comprehensive and consistent manner. There are only three such systems – collective bargaining (followed, perhaps, by arbitration), indexation and the process of review. In this country we have managed to create a situation in which we have a bit of all three. To extend the review body system to everybody would require the police and the firemen to give up their indexation, civil servants, ambulance staff and other parts of the NHS to give up collective bargaining, and the school teachers to sacrifice their ambition for a return to that process. Government, too, would have to accept that no-strike commitments have to be earned, and that employees and their unions are unlikely to change their attitude to the use of the strike weapon until they are confident that a new system produces results that they perceive to be more fair and equitable.

None of which is likely to happen in the short term.

4 Individual Conciliation

We may not all know precisely what they are but each and every one of us in civil employment enjoys a number of rights. Some of these rights may derive from terms which we have personally agreed with our employer or which have been negotiated through collective bargaining carried out by a trade union acting on our behalf; some rights derive from the common law; others are statutory employment rights laid down in various Acts of Parliament. If we think that our employer is failing to observe one of our employment rights we can seek redress in one of a number of ways, for example, through the grievance procedure which should be available to us or to our trade union; through the county or sheriff courts; and in the case of most breaches of our statutory employment rights, to bodies called industrial tribunals.

It is to the resolution of cases that are alleged to or might involve a breach of statutory employment rights that we now turn our attention.

Development of Statutory Employment Rights

During the past 20 years the number of these rights has increased considerably. A large part of this increase took place after a Labour Government took office in 1974. Many provisions of the Employment Protection Act of 1975 (the same Act that put ACAS on to a statutory footing) were characterised by its critics as the rewards which the trade unions felt to be their due for having assisted the political cause of the Labour Party to such good effect. They can also be seen as the trade-off for pay restraint under the Labour Government's social contract. But other legislation, for example, in the field of sex and racial discrimination, was enacted to meet what were perceived to be the social needs of the age.

When the Conservative Party returned to power in 1979, major features of the new government's policy were the reform of industrial relations and trade unions and the deregulation of the employment market. A number of measures were taken to achieve the latter, including the removal of some established employment rights and the modification of others. The pay provisions of Schedule 11 of the 1975 Act, for example, were totally repealed; and the very important employment right concerning unfair dismissal was modified by lengthening the service qualification before a worker was entitled to lay a complaint of unfair dismissal against his employer. A number of new provisions were also enacted, mainly but not wholly in the field of trade union membership.

Today statutory employment rights basically take one of three forms, namely, rights owed by the employer to his employees either individually or collectively; rights owed by the trade union to its members; and rights owed by the employer to a trade union.

Table 4.1 summarises the industrial tribunal jurisdictions divided between those for which ACAS has the responsibility for trying to dispose of an employee's claim without the need for a reference to a tribunal, and those in respect of which there may be a direct reference to a tribunal, without any prior ACAS involvement.

Although the number of jurisdictions is high, Table 4.2 shows that the overwhelming proportion of cases received year in, year out, by ACAS is concerned with cases of unfair dismissal.

Some Typical Cases

But details of the jurisdictions and the number of complaints received each year are but cold facts and figures. What about the strength of the actual complaints? How fair was it, for example, that the worker who was caught asleep on the nightshift should have been dismissed? 'I know that other workers previously caught like me have received nothing more than a warning!'

And what about the office secretary who for years has felt that the work she does in the office is under-valued by her employer?:

> I had to be trained before I could apply for the job and I have to keep on updating my skills. The production workers are all members of a union but, unlike me, they receive little or no training; they don't have to use much by way of initiative or judgement. I think my work is of equal value to theirs but I'm paid much less.

And what about the worker who recently applied for a vacant supervisor's job?:

> I am well-qualified and I have worked here for ten years and neither my work or my conduct has ever been questioned. With the training that is given here I'm sure I could do the job. I think the management turned me down because I'm black.

Table 4.1 Summary of industrial tribunal jurisdictions, as at December 1988

(a) in which ACAS has an individual conciliation responsibility

Equal Pay Act 1970
- Equal pay

Employment Protection Act, 1975
- Consultation with trade union on redundancy
- Non-payment of protective award

Sex Discrimination Act, 1975
- Discrimination on grounds of sex or marriage in the employment field

Race Relations Act, 1976
- Race discrimination in the employment field

Employment Protection (Consolidation) Act, 1978
- Itemised pay statement
- Guarantee payments
- Suspension from work on medical grounds
- Trade union membership and activities
- Time off for trade trade union duties
- Time off for trade union activities
- Time off for public duties
- Time off to look for work or make training arrangements
- Time off for ante-natal care
- Return to work after pregnancy
- Written statement of reason for dismissal
- Unfair dismissal

Employment Act, 1980
- Unreasonable exclusion or expulsion from trade union

Transfer of Undertakings (Protection of Employment) Regulations, 1981
- Failure to inform or consult trade union on transfer
- Non-payment of compensation

Wages Act, 1986
- Unlawful deduction from wages and payment by workers to their employers

Employment Act, 1988
- Union members unjustifiably disciplined by their unions
- Continued deduction of union dues after termination of union membership

(b) in which ACAS has no individual conciliation responsibility

Sex Discrimination Act, 1975 and *Race Relations Act 1976*
- Discriminatory advertisements
- Instructions to discriminate
- Pressure to discriminate

Employment Protection (Consolidation) Act, 1978
- Written particulars of the terms of employment
- Redundancy payment
- Rights in the event of insolvency
- Interim relief for employee claiming unfair dismissal on grounds of union membership/non-membership or union activities

Safety Representatives and Safety Committee Regulations 1977
- Time off with pay for safety representatives

Table 4.2 Jurisdictional analysis of industrial tribunal applications received by ACAS, 1982–8 (% of total)

	Year						
Jurisdiction	*1982*	*1983*	*1984*	*1985*	*1986*	*1987*	*1988*
Unfair dismissal	88.1	86.4	86.6	89.2	87.9	84.7	81.8
Equal pay	1.8	3.1	0.9	1.2	3.3	4.8	1.2
Sex discrimination	1.1	0.9	0.9	1.2	1.2	1.6	2.3
Race relations	1.1	1.2	1.5	1.6	1.3	1.8	2.0
Others	7.9	8.4	10.1	6.8	6.3	7.1	12.7

Source: ACAS, *Annual Reports*, 1982–8

Any breach of any employment right is understandably a matter of individual concern, but because cases involving unfair dismissal, equal pay and discrimination in employment account for nearly 90 per cent of all complaints, it is on these that the remainder of this chapter largely concentrates.

The Development of Law – Unfair Dismissal

During the 1960s Great Britain can be seen in retrospect to have been moving inexorably towards statutory provisions under which employees who felt themselves to have been unfairly dismissed would have some right of external appeal. Whatever their record, the procedures agreed between employers, their associations and trade unions were increasingly regarded as insufficient. Trade unions at times pointed to the unfairness of a system which not only allowed the employer to take the decision to dismiss but also put him in the position of 'judge and jury' when the appeal was heard. But at times they themselves were not averse to using their muscle to seek the re-employment of a member (perhaps a shop steward) who they thought had been wrongly dismissed or 'victimised' for his union activities. A further inadequacy of the system lay in the fact that workers who were not members of a trade union had even less means of redress.

In 1964 the government of the day announced that subject to certain reservations, it accepted a Recommendation of the International Labour Conference of 1963, the underlying principle of which was that 'termination of employment should not take place unless there is a valid reason ... connected with the capacity or conduct of the worker or based on the operational requirements of the undertaking, establishment or service'.[1] In 1967 a committee of the National Joint Advisory Council to the Minister of Labour (a long-defunct tripartite body), reporting on dismissals procedures, did not go so far as to recommend the introduction of statutory machinery but did nevertheless outline a possible approach that had some similarities to the one that was eventually introduced.

In 1968 a majority of the Donovan Commission recommended early legislation 'to establish statutory machinery to safeguard employees against unfair dismissal'.[2] The recommendations were picked up by the Labour Government in 1969 in its ill-fated white paper, *In Place of Strife*. Although as a result of passionate trade union resistance a number of the proposals of that white paper were eventually dropped, the Labour Government tabled an industrial relations bill in 1970 which, amongst other things, would have provided for statutory protection against unfair dismissal. This bill never became law but it is an indication of the extent to which protection of this kind had by now become politically non-controversial that, when the Labour administration of Harold Wilson was replaced by Edward Heath's Conservative administration, the latter's Industrial Relations Act of 1971 contained provisions for protection against unfair dismissal which were not dissimilar to those contained in the 1970 bill.

With the return of a Labour Government in 1974, the Industrial Relations Act was repealed but on the strong representation of the trade unions, the unfair dismissal provisions of that Act were salvaged and, with some changes were incorporated into the Trade Union and Labour Relations Acts 1974–6 and the Employment Protection Act of 1975.

The basic law on unfair dismissal is now contained in the Employment Protection (Consolidation) Act of 1978, as amended by the Employment Acts of 1980, 1982 and 1988. Section 54 of the 1978 Act is the key provision and states that 'every worker shall have the right not to be unfairly dismissed by his employer'. This general provision does, however, have a number of qualifications of which, perhaps, the most important relates to length of service with the employer. The law, as amended by a statutory order in 1985, now provides that, before the statutory protection applies, a worker must have had two years' continuous service with his employer. In the case of dismissal on grounds of sex, racial discrimination, trade union membership or activities, or non-membership of a trade union, no qualifying period of service is required. A complaint of unfair dismissal must be made either during the period of notice or within three months of the dismissal.

Perhaps the most widely-publicised delinquent in respect of late application was Derek ('Red Robbo') Robinson, the Longbridge convenor of shop stewards who had been dismissed in November 1980 following his refusal to withdraw his name from a pamphlet which pledged opposition to the British Leyland recovery plan despite an overwhelming vote of support for the plan from the work-force. Mr Robinson did not lodge a complaint, presumably acting (or, more accurately, failing to act) on the assumption that a strike could be called and successfully prosecuted. In other words, his reinstatement by British Leyland could be secured by industrial action so there would be no need to resort to a tribunal at all. When this tactic failed Mr Robinson invoked that part of Section 67 (2) of the Employment Protection (Consolidation) Act which allows a tribunal to extend the three months' period 'if it is satisfied that it was not reasonably practicable for the complaint to be presented before the end of the period of three months'. Not surprisingly, Mr Robinson's application was refused.

Another significant exclusion related to the position of employees who were either locked out or on strike.

The 1971 Industrial Relations Act of Mr Heath's Conservative administration laid down that the dismissal of an employee by way of a lock-out was not to be regarded as unfair if the employee was offered re-engagement when work was resumed. Similarly, if an employee was dismissed for taking part in a strike or other industrial action, the dismissal was not to be regarded as unfair unless other employees involved in the strike were not dismissed or other employees who were dismissed were offered re-engagement at the end of the dispute.

When the 1971 Act was repealed and ammended, unfair dismissal provisions were incorporated into the Employment Protection (Consolidation) Act of 1978, and the same principles were maintained but industrial tribunals were debarred from considering any other claims of unfair dismissal in the context of strikes or lock-outs. Under Section 9 of the Employment Act of 1982 the employer was permitted to exercise some selectivity without running the risk of complaints of unfair dismissal on the part of those not re-employed. (In late-1989 the Conservative government announced its intention of withdrawing all protection from those involved in unofficial industrial action.)

It is interesting to speculate why a Labour government that was under such strong trade union influence should have decided to bar the industrial tribunals in the way it did. It can only be assumed that the unions preferred to keep the law out of industrial disputes. They didn't want the courts to use individual cases as the pretext for examining the substance of a dispute and deciding on its reasonableness. Given their strength at the time, they much preferred the use of industrial muscle should any employer be foolhardly enough to take what was then the very exceptional course of dismissing his employees during the course of an industrial dispute.

Their inability to secure the re-employment of the print workers dismissed by News International in 1986 (by which time the trade union movement was much weaker) brought about a change of heart and perhaps, for the first time, made unions aware of the legal position. In a joint document (*People at Work: New Rights, New Responsibilities*) agreed before the 1986 general election, the TUC and Labour Party foreshadowed 'strengthening individual workers' legal rights in respect of dismissal for taking industrial action'. In its 1989 Policy Review for the 1990s (*Meet the Challenge, Make the Change*) the Labour Party elaborated by stating: 'Workers will no longer be sacked for taking legitimate industrial action . . . both the employer's and the employee's contractual duties will be suspended for the duration of any industrial action.' Dismissal would be unlawful.

By law, some reasons for dismissal (race, sex, married status, pregnancy and selection for redundancy in breach of custom or agreed procedure) are automatically unfair. So too is dismissal for reasons of trade union membership, trade union activities and non-membership of a trade union. Other reasons (for example, capability, conduct and redundancy) are potentially unfair. From time to time the law is changed and as precedents are handed down it becomes increasingly complex. It is one of the conciliator's responsibilities to keep abreast of all these changes so that he can give up-to-date and accurate advice both as to the provisions of the statutes and their likely interpretation.

The Law on Equal Pay

The disparity in pay between the sexes has for long been a controversial issue. For generations employers and trade unions involved in the collective bargaining process deliberately distinguished between men's work and women's work and differentiations in pay were invariably agreed to the disadvantage of the women. The industries and services in which the principle of equal pay for equal work applied were very much the exception.

It will for ever be a matter for speculation as to whether much progress would have been made in the equal pay field if the United Kingdom had decided not to enter the European Community. Employers have always been (and indeed, still are) quick to argue the economic cost of moves towards equal pay, and despite a TUC resolution dating back to 1888 in favour of the principle of equal pay and much subsequent lip service paid to the women's cause, the priorities of the trade union movement have all too often lain elsewhere. Mary Redmond has drawn attention to the importance of European law and has commented that the 'influence of EC law on sex discrimination in employment and equal pay is increasing, affording rights more extensive than national law'.[3]

Article 119 of the Treaty of Rome which is binding on the UK, lays down the principle of equal pay for equal work and an EC directive on equal pay issued in 1975 amplified this to mean 'for the same work or for work to which equal value is attributed, . . . the elimination of all discrimination on grounds of sex with regard to all aspects and conditions of remuneration'.[4]

The British statute, the Equal Pay Act, dates from 1970, but did not come into full effect until 1976. In summary the Act established the right of a woman to equal treatment in respect not just of pay, but all the terms of her contract of employment when she was employed on work of the same nature as, or which was broadly similar to, that of a man, or work established under a job evaluation study, and there was no material difference other than the difference of sex between her case and his. A woman could only draw a comparison with the job of a man employed by the same employer or associated employer. The Act also gave the same right to a man *vis-à-vis* work done by a woman.

The means of enforcing the Act were to be as follows:

- the Secretary of State for Employment could refer a question to an industrial tribunal where, in the words of Section 2 (2) of the Act, it was 'not reasonable to expect the parties to take steps to determine the question';
- individual complaints could be referred to an industrial tribunal;

- the Central Arbitration Committee was empowered to remove discrimination in collective agreements, employers' pay structures and statutory wage orders which contained any provisions applying specifically to men only or to women only.

The maximum amount that a successful claimant could receive from an industrial tribunal was two years' back pay and any claimant had to have been employed in the employment concerned within six months preceding the date of the reference to the tribunal.

In practice, the first option (action by the Secretary of State) has not been used. The third option empowered the CAC:

> to declare such amendments, if any, as need to be made in the agreement to extend to both men and women provisions applying specifically to men only or to women only; and to eliminate any resulting duplication in the agreement in such a way as not to make the terms and conditions agreed for men, or those agreed for women, less favourable in any respect than they would have been without the amendments.[5]

In its 1977 report the CAC stated that once discrimination was seen to exist (not always an easy task), it had found the informal approach and its determination to use the goodwill of the parties to achieve a sound solution to be invaluable. Joint job evaluation was very often found an essential prerequisite to settlement. The Committee then went on to question the view that under the Equal Pay Act it was only those rates that were 'female only' that must be raised to the lowest male rate irrespective of job content:

> This is a view which is hard to reconcile with the concept of equality and leads to the extinction of differentials which may still be necessary if a grading structure showing the relative assessment of jobs free from discrimination based on sex is to be maintained.[6]

In other words the Committee had been 'willing to carry out a general wages review, determining pay rates of grades resulting from a job evaluation where the parties disagreed on such rates'.[7]

Unfortunately for the CAC its approach was blunted as a result of R. v. CAC *ex parte* Hy-Mac Ltd. In October 1979 it was held on appeal by the Divisional Court that in amending an agreement which did not contain a provision referring specifically to men only or to women only, the CAC had acted beyond its statutory powers. The

CAC, in other words, should not have carried out a general wages review. It was hardly surprising that in its 1979 report the CAC stated that it appeared 'that the usefulness of the provisions upon which the Committee's jurisdiction is based is nearly over'.[8] In that year the CAC had received only 2 equal pay cases compared with a peak of 35 cases received in 1976. The powers of the CAC in this area were removed by the 1986 Sex Discrimination Act.

This left the second and possibly more tortuous option of references of individual complaints through the industrial tribunal procedure, including ACAS conciliation.

Unfortunately the UK statute enacted in 1970 did not reflect the equal value requirement of the subsequent (1975) directive of the European Commission and in 1979 the Commission raised the issue with the UK government. Eventually the European Court of Justice agreed with the Commission that the UK was in breach of the EC directive because women in the UK were not entitled to equal pay for work of equal value unless their employer had chosen to undertake a job evaluation study.

This clearly put the UK government on the spot and with no great show of enthusiasm the decision was taken to introduce regulations which as from 1 January 1984 allowed claims for equal pay to be made on the basis of equal value. A woman's job could now be compared with a man's job (or vice versa) even though the jobs were quite dissimilar. Unfortunately, but perhaps understandably, although the statute referred to demands, for instance, under such headings as effort, skill and decision (which indicated the need for factor-based, analytical job evaluation), little or no other guidance was given as to what might constitute work of equal value.

The Law on Sex and Race Discrimination

The basic laws relating to discrimination on grounds of sex and race were enacted at about the same time and are structured similarly. The Sex Discrimination Act was passed in 1975 and applies to discrimination on the basis of both sex and marital status. The Race Relations Act was passed in 1976. The Acts outlaw both direct and indirect discrimination. Direct discrimination occurs when an employee is treated less favourably than a person of the opposite sex or of another racial group. Indirect discrimination takes place against a woman in circumstances where somebody applies an apparently equal requirement or condition to men and women but which is such (so states Section 1 (1)(b) of the Sex Discrimination Act):

> (i) that the proportion of women who can comply with it is considerably smaller than the proportion of men who can comply with it, and (ii) which he cannot show to be justifiable irrespective of the sex of the person to whom it is applied, and (iii) which is to her detriment because she cannot comply with it.

Section 1 (1)(b) of the Race Relations Act refers to racial groups instead of women and an employer has to demonstrate that the requirement or condition is 'justifiable irrespective of the colour, race, nationality or ethnic or national origins of the person to whom it is applied'. Arguably, it is harder to prove indirect than direct discrimination.

The scope of the Acts is such as to outlaw discrimination on the grounds of sex or race against applicants in selection arrangements and job offers and against those employed in access to promotion, transfer or training or as regards other benefits, facilities or services, and by dismissal or subjection to any other detriment. The Acts place the primary liability on the employer, but the burden of proof of discrimination lies on the claimant.

Under both Acts the entitlement to seek a remedy to alleged unlawful discrimination rests with the individual. Both the Equal Opportunities Commission and the Commission on Racial Equality may assist a complainant by way of advice or representation. Failing a prior settlement in conciliation (in cases where conciliation is provided for), complaints, unless withdrawn, are determined by an industrial tribunal.

The tribunal remedies for proven discrimination are to make an award declaring the rights of the parties, to award compensation, or to recommend that within a specified period of time the respondent takes action for the purpose of obviating or reducing the adverse effect on the complainant of the act of discrimination. The amount of compensation awarded must not exceed the maximum compensatory award applicable in cases of unfair dismissal.

Conciliation – the Prelimimary Stage

As already noted, complaints of breaches of statutory employment rights do not all go directly to an industrial tribunal. For the vast majority of cases there is provision for a conciliation stage. The Donovan Commission in its report envisaged that the tribunal itself would fill this role but it was, in fact, Department of Employment officials and subsequently ACAS conciliation officers who were charged with the task of trying to bring about a conciliated settlement between employer and employee so as to obviate the need for a reference to a tribunal other than for the formal recording of any settlement that might have been reached in the conciliation process.

But that is not all. ACAS also has the responsibility for dealing with certain kinds of case where no formal complaint has been made to a tribunal but where the potential for such a complaint exists. These cases are almost exclusively brought to the attention of ACAS by employers who are about to dismiss one or more of their employees, but who wish to do so on agreed terms which will preclude any subsequent tribunal complaint. ACAS describes these as 'non-ITI cases' thereby distinguishing them from cases in which a formal complaint has been made. The latter are classified as 'ITI cases' (so called because of the reference number of the statutory form on which the written complaint is made).

In recent years individual conciliation, as it is called by ACAS, in both ITI and non-ITI cases has represented about 50 per cent of the Service's total operational workload. This compares with a figure of about 8 per cent for the much more widely-known collective conciliation role. The individual conciliation process acts as an invaluable and cost-effective filter. It not only eliminates those cases that with ACAS assistance, can be settled between employer and employee; it also removes those in which the employee decides for one reason or another to withdraw the complaint (perhaps because of a belated appreciation, based on ACAS advice, either that the legal grounds for the complaint are not as strong as he once thought, or that he is unlikely to win at a tribunal hearing).

The filter thus saves the time and expense of a tribunal hearing. And whereas a tribunal hearing and its decision are public property – a feature not invariably welcome to the parties – the conciliation process is private and confidential. It is a successful filter as well. Table 4.3 shows the number of cases in all jurisdictions (ITI and non-ITI combined) that were received and disposed of by ACAS during the years 1982 to 1988 inclusive.

Year on year comparisons based on the figures in Table 4.3 must be made with care. Over the period new jurisdictions were introduced, the length of the quaifying period of employment (for example, in

Table 4.3 Individual conciliation cases received and dealt with in all jurisdictions, 1982–8

Number of Cases	*1982*	*1983*	*1984*	*1985*	*1986*	*1987*	*1988*
Received	46 996	42 943	42 723	42 887	51 431	40 817	44 443
Settled by ACAS	17 211	16 617	17 375	19 283	25 288	26 094	25 654
Settled privately	1 477	1 432	1 364	*	*	*	*
Withdrawn	12 253	10 588	10 047	9 832	11 198	8 266	8 220
To industrial tribunal	14 911	14 323	12 454	10 682	12 928	9 664	8 297
Total completed	45 852	42 960	41 240	39 797	49 414	44 024	42 171
Cases settled or withdrawn as percentage of cases completed	67.5	66.7	69.8	73.2	73.8	78.0	80.3

Note:
Since 1985 the cases settled privately have been combined with cases withdrawn.
Source: ACAS, *Annual Reports*, 1982–8

relation to complaints of unfair dismissal) was changed, and the ratio of ITI cases to non-ITI cases each year varied (as will be shown later almost all of the latter are settled without the need to refer them to a tribunal for hearing). Nevertheless, the proportion of all cases that are disposed of either by settlement or withdrawal is consistently high.

Development of Industrial Tribunals

The industrial tribunal system started in 1964 from very modest beginnings. It was in that year that the Industrial Training Act was passed and industrial tribunals were established to adjudicate on disputes arising out of levies imposed on employers by the newly-created industrial training boards.

A significant change in the role of the tribunals took place a year later. The 1965 Redundancy Payments Act made general provision for redundant employees to receive a lump sum payment by way of compensation. For the first time tribunals could be called upon to adjudicate not on disputes between the individual and the state (or one of its agencies) but on those between employer and employees. Another significant change took place under the Employment

Act of 1980 when tribunals were required to adjudicate in disputes between union member (or ex-member) and his union.

The advantages of tribunals over conventional courts were stated in the 1957 report of the Franks Committee on Administrative Tribunals and Enquiries to be 'cheapness, accessibility, freedom from technicality, expedition and expert knowledge'.

If any one single body can be held responsible for the extension of the industrial tribunal system it is the Ministry of Labour (now the Department of Employment). In its evidence to the Donovan Commission the Ministry invited the Commission 'to consider whether the jurisdiction of the existing industrial tribunals should be enlarged so as to comprise all disputes between the individual worker and his employer'.[9] The Commission concluded that subject to certain limitations, this should be done. The Commission thought it:

> desirable that provision should be made by statute so as to improve the present machinery for the judicial determination of disputes between employers and employees arising from and in connection with contracts of employment and statutory claims arising between employers and employees.[10]

In the event, however, the areas of tribunal jurisdiction were not widened to the extent recommended by Lord Donovan and his colleagues. They were restricted to dealing with complaints arising from alleged breaches of statutory employment rights. Nevertheless the scope of this activity is now considerable.

Any appeal on a question of law arising from an industrial tribunal decision is made initially to the Employment Appeal Tribunal set up under the 1975 Employment Protection Act. Cases may subsequently be referred to the Court of Appeal (Court of Session in Scotland) and the House of Lords.

Bringing Conciliation into Play

How then does the worker who thinks he was unfairly dismissed, the office secretary who thinks she should be paid the same as men and the black worker who thinks he is being discriminated against go about getting their grievances examined? The answer is that they get hold of a copy of form ITI (for example, from a local Job Centre), fill it in and send it off to the Central Office of the Industrial Tribunals (COIT) in London if he or she is employed in England or Wales or to

COIT (Scotland) in Glasgow if he or she works in Scotland. After the form has been checked to ensure that the applicant appears qualified to bring the claim, a copy of it is sent to the employer and the appropriate regional office of ACAS.

The Conciliation Objective

Under Section 2 (4) of the Employment Protection Act of 1975 ACAS is required 'to designate officers of the Service to perform the functions of conciliation officers . . .'. It is to one of these officers that each case received from COIT or COIT (Scotland) is allocated. Section 133 (2) of the 1978 Employment Protection (Consolidation) Act states:

> Where a complaint has been presented to an industrial tribunal, and a copy of it has been sent to a conciliation officer, it shall be the duty of the conciliation officer –
> (a) if he is requested to do so by the complainant and by the person against whom the claim is presented, or
> (b) if, in the absence of any such request, the conciliation officer considers that he could act under this subsection with a reasonable prospect of success,
>
> to endeavour to promote a settlement of the complaint without its being determined by an industrial tribunal.

Similar provisions relating to unfair dismissal complaints are contained in Section 134 (1) of the 1978 Act.

Such is the overriding statutory duty of ACAS – 'to endeavour to promote a settlement of the complaint without its being determined by an industrial tribunal' – and it is this provision which brings conciliation (or 'the invisible stage in the industrial tribunal system'[11] as it has been called) into play. As a matter of practice where a request for conciliation has not been received from both parties, ACAS normally acts on the assumption that there is a 'reasonable prospect of success'. The Service therefore tries to conciliate in all cases.

The objective of conciliation is to bring about a settlement between two parties who are in dispute. It must never be forgotten that once both sides have agreed to a settlement under ACAS, any right of subsequent access to an industrial tribunal is lost. ACAS must never forget, too, that as its individual conciliation duties are imposed by law, any failure by a conciliation officer properly to discharge these duties exposes the Service to the risk of action in the civil court. Of equal importance is the fact that unless a conciliation officer acts in accordance with the statutory duty, a conciliated settlement is not generally binding.

Before proceeding to try and conciliate, the conciliation officer will wish to confirm not just that the complaint is of a kind in which ACAS actually has a statutory duty to conciliate, but that if there are internal grievances or appeals procedures within the organisation that have not been fully used, the parties are first encouraged to use them.

The Responsibility of the Conciliation Officer

In general, there seems to be little misunderstanding among employers and trade unions as to the ACAS role in collective disputes. The ACAS conciliator is not normally expected or asked to make known to the parties his judgement as to whether a particular claim is just or a particular response is reasonable. Mistakenly, however, in an individual case involving an alleged breach of a statutory employment right, the conciliator is sometimes asked to pronounce to one party or the other on the merits of the complaint. If he declines to act as a judge he may stand accused of being less than helpful or, worse, his silence is interpreted as favouring one party at the expense of the other.

The employee probably feels more strongly about this than the employer. To both sides the provisions of the law and the procedures that have to be followed may be something of a mystery, but the employee often feels more disadvantaged because he lacks the same resources as the employer to obtain experienced advice and assistance. He feels that both knowledge of the legal process and the skills of advocacy are far from equal and so expects the ACAS conciliator to be much more positive and judicial than in fact he is allowed to be.

In the words of ACAS itself:

> the duty to seek to promote a settlement without its being heard by an industrial tribunal has to be seen in the context of a complainant's right to take a case to an industrial tribunal. A judgement on the merits of the case is for an industrial tribunal, not for ACAS, and the Service must never therefore take sides, or act as a representative of one side or the other, or apply pressure for a settlement against the will of the parties.[12]

Who are the Conciliators?

Individual conciliation is carried out by full-time members of the ACAS staff classified by the Service as industrial relations officers (the Civil Service grade is that of higher executive officer). Typically within ACAS (there are limited exceptions) the work of a number of industrial relations officers is managed and controlled by a senior industrial relations officer (a controller).

Individual conciliation is usually the first operational work performed by new recruits; they may subsequently move on to advisory work or collective conciliation. The general practice is to recruit from within the Civil Service, normally from the DE group, from such areas as the Employment Service and the Unemployment Benefit Service.

Although much of the training is gained 'on the job' under the close supervision of one of the controllers, there is some formal 'off the job' training. A six-week induction training course is carried out within each of the ACAS regions and a reinforcement course is later carried out centrally.

The length of time that industrial relations officers carry out individual conciliation varies considerably. Some may move after two or three years but many remain in the job for ten years or more. Supplementary training includes not just occasional seminars on new legislation but refresher courses of a more general kind as well. Special training in the handling of discrimination cases is given to officers selected specifically to handle these kinds of case but all conciliation officers are made aware during their training of the sensitive nature of these cases.

During the 1970s and 1980s there was a big increase in the number of jurisdictions involving conciliation by ACAS. From time to time important precedents are laid down by the Employment Appeal Tribunal, the Court of Appeal (Court of Session in Scotland), or the House of Lords. New codes of practice may be published. All of this means that ACAS has a major responsibility in keeping its conciliation officers up to date with all that is happening. The staff themselves have to absorb and apply these changes as and when they occur.

Each individual conciliator probably carries out something like 300 cases a year. Perhaps the greatest challenge he faces is never to give the impression that he is engaged on a repetitive and mechanistic task. To him one dismissal may be just like any other and the law and the legal precedents may be identical. But to the individual complainant his case is special, in his eyes it is different from any other and the injustice is greater. The neutrality of an ACAS conciliator is all important, but he must always bear in mind that it does not have to be impersonal. Tactfulness and impartiality are not mutually exclusive.

A Change of Role for ACAS?

In their exhaustive and painstaking study of unfair dismissal and the industrial tribunal system, *Dismissed*, Linda Dickens, Michael Jones, Brian Weeks and Moira Hart pointed to ACAS's refusal in collective disputes to involve itself in the merits of any outcome. But in view of the different context within which individual conciliation occurred they suggested that there was a precedent 'for a form of conciliation which might be thought more appropriate in individual rights cases'. They called this 'committed conciliation'[13] and described it as 'conciliation designed to bring about agreed settlements promoting certain desired substantive ends'.[14] The precedent which the authors had in mind was that part of the Employment Protection Act of 1975 under which trade unions seeking recognition from an employer for collective bargaining purposes could invoke a procedure involving ACAS. Dickens *et al.* pointed out that conciliation in these cases took place within the context of the general duty placed on ACAS under Section 1 of the Act 'of encouraging the extension of collective bargaining'. They suggested that ACAS had been required to adopt a positive approach when conciliating in recognition claims and that by analogy 'one might argue that conciliation in cases where individuals are seeking to pursue their legal rights could seek to promote those rights, ensuring they are not abandoned or compromised below their value'.[15]

For reasons that are not relevant to the purpose of this chapter, the recognition provisions of the Employment Protection Act were repealed in 1980. The precedent of those provisions would not be a happy one, however, for it was the ACAS experience that their very nature, and the way they had to be applied, tended to call into question the impartiality and neutrality of the Service on which its success in every area of its work depends. This was recognised by Dickens *et al.* who suggested that if a rights enforcement role was required, ACAS was not the appropriate body to provide it.

The Conciliation Process

'Committed conciliation' would require legislative change. ACAS conciliators have to comply with the law as it stands. In assisting the parties in the strictest confidence to reach a settlement they therefore see their tasks as:

- providing information on the legislation, on similar cases which have previously been heard and on tribunal procedure;
- helping to establish the facts and to clarify the views of each side;
- without giving a direct answer to such questions as 'How good is my case?' or 'What are my chances at the tribunal?', drawing attention to relevant precedents such as case law which might have a bearing on the issue;
- pointing out any relevant guidance in the Codes of Practice published by the Department of Employment, ACAS and other bodies.

ACAS states that in these various ways:

> the conciliation officer can help the parties reach their own informed decisions about how to proceed. The information they have had from him may lead either or both parties to seek a conciliated settlement; alternatively, at one extreme it could strengthen the convictions of either to pursue the matter to the tribunal; or, at the other, the complainant might decide to withdraw the complaint altogether.[16]

The actual conciliation process over complaints of infringed statutory employment rights shares some common features with conciliation over collective issues. Thus the processes are confidential and they are both as flexible as is necessary. If the parties agree to settle, the responsibility for the terms is theirs. There are, however, certain differences, for example, individual conciliation rarely involves joint meetings of the two parties, and much of the work is done by telephone or through separate meetings with the employer and the aggrieved employee (or their representatives).

There is no requirement as to which of the two parties should be approached first. Some conciliation officers perceive an advantage in meeting the complainant and obtaining as much information as possible before approaching the employer. Others will approach the employer first, realising that if the issue has already been fully discussed within the internal grievance or appeals procedure and has involved various levels of management, the scope for conciliation may be very small. Indeed, many employers believe it so vital to uphold the credibility of their internal procedures that they will resist as a matter of principle any third party offer of conciliation.

So far as is possible, however, a conciliation officer will make contact with or meet each of the parties or their representatives at least once. He will certainly regard it as a special responsibility to ensure that all complainants who are unrepresented are visited as far as possible. He will take particular care always to explain the implications of a settlement reached under ACAS.

If out of the process of clarification, explanation and discussion an agreed settlement is reached, the conciliation officer, having first acted as an intermediary, now helps the parties to record the agreed terms formally. Both parties will be asked to confirm that they fully understand and accept the terms of the settlement and also its implications. The complainant, in particular, must understand that once agreement has been reached under ACAS auspices, he will no longer have the right to proceed to a tribunal.

ACAS provides each party with a copy of the signed agreement and sends the original to the tribunal so that the complaint can be recorded as having been settled by conciliation. The fact of a settlement is eventually promulgated in the form of a tribunal decision.

The Growth of 'Legalism' and Formality

The Donovan Commission expressed the view that the industrial tribunal procedure should be easily accessible, informal, speedy and inexpensive.

The procedure is certainly accessible at present (although from time to time the idea of some form of 'entrance fee' is proposed). Speediness, however, is a matter of opinion. ACAS states that most cases coming to a tribunal hearing 'do so within a period of five to 12 weeks of the complaint being lodged . . .'.[17] Taking into account the additional period of time that may have been involved in the prior use of internal grievance or appeals procedure, this means that the average complaint will probably take anything up to three months before it comes to a tribunal hearing (assuming, of course, that conciliation has failed). The exceptional case that is appealed before the Employment Appeal Tribunal, the Court of Appeal (Court of Session in Scotland), and perhaps even the House of Lords would, of course, take much longer. One of the leading cases concerning equal pay (*Ms Hayward* v. *Cammell Laird Shipbuilders Ltd*) was first summarised in an ACAS annual report of 1985. It was 1988 before the judgement of the House of Lords was handed down.

But it is the demise of informality and the development of what ACAS has called 'legalism' that are more serious. The original idea that an aggrieved employee could informally confront his employer before the 'three wise men' of an industrial tribunal was perhaps more romantic than realistic. It was no surprise that lay (as distinct from legally qualified) officials of trade unions and of employers' associations saw it as a logical development of their representational role to appear before tribunals on behalf of their respective memberships.

But of much greater concern has been the arrival of the legally qualified representative, inevitably bringing in his train greater formality, attachment to legal process and precedent, demands for the revelation of what occurred in the course of confidental conciliation proceedings and, of course, cost. A secondary industry has also developed which devotes itself to reporting on and analysing cases involving employment rights.

ACAS first drew attention to its concern over this development in its report for the year 1983.

> It became evident during the year that there was concern amongst both trade unions and employers about the increasing 'legalism' which they felt was creeping into the handling of complaints concerning individual employment rights. Concern was expressed particularly about the growing practice of legal representation at tribunal hearings . . .[18]

In its report for 1984 ACAS developed its concern further. 'The growth of legalism in relation to the processing of employment rights complaints is clearly reflected in the growth of legal representation, both in conciliation and at tribunal'.[19] An ACAS study had revealed:

> that there has been significant growth in the extent of representation in recent years. Thus whereas in 1974 over half of all unfair dismissal applications involved self-represented applicants on one side and employers represented by line or personnel managers on the other during conciliations, by 1984 this was true of no more

than one-fifth of cases. Looked at another way in between one-fifth and one-quarter of conciliation cases both applicants and respondents are now legally represented.[20]

Of solicitors, ACAS stated that in its experience their involvement:

can hinder the informal, speedy, inexpensive and amicable settlement of employment rights disputes. Our conciliation officers endeavour to make rapid contact with each side in such disputes but when solicitors are involved this often proves very difficult. Indeed, they sometimes appear only to become interested in resolving cases when the hearing date is imminent. This can seriously inhibit the conciliation process, reduce the possibility of promoting a voluntary settlement and virtually eliminate any possibility of securing re-employment.[21]

Legal representation has now developed to such a stage that any return to informality is unlikely. It is easy to blame employers and to a lesser extent employees for having allowed such a situation to develop, but this does not mean that the attempt should not be made to keep legalism under some kind of control. The Court of Appeal itself frowned upon the attempt of the Employment Appeal Tribunal to lay down guidelines for general application by tribunals in handling redundancy questions.

But it is difficult to dissent from Dickens *et al.*'s view that:

the characteristics of the parties and the context in which the tribunals have to operate, the fact that they are court-substitute bodies applying complex law rather than non-court bodies, constrains the extent to whch skilled advice and representation will ever be seen as irrelevant or unimportant.[22]

Once 'skilled advice and representation' are seen as necessary in the industrial tribunal process, so too do they become increasingly inevitable in the conciliation process as well.

The Remedies in Dismissal Cases

In dismissal cases it is in the area of remedies that ACAS finds itself under the greatest criticism. Section 134 of the Employment Protection (Consolidation) Act lays down that in promoting a settlement:

(a) the conciliation officer shall in particular seek to promote the reinstatement or re-engagement of the complainant by the employer, or by a successor of the employer or by an associated employer, on terms appearing to the conciliation officer to be equitable; but

(b) where the complainant does not wish to be reinstated or re-engaged, or where reinstatement or re-engagement is not practicable, and the parties desire the conciliation officer to act under this section, he shall seek to promote agreement between them as to a sum by way of compensation to be paid by the employer to the complainant.

In practice the remedies can be:

- reinstatement or re-engagement – (reinstatement means treating the employee in all respects as if he had not been dismissed, for example, payment of arrears of pay and retention of seniority and pension rights; re-engagement means that the employee is engaged by the employer, or by a successor of the employer or by an associated employer, in employment comparable to that from which he was dismissed or other suitable employment on terms that have to be agreed);
- financial compensation;
- a non-financial settlement such as the provision of a reference or a benefit in kind, for example, retention of the company car.

The conciliator's priority is, however, quite clear. He must first seek to promote reinstatement or re-employment and only if this fails can he then attempt to promote a monetary settlement. If everything else fails he can try and promote a non-monetary settlement even though the statute does not provide expressly for this.

In the vast majority of dismissal cases settled through conciliation the settlement is one involving a monetary payment. The ACAS annual report for 1987 informs us that out of 24 676 settlements that were reached in that year in dismissal cases there were only 385 (1.6 per cent of the total) that involved re-employment (namely, reinstatement or re-engagement).

Problems of Re-employment

Dickens *et al.* have pointed to the way in which over the years the proportion of conciliated settlements in dismissal cases which involve re-employment has declined. Their figures show that in 1972 the figure was 15.4 per cent, in 1973 it was 9 per cent but by 1980 it had declined to 3 per cent. In 1981 it was 3.7 per cent, and in 1982, 4 per cent. A number of commentators maintain that re-employment should be possible in a greater number of cases. Dickens *et al.*, for example, point out that according to a survey carried out by the Industrial Relations Research Unit at Warwick University (hereafter referred to as the Warwick Survey), just over a quarter of the employers who made a settlement did so because they agreed that the dismissal had been unfair or thought that their case was weak or admitted that they had not followed the proper procedure. They suggest[23] that this 'indicates there is some scope for pursuing the re-employment option: if the employer agrees the dismissal was unfair, or at least "contrary to statute" why not erase it by reinstatement?' They go on to point out that, according to the same survey, 42 per cent of employers settled in conciliation rather than go to a tribunal hearing because it was 'the cheaper option'. They suggest that, in fact, reinstatement could have been cheaper than compensation for loss of a job. The employer has to pay for loss of earnings between dismissal and reinstatement but he 'obtains the reinstated worker's labour'. If re-engagement is agreed he 'may even avoid having to pay loss of earnings'.

The nature of the case, Dickens *et al.* go on, 'will obviously have a bearing on the employer's willingness to consider re-employment', for example, the case of the employee who is dismissed for something uncharacteristic and who might be given a second chance, the case of the employee who is dismissed for ill-health absence, lateness or absenteeism in circumstances that are unlikely to be repeated in future, or the case of constructive dismissal in which the complainant can be assured that the circumstances which led to the resignation have changed or will change. (Constructive dismissal can be described as resignation which is forced upon the employee through conduct by the employer of a kind which demonstrates that he no longer intends to be bound by one of the essential terms of the contract.)

The essence of Dickens *et al.*'s charge against ACAS was that 'conciliation officers are aware that the question of re-employment has to be raised, but the research evidence indicates that this may be done in such a low-key fashion that the parties fail to recognise it'. Indeed, they argue, the training of conciliation officers is directed less at the re-employment and more on the monetary option, and the emphasis in conciliation itself is first and foremost to promote settlements, and that the nature of the settlement is of secondary importance.

ACAS itself has become increasingly sensitive to this and similar charges. In its annual report for 1983, for example, the Service set out the following factors which in its view contributed towards the small number of re-employments recorded:

(a) the fact that re-employment is neither sought by nor acceptable to many applicants;
(b) that it is sometimes impracticable, e.g. where the employer has no suitable vacancies;
(c) many employers have improved their disciplinary procedures in recent years and either resolve more dismissal cases internally or are unwilling to re-employ if this would undermine the disciplinary action they have taken and thereby undermine the credibility of their procedures;
(d) personal relationships may be seriously damaged rendering restoration of a businesslike relationship impracticable, especially in small companies;
(e) in circumstances of redundancy, re-employment would simply mean someone else being made redundant;
(f) employers' awareness of the low number of re-employment orders at tribunal;
(g) general willingness on the part of employees to exchange employment for a sum of money;
(h) the involvement of representatives, especially solicitors, may tend to impede discussion of the possibility of re-employment.[24]

In a pamphlet published in 1987 (*Individual Employment Rights – ACAS Conciliation between Individuals and Employers*) ACAS stated that the conciliation officer will keep the objective of re-employment in mind throughout the process, but he must 'use discretion so as not to pursue or press such enquiries to a point where the prospect of promoting any other forms of settlement is prejudiced by his offending either party'.

Perhaps the one factor more than any other that makes re-employment so difficult is the way in which the dismissal process destroys the personal relationship between employer and employee. An employee who feels that his dismissal is unjustified may well give vent to his feelings in an unrestrained way. He may regard it as a poor reward for years of loyal service. The manager who may have agonised long and hard before deciding that dismissal is the only course of action may feel confirmed in his decision if he is subsequently abused by the employee. The need to avoid loss of face or to support managerial subordinates is all important.

And so both parties begin tacitly to accept that re-employment is out of the question ('If that's what they think of me, they know what they can do with the job' or 'I wasn't sure whether he really deserved the sack but after what he said, I'll never have him back').

And so even the employee who might have stated on his ITI that he wanted his job back may subsequently decide that realistically he should settle for a lump sum payment. The Warwick Survey in fact, revealed that only 24 per cent of the applicants covered indicated on their ITI a preference for re-employment, compared with 69 per cent who opted for compensation.

For his part, the employer may decide that although the dismissal was totally justified and could be defended before a tribunal, he should make a 'convenience payment' ('Find out how much he wants to go away'). In this way he can save time and trouble and avoid publicity.

One final point. For generations the courts have refused to order what is called 'specific performance' on a contract of employment. Professor K. W. (now Lord) Wedderburn tells us how even during the years of the Second World War when an order was in force which forbade strikes and lock-outs and required compulsory arbitration of disputes, the House of Lords refused to construe the order as giving even the National Arbitration Tribunal the power to grant what Lord Chief Justice Goddard called 'a remedy which no court of law or equity has ever considered it had power to grant. If an employer breaks his contract of service with his employees . . . the workmen's remedy is for damages only'.[25] It was an awareness of this principle that led the Donovan Commission to move away from reinstatement as the prime remedy.

Dickens *et al.* observe that the present legislation 'has attempted to overcome this hesitancy but the tribunals have not'. They go on to say that 'it is clear that there is a reluctance on the part of tribunals to exercise their discretion in favour of ordering employers to re-employ those whom they dismissed unfairly'.[26]

As ACAS pointed out in its 1983 report, employers who are increasingly choosing to be represented by solicitors even at the conciliation stage will presumably be aware of the reluctance of tribunals to award re-employment and will thus turn more readily to the alternative of a monetary settlement. The tribunals, in turning away from ordering reinstatement, will presumably act on the assumption that if an ACAS conciliator has tried and failed to secure the employer's agreement to re-employment, it is useless for them to pursue that option further.

Given this background, the failure of ACAS conciliators to secure a greater number of settlements which provide for the reinstatement or re-engagement of the dismissed employee becomes more understandable.

Re-employment through Arbitration

But what is difficult to secure by law can sometimes be more readily achieved through voluntary agreement. That is why, despite the statutory remedies that are now available against unfair dismissal, there are those who regard voluntary arbitration as the more acceptable process. After all, the agreed terms of reference can expressly provide that if the arbitrators find that the dismissal was unfair or unjustified, the worker will be re-employed.

The Electricity Supply Industry is a case in point. Industrial and technical engineering staff in that industry are covered by agreed procedures under which a penalty of suspension without pay, transfer or dismissal may be referred to independent arbitration if appeals within the internal procedure have not produced an outcome acceptable to the employee concerned. Table 4.4 shows the annual number of arbitrations in respect of industrial staff (they do not include the very small number of cases involving technical engineering staff).

It is noteworthy that although the agreed procedures in Electricity Supply place no restriction on the right of an employee who is

Table 4.4 Electricity supply industry: disciplinary cases referred to arbitration

Year	*Number*
1983	27
1984	32
1985	26
1986	46
1987	47
1988	40
1989 (to August)	25

Source: The Electricity Council.

dissatisfied with an arbitrator's award to exercise his statutory right of subsequently referring the issue to an industrial tribunal, this rarely happens. The trade unions are not keen to support a member who wishes to proceed further and subsequent appeals by unrepresented employees (or ex-employees) are equally rare.

Parallel procedures (which differ in some important points of detail, but which all contain the principle of an arbitration stage) apply to clerical, administrative, professional, sales and managerial staff in Electricity Supply. Very few cases reach the arbitration stage.

A well-publicised case of a reference to arbitration in another industry occurred in 1983 when there was a major dispute in Ford's Halewood plant following the dismissal of an employee (Kelly) for allegedly causing malicious damage by bending a bracket in a car on the assembly line. Like so many strikes in the motor industry, this one escalated rapidly so that by the end of a month (the strike lasted that long) 4500 Ford employees were on strike and a further 4100 had been laid off due to non-availability of work.

The case could, of course, have been referred to an industrial tribunal, but this was a course that the employee's union (the Transport and General Workers' Union) flatly declined to adopt. They felt that there were wider issues involved than just the dismissal. The Company's disciplinary procedure, in fact, provides that as a final stage a dismissal decision may, by joint agreement, be referred to arbitration and in this case, as a result of conciliation by ACAS, it was eventually agreed that if those on strike returned to work the issue would be referred to a panel of arbitration with a legally qualified chairman.

If an industrial tribunal had heard the employee's complaint it would probably have confined itself to the narrow issues of whether the company had met its legal and procedural obligations and whether in the circumstances the dismissal was fair. The agreed terms of reference for the arbitration were broader. They required the arbitration panel 'to consider the background events and evidence leading to the dismissal of Mr. Kelly and to determine whether the company acted reasonably in dismissing him in those circumstances'.

It was the gravamen of the company's case that an act of deliberate vandalism had occurred and that on the basis of the evidence Mr Kelly had been responsible. The appropriate penalty was dismissal, and after a thorough and objective investigation of the circumstances of the events of that day and for no other reason, he had been dismissed. For Mr Kelly, the union argued that, in a general atmosphere of management anxiety about vandalism in which Mr Kelly had been disadvantaged because of anonymous and unproven allegations of previous misbehaviour, and in the light of circumstantial evidence of a less than satisfactory nature, the decision to dismiss was neither fair nor reasonable. In the interests of natural justice he should be reinstated.

In its report the arbitration panel concluded that the company had been justified in deciding that Mr Kelly was responsible for the damage and that, as far as it could tell, the management had followed the disciplinary procedure in the usual manner. As to the reasonableness of the penalty of dismissal the panel was obviously concerned that the background of the company's prevailing concern about acts of vandalism might have adversely affected Mr Kelly. They were not certain whether the single act of wilfully bending a bracket (which could subsequently be repaired) fell clearly under that part of the company's definition of gross misconduct which warranted dismissal for a first offence ('wilful destruction . . . of property belonging to the Company' or vehicles 'deliberately damaged, i.e. vandalised and now require major paint and metal repairs to make them saleable').

Be that as it may, the panel's final conclusion was to 'venture to express the view' that once the company was convinced that Mr Kelly had been responsible for the incident a more reasonable decision would have been a period of suspension without pay of 10 working days, a clear written warning and transfer to another area.

Mr Kelly was, of course, re-employed by Ford, on this basis.

The reference of a dismissal case to arbitration does not even require a standing provision for arbitration in the disciplinary procedure. It can be agreed on an *ad hoc* basis.

We have already noted that some observers prefer arbitration to the industrial tribunal system as the basis for deciding unfair dismissal cases. They believe that an arbitral procedure which is inquisitorial rather than adversarial, which could put a dismissal case into a wider context than narrowly-defined 'fairness', and which would involve not a legally qualified chairman but an arbitrator both knowledgeable about and experienced in industrial relations, is to be preferred. They also believe that employees are likely to be better served by arbitration because when the employer is found to have been at fault, re-employment will not just be awarded but will actually take place.

But for all the resentment they may feel against a system which qualified their 'right to fire', employers, in general, would be unlikely now to accept willingly the compulsion of an alternative system which, as had already been suggested in Chapter 2, many of them dislike and distrust (even though some of them use it voluntarily). Arbitration on the US pattern as a means of applying the whole of a legally enforceable collective agreement, including dismissal cases, would perhaps be one thing, but arbitration as the means for deciding the single issue of dismissals would be something quite different.

Perhaps, too, employers are now becoming less hostile to the tribunal system. They are certainly becoming increasingly sophisticated in handling it. If we take as an example the 12 months from mid-1984 to mid-1985, there were 577 000 terminations of all kinds (including redundancy) during that period. Over the same period some 35 000 complaints of unfair dismissal were lodged, that is, only 6 per cent of the total. Thus, for whatever reason (for example, settlement of the issue within internal appeals procedures, not being within scope of the law, ignorance of its provisions or acceptance of the employer's decision), 94 per cent did not complain. Of the 35 000 complaints that were lodged only about one-third (say, 12 000) found their way to a tribunal (the remainder having been disposed of during the conciliation stage), and in only about 30 per cent of those 12 000 cases (say, 3600 or 0.6 per cent of the total number of dismissals) was dismissal actually found to have been unfair.

It is perhaps because of their dissatisfaction with figures like these that the TUC and Labour Party are in favour of change. In their joint document[27] (*People at Work: New Rights, New Responsibilities*) agreed in 1986 they agreed that an incoming Labour government would 'improve the protection available against unfair dismissal' by, among other steps, 'reviewing the present industrial tribunal system and exploring the scope for express procedures based on arbitration'. The TUC and Labour Party are not the only two bodies calling for change.

The Labour Party did not win the 1986 election. If it had, a new Secretary of State for Employment would doubtless have had his attention drawn to Section 65 of the Employment Protection (Consolidation) Act of 1978. This clause provides an escape hatch from the industrial tribunal system if there is an agreed dismissals procedure agreement in place which meets certain criteria including, as a last resort, 'arbitration or adjudication by an independent referee'.

In fact only one industry has so far sought and obtained the required approval of the Secretary of State for Employment for exemption from the statutory provisions. This is the Electrical Contracting Industry. The final stage of the dismissals procedure agreement between the Electrical Contractors' Association (ECA) and the EETPU provides for appeal to a legally qualified arbitrator appointed by ACAS who is assisted by two advisors, one nominated by the ECA and one by the EETPU. In fact, the final stage is rarely invoked, an indication, perhaps, of the effectiveness of the preceding stages of the procedure.

Financial Compensation

We have already seen that the number of conciliated settlements in dismissal cases that actually provide for re-employment is very small indeed. Compensation is the most frequent remedy. It is a possible remedy in other cases too, for example, unreasonable exclusion or expulsion from a union (payable by the trade union) and discrimination on grounds of race or sex.

The basis for calculating compensation for unfair dismissal which can be awarded by an industrial tribunal was laid down in the Employment Protection (Consolidation) Act of 1978, but the maxima are varied from time to time by statutory order. There can be three elements, namely, the basic award which is based on age and length of service, the compensatory award which relates to the loss sustained by the employee because of the dismissal, and an additional award for failing to comply with the terms of a re-employment order.

Additionally, under the Employment Act of 1982 a substantially increased level of compensation was introduced for a worker dismissed for exercising his right not to be a member of trade union. Where the dismissal was found to have resulted from union pressure, so-called joinder provisions enabled the compensation to be obtained from the trade union rather than the employer.

The detailed provisions laid down for calculating the compensation awarded by tribunals in dismissal cases are complex but it is an important part of the conciliation officer's role to advise both the applicant and the employer of the possible levels of compensation that might be awarded should the case go against the employer at the tribunal. The calculation is made more complex by virtue of (a) the common law duty on the applicant to mitigate his loss (the duty is, in fact, written into the Employment Protection (Consolidation Act), and (b) the extent to which the applicant was regarded by the tribunal as having contributed to his own dismissal.

The following figures of the compensation awarded by tribunals during the two periods 1 April 1985 to 31 March 1986 and 1 April 1986 to 31 March 1987 were published in the *Employment Gazette* for October 1987:

	No. of cases	*Median award*
1 April 1985 to 31 March 1986	1 540	£1 674
1 April 1986 to 31 March 1987	1 394	£1 805

Details of the sums of money agreed in conciliated settlements over dismissal cases are not so readily available but, apart from a belated acknowledgement that the action taken was unfair, the main reason that prompts employers to settle for a sum of money at the conciliation stage is to save the time and expense involved in going to a tribunal hearing (the so called 'convenience payment'). Indeed there are some cases in which managers choose this course even though, to preserve the effectiveness of the disciplinary procedure and their own reputation for firmness and consistency, they should have allowed the issue to be contested right through to a tribunal hearing. Financial compensation can be at any level the parties care to agree, regardless of the levels laid down by statute.

The employee's reasons for settling at the conciliation stage are probably a mix of apprehension about appearing before a tribunal, uncertainty as to the outcome, difficulty in finding witnesses prepared to testify and even satisfaction with the amount of money on offer. He may even have found another job as a result of which his motivation to take action against his former employer has largely disappeared. The sums agreed are often relatively low.

In the final analysis, the amount agreed by way of settlement is a matter for the applicant and the employer. Even if the individual wishes, for whatever reason, to settle for less than his statutory or contractual entitlement, that is his affair, although naturally the conciliation officer should try and ensure that the individual understands what he is doing.

From the standpoint of the conciliation officer the important fact always to bear in mind is that, unlike tribunal awards, conciliated settlements are not intended to compensate for the loss sustained by the employee. They are merely sums of money agreed between the parties. The conciliation officer may offer advice as to what a tribunal might award, but his responsibility is to bring the parties to the point of settlement and not with equity, fairness or the reasonableness of the sum actually agreed.

It might be thought that once a conciliation officer has sought and failed to achieve a conciliated settlement, and the case has passed to a tribunal, he could close the file. This is not necessarily so. Some tribunals (with the notable exception of those in Scotland), having found a dismissal to be unfair, have adopted the practice of referring the question back to ACAS with a view to the remedy being agreed in a further conciliation.

In the words used in its 1986 report – 'For some years it had been ACAS policy to provide only advisory assistance in these circumstances. This was based on the belief that the Service's statutory duty ceased once the complaint had reached a tribunal and the merits of the case had been determined. In the judgement of the EAT [*Keys* v. *Courage Take Home Foods*, 1986] the Service's interpretation of its duty was wrong in so far as a complaint is not determined until both merits and remedy have been decided by an industrial tribunal'.[28]

ACAS had no option but to comply with this ruling but it did so with some misgivings. It felt, for example, that once applicants knew that a tribunal had decided in their favour, they might be unwilling to embark on conciliation over the remedy 'with its possibilities of a measure of compromise'.[29]

The Non-financial Settlement

On the third option available during the conciliation process, that is, the non-financial settlement, little needs to be said. We have already noted that this option should not be canvassed by the conciliator until after the possibilities of re-employment or a financial settlement have first been explored without success. The value to an ex-employee of a non-financial settlement should not, however, be discounted. In a difficult job market, for example, the willingness of an employer to provide a reference to a dismissed employee may be more valuable than a few hundred pounds of compensation.

The non-financial settlement is not specifically provided for in the statutes but happily this is an instance where common sense and the wishes of the parties are clearly regarded as being of more significance than some relatively petty legislative detail. It will be a sad day if the principle of a non-financial settlement is challenged in the courts, but the uncertainty of the true legal position is one which the wise conciliator will always bring to the notice of the employer and former employee.

Conciliation in Equal Pay Cases

Before the new regulations relating to equal value cases came into effect in 1984, the procedure for dealing with complaints was relatively simple. The applicant registered a claim on our old friend, ITI; ACAS attempted to conciliate, and if conciliation failed, the case could proceed to an industrial tribunal for decision. There were only two possibly complicating factors:

- the extent to which a job evaluation scheme might be sex biassed;
- the right of the employer to show that any variation in pay between the man and the woman was genuinely due to a material factor which was not the difference of sex, for example, higher performance or greater productivity.

The new equal value procedure was to be much more complex. The following is but a brief summary of what has to be done:

- the applicant registers a claim;
- ACAS tries to conciliate;
- if conciliation fails, the case proceeds to an industrial tribunal. The tribunal has to decide whether the case falls under the 1970 provisions relating to like work or work rated as equivalent or under the equal value provisions;
- if the case involves an equal value claim, the tribunal must offer an adjournment to the parties. If both parties agree, the adjournment must be granted for the purpose of seeking a settlement. In the event of no adjournment or settlement the procedure continues;
- a tribunal is not empowered to decide an equal value claim unless it is satisfied that there are no reasonable grounds for determining that the work is of equal value (for example, it is blatantly obvious that the jobs are not of equal value) or it has commissioned a report from an independent expert. Thus even at the preliminary stage the employer can argue that there are no reasonable grounds for the claim. The regulations require ACAS to appoint a panel of independent experts for equal

value claims. This panel is appointed by, but is in no sense controlled by, ACAS. Each expert operates as he sees fit. He is appointed to a case by an industrial tribunal;

- in due course the expert completes his report and copies are sent to the parties;
- at a resumed tribunal hearing the report is submitted as evidence unless the tribunal has grounds for rejecting it, for example, the expert has failed to act fairly or his conclusions were wrong in the light of the evidence;
- if the report is accepted and admitted in evidence, the expert may be cross-examined and each side is also free to call one expert witness of its own;
- the employer can again raise the 'genuine material factor' defence (he may have done so earlier at a preliminary hearing). In equal value cases wider considerations can be introduced than in other equal pay cases, for example, market force arguments;
- the tribunal reaches its decision.

This procedure is complex. Indeed, if anybody had been instructed to draw up a procedure expressly designed to discourage workers from coming forward with an equal value complaint, this one could hardly have been bettered.

If, for the period 1979 to 1988 inclusive, one examines the number of cases which involved in one form or another the principle of equal pay it can be seen that they were no more than 7700 or only 1.7 per cent of the total number of individual conciliation cases in which ACAS was involved. Even this figure is distorted by virtue of the fact that as many as 3336 applications related to two claims, canteen assistants employed by the National Coal Board (now British Coal) and speech therapists employed by district health authorities. As for equal value complaints, ACAS stated in its 1987 report that discounting these two multiple cases 'the equal value caseload . . . remained fairly stable at about 340 cases per year from 1985–87. The number of employers cited . . . has fallen from just over 60 in 1985 and 1986, to just under 50 in 1987'. In its 1988 report ACAS quoted a figure of only 120 equal value cases received in that year.

There is obviously more than one reason for this relatively low level of complaints. Equal pay has not been achieved. The procedure is certainly complex but apathy among women workers, ignorance, concern about the consequences of raising one's head above the parapet during a period of uncertain job opportunities, the preferred union approach of making progress through collective bargaining, and, as ACAS itself said in its 1987 report, 'continuing uncertainty about how the law is to be interpreted and a number of caselaw questions . . . undecided'[30] are the most likely reasons for the lack of progress.

Given the complex nature of the equal value regulations it was inevitable that there would be problems of interpretation, and that given the importance of the issues involved, these would eventually require final determination by the courts.

So it was that the case of the cook, the 'token man' and the nursery nurse found their way to the House of Lords.

Julie Hayward is a cook employed by Cammell Laird Shipbuilders Ltd. She claimed to be carrying out work of equal value to a painter, a joiner and a thermal engineer employed in the shipyard. The application went through the procedure described earlier and the independent expert reported that the work of Julie Hayward and that of her comparators were, indeed, of equal value. The tribunal duly decided in her favour. Unlike her comparators, however, Ms Hayward enjoys staff status and the company now claimed that these terms should be given a monetary value and be taken into account in determining the pay due to Ms Hayward. The tribunal found for the employer as, too, on appeal, did the Employment Appeal Tribunal and the Court of Appeal. The House of Lords, however, held that as a matter of statutory construction, the words of the Equal Pay Act of 1970 provided that an employee was entitled to the same rate of pay as her comparator and not merely an 'equivalent overall package'. The case was thus referred back to the industrial tribunal to decide on the money due to Julie Hayward.

By any standard this was a famous victory for the equal pay cause. Ms Hayward's reputation as a cook may perhaps not be as famous as that of Mrs Beaton, but whatever her culinary skills, she has undoubtedly carved a name for herself in British industrial relations history.

The spectre of the 'token man' raised its head in the case of *Pickstone and others* v. *Freemans plc* (the token woman is a quite different species; her natural habitat has been largely confined to royal commissions and government-appointed agencies). In the Pickstone case the Employment Appeal Tribunal agreed with an industrial tribunal that, because a man was doing like work to five women complainants (warehouse operatives), an equal value complaint in which the comparator was a male checker warehouse operative, was prohibited on a strict interpretation of the legislation. The Court of Appeal decided that the applicants had an enforceable right to equal pay with the checker for work of equal value. On appeal to the House of Lords, their lordships agreed.

This was another decision that was fundamental to the cause of equal pay. If the House of Lords had ruled for the employers, any claim by a group of women for equal pay on grounds of work of equal value could have been frustrated by the employer ensuring that a man (the 'token man') was employed on the same work as the women.

Mrs Leverton is a nursery nurse employed by the Clwyd County Council. She claimed that she was employed on work of equal value to that of eleven male comparators employed by the Council. The Council resisted her claim on two principal grounds, firstly, that none of the comparators was a man in the same employment and, secondly, that the variations between the applicant's contract and those of the comparators were genuinely due to a material factor which was not the difference in sex.

None of the comparators was employed at the same establishment as Mrs Leverton. They were all employed under the same national agreement but Mrs Leverton and her comparators were paid different salaries. Mrs Leverton also worked a shorter basic week (32½ hours against 37 hours – in one case, 39). Holiday entitlements, too, were different.

The effect of these differences was that each of the comparators had to work many more hours to earn his annual salary than Mrs Leverton worked to earn hers.

A majority of the industrial tribunal held that Mrs Leverton was not in the same employment as her comparators and that the difference in working hours and length of holidays was a material factor. Mrs Leverton's application was accordingly dismissed.

The case was appealed to the House of Lords via the Employment Appeal Tribunal and the Court of Appeal. Their Lordships dismissed Mrs Leverton's application on the grounds that although common terms and conditions were observed within the meaning of the Equal Pay Act, the difference in pay was due to a material factor other than sex, namely the difference in working hours and holiday entitlements.

Commenting on this case in EEF News in February 1979 the Engineering Employers' Federation suggested that the outcome of the Leverton case:

confirms the view that Hayward v. Cammell Laird might have been decided differently if Cammell Laird had raised the defence that there was a 'material factor' explaining the fact that Julie Hayward was paid less than the male shipyard workers – namely her paid meal breaks and more favourable holiday and sick pay entitlements.

These three cases are but the first of a number which will have to be determined by the House of Lords before there is reasonable clarity as to the way in which the regulations should be applied. Pressure from employers for amendment of the regulations cannot be ruled out, but any government, however sympathetic to the employers' cause, will have to move carefully for fear of yet another 'thumbs down' from the European Court of Justice. Even though the regulations providing for equal pay for work of equal value were approved by the House of Lords in December 1983, their Lordships at the same time adopted an opposition amendment which stated that 'this House believes that the Regulations do not adequately reflect the 1982 decision of the European Court of Justice and Article 1 of the EEC Equal Pay Directive of 1975'.

As with unfair dismissal cases, equal pay complaints are not invariably determined through the industrial tribunal procedure. A case in point was the affair of the sewing-machinists employed by the Ford Motor Company.

The dispute had a long history dating back to 1967 in which year the company agreed with its trade unions that an old four-grade structure should be replaced by five new grades, and that women's jobs should be slotted into the appropriate grades, as determined by job evaluation and without sex discrimination. Prototype machinists were allocated to Grade C; production sewing-machinists were placed into the lower Grade B.

An appeal from the production sewing-machinists to be placed in Grade C was rejected and a highly damaging strike over the issue lasted for three weeks. After the return to work the company agreed to increase its women's rates from 85 per cent to 92 per cent of the men's equivalent rate for each grade and a court of inquiry, chaired by Mr (later Sir) Jack Scamp, examined the issue of grading and alleged sex discrimination. The court of inquiry dismissed the allegation of sex discrimination and the sewing-machinists were not regraded.

But this strike was nevertheless a momentous one. Given the practice of the day, it was not surprising that, despite the highly skilled conciliation staff who were then operating within the Department of Employment, the Secretary of State, Mrs Barbara Castle, should have intervened personally (her cup of tea with representatives of the strikers has now become part of British industrial relations history). But of much greater significance was the fact that the strike accelerated the decision of the Labour Government then in power to legislate on equal pay as quickly as possile. The Equal Pay Act duly arrived in 1970.

Ironically, the Act was of no benefit to the sewing machinists because there was no evidence to show that the Ford job evaluation was discriminatory and at this stage the Act only applied where women were doing the same or broadly similar work as men, or work equally rated under a job evaluation scheme. The women's grievance thus remained unsettled and it was to be almost another 15 years before the next steps were taken which were to bring the matter once more to crisis point and, this time, to final determination.

In 1983 an application was submitted by three of Ford's sewing-machinists to the London North Industrial Tribunal complaining that the company's job evaluation scheme was discriminatory. After the equal value regulations came into effect in January 1984 the complaint was changed to one relating to equal value. In June 1984 the tribunal published its (majority) decision that there 'are no reasonable grounds for determining that the work of the applicants is of equal value to that of the male comparators . . . and their applications are therefore dismissed'. The sewing-machinists then renewed their claim for upgrading and this became part of the unions' 1984 pay claim against Ford. The women's union (the TGWU) suggested that the company should allow independent assessors to examine the women's claim for upgrading and also expand the content of the women's job to justify the regrading of their jobs. Both suggestions were rejected by the company and the women started their second strike on the regrading issue. This time the strike lasted for seven weeks before agreement was reached that the sewing-machinists' job should be re-examined by an independent panel appointed by ACAS. The panel reported in April 1985. In their reassessment of the job 'the Panel uprated the machinists on 11 of 28 characteristics and raised the job score . . . which brought it comfortably within Grade C'.[31]

The struggle of the sewing-machinists was over. Significantly in yet another question affecting the Ford Motor Company a union victory was achieved, not through the industrial tribunal procedure, but by a strike followed by what was in all but name, arbitration.

In its 1985 report ACAS pointed out how difficult conciliation was in equal value cases:

> because of the sensitivity of the issues involved, the potential collective repercussions and a desire on all sides to await developments in case law. However there are signs that an increasing number of companies are looking to negotiated settlements and this was reflected by a significant increase in the proportion of conciliated settlements in equal pay cases in 1985 from 23 per cent to 42 per cent.[32]

Unfortunately this optimism was not supported by the figures for 1986 and 1987 when conciliated settlements fell to 10 per cent and 21 per cent respectively. ACAS was thereupon constrained to write in its 1987 report that equal value cases took a long time to progress and the results of individual conciliation in this jurisdiction were best analysed over a longer period than a single year. It was also necessary to discount the distorting effect of multiple cases. Over the period 1985–7, of the cases where a conclusion was reached:

> 28 per cent had been settled, 50 per cent withdrawn and 22 per cent were decided by tribunals. As well as producing settlements, ACAS conciliation has a likely effect on a number of withdrawals (including some private settlements) and has thus played a significant part in the operation of the equal value provisions.[33]

Critics of the high level of withdrawals associated with equal pay (and indeed racial discrimination) cases are less happy with this conclusion.

Conciliation in Discrimination Cases

Under both the Sex Discrimination Act and the Race Relations Act ACAS is charged with the responsibility of conciliating in order to try and settle a complaint without the need for its determination by a tribunal.

It is generally accepted that these cases, along with those involving equal pay, present special difficulties and problems. This is also an area in which the ACAS individual conciliation role is particularly misunderstood and in which, as the research findings summarised later in this chapter show, the Service has come in for some criticism. Accordingly ACAS now organises specialist training courses for

Table 4.5 Individual conciliation: cases settled and withdrawn as percentages of cases dealt with, 1983–8

	1983	*1984*	*1985*	*1986*	*1987*	*1988*
Dismissal cases						
Settled	40	44	51	54	63	67
Withdrawn	27	25	24	21	16	15
Sex Discrimination Act						
Settled	25	28	31	23	22*	19*
Withdrawn	28	33	36	38	42*	55*
Race Relations Act						
Settled	16	12	15	15	*	*
Withdrawn	33	42	42	40	*	*

Note:
*All discrimination complaints combined.
Source: ACAS, *Annual Reports*, 1983–8.

those conciliation officers who are specially selected to undertake discrimination casework. Speakers from both the Equal Opportunities Commission and the Commission on Racial Equality contribute towards these courses.

For some years ACAS has recognised that discrimination cases need particularly sensitive handling and keeps under review the criteria for selecting staff for this work. In the light of some of the research findings ACAS has also accepted the need to publicise its role and that of the agencies more effectively.

The conciliation process itself differs little from that followed in other types of complaint, but as Table 4.5 shows, there is a marked difference in the numbers of settlements and withdrawals as between dismissal cases and discrimination cases, even after making allowance for the fact that the dismissal complaints were influenced by the steadily increasing number of non-ITI cases.

The experience of ACAS and the results of some of the research summarised later in this chapter suggest two reasons in particular for the low disposal rates in sex and discrimination cases:

- the issues are seen by one side or the other to involve matters of principle which do not lend themselves so readily to monetary compromise as dismissal cases:
- it is only after they have lodged a complaint that employees begin to realise the enormity of the pressures to which they are exposed in pressing it to a conclusion – hence the high number of subsequent withdrawals.

In summary, although ACAS is required by law to seek to achieve settlements which avoid the need for a tribunal hearing, the whole process of conciliation over discrimination cases lies uneasily with the underlying principles of the legislation. The principles themselves are questioned in the Labour Party's 1989 Policy Review (*Meet the Challenge Make the Change*). An incoming Labour government would not only change the law, it would establish equality tribunals to assume the role presently discharged by industrial tribunals in sex and equality cases.

The Special Problems of Non-ITI Cases

We have already noted that ACAS has a responsibility for dealing with cases where no formal complaint has been made but where the potential for such a claim exists. These are the so-called non-ITI cases.

The statutory obligation under which ACAS acts in these cases is to be found in Sections 133 (3) and 134 (3) of the 1978 Employment Protection (Consolidation) Act, in Section 64 of the Sex Discrimination Act 1975 and in Section 55 of the Race Relations Act of 1976. Section 134 (3), for example, provides that where action has been taken against a worker in respect of which he could have made a complaint (that is dismissal) but before a complaint has actually been made to a tribunal, a conciliation officer may be asked to act as if a complaint has been made.

The vast majority of these cases are concerned with dismissal. The reason why the services of a conciliation officer are regarded as essential is because, before the employer agrees the terminal arrangements (for example, special enhanced payments) to be made, he wants to be sure that even if the employee does have second thoughts, any subsequent complaint to an industrial tribunal would be excluded. Section 140 of the Employment Protection (Consolidation) Act lays down that any agreement which seeks to preclude any person from proceeding to an industrial tribunal is void *unless a conciliation officer has taken action*.

Typical of these cases are the following:

- the employer who has declared a redundancy and who wishes to agree terms with those to be dismissed (which may be higher than legal entitlement);
- the employer who wishes to part company with a member of his

staff whose services are no longer required but who deserves special consideration for past performance;

- the director or senior manager whose contract is to be terminated before the due date. The financial terms envisaged in these cases are nearly always in excess of the statutory maxima but a declaration by a tribunal that the dismissal was unfair could be useful in subsequent proceedings in the civil courts, for example, wrongful dismissal;
- the employer who is not prepared to re-employ workers who were dismissed during an industrial dispute but who is prepared to make some kind of severance payment.

In these kinds of case the employer frequently demands rapid ACAS action but the conciliator has to bear in mind that unless he discharges his statutory responsibilities correctly, any agreement that he does witness would not debar an applicant's right to go to a tribunal. In addition, ACAS might find itself subject to action in the courts. And he must also bear in mind that if in any particular case a trade union is recognised for collective bargaining purposes, his neutrality may be challenged if the union feels that he is bending over backwards to help the employer deal expeditiously with, say, a redundancy even before the union has had the fullest opportunity to raise directly with the employer either the need for the redundancy or his method of giving effect to it.

In its 1982 report ACAS pointed out that where both sides arrive at a provisional settlement, whether through ACAS conciliation or not, the conciliation officer must ensure that they fully understand the terms of the settlement:

> In particular, the complainant must be made aware that the right to pursue a claim to an industrial tribunal is removed by signing an ACAS conciliated settlement. The conciliation officer cannot thus discharge his statutory responsibilities simply by 'rubber stamping' a previously agreed settlement between the parties.[34]

In its 1983 report ACAS returned to the point by stressing that unless 'a conciliation officer is able to take action as prescribed by Parliament in the legislation, any subsequent settlement may not be excluded from the jurisdiction of the industrial tribunals'.[35]

But it was in its 1985 report that ACAS entered into its fullest explanation. Before an agreement reached under ACAS auspices would debar a reference to a tribunal:

various conditions must be satisfied and a conciliation officer needs to have taken certain minimum action to promote a valid settlement. Two conditions relating to unfair dismissal complaints are first, that individuals must be under notice of termination (or have left) and second, be claiming that action has been taken in respect of which they could complain to a tribunal. Conciliation officers need to establish that these two conditions are satisfied. It is also necessary to ensure that the parties understand the Service's role, their statutory rights as appropriate and the implication of coming to an agreement. Conciliation officers also need to offer them reasonable time to reflect and seek advice if required. It can take time to complete this minimum action, which will necessitate private discussions with the employees affected, or their representatives. These could in turn result in employees seeking to improve the terms on offer and this possibility has caused employers to change their decision to involve ACAS, especially where employees have volunteered for redundancy and were presumed to be satisfied with the terms already offered. It is therefore advisable for employers not to assume ACAS involvement without first discussing the implications with the Service.[36]

Table 4.6 shows how dramatically the number and proportion of non-ITI cases has increased.

Table 4.6 Total cases received by ACAS and number and percentage of non-ITI cases, 1976–88

Year	*Total cases received*	*Non-ITI cases received*	
		Number	*% of total*
1976	41 930	752	2
1977	43 899	2 388	5
1978	44 713	3 071	7
1979	43 406	3 627	8
1980	46 447	8 648	19
1981	47 040	5 438	12
1982	46 996	6 132	13
1983	42 943	6 102	14
1984	42 723	6 693	16
1985	42 887	8 774	20
1986	51 431	12 825	25
1987	40 817	13 014	32
1988	44 443	16 206	36

Source: ACAS, *Annual Reports*, 1984–8.

The reasons for this enormous increase in non-ITI cases are not immediately apparent. One reason undoubtedly lies in the increasing number of cases in which the employer is legally represented. Even though the terms for settling say, a redundancy may be no more than those provided by statute or collective agreement and even though the redundancy may not even be contested, the lawyers are increasingly demanding that individual settlements should be reached under ACAS auspices so as to ensure a bar to subsequent industrial tribunal proceedings.

Every non-ITI case in which the conciliation officer assists the parties to conclude a settlement is recorded in the statistics as a conciliated settlement. This means that if ITI and non-ITI cases are combined the figure of conciliated settlements expressed as a percentage of all dismissals cases handled, can be misleading. Because of this, the ACAS report for 1987 and 1988 recorded the figures for ITI cases only as well as for the combined caseload. For ITI and non-ITI cases combined, conciliated settlements amounted to 63 per cent of all unfair dismissal cases completed in 1987 and 67 per cent in 1988. For ITI cases only, the figures were 47 per cent and 41 per cent. Figures contained in the same reports enable us to calculate a 96 per cent and 98 per cent settlement rates for non-ITI cases in 1987 and 1988. The fact that all the non-ITI cases did not result in recorded settlements suggests that ACAS conciliation officers were properly discharging their statutory responsibilities of explanation and clarification.

Concerns of the TUC

Any action, whether by ACAS or others, that could weaken the collective bargaining position of the trade unions is always a matter of concern to the TUC.

In 1985 the TUC became concerned that individual dismissal settlements reached under ACAS auspices were being used by an employer to undermine collective bargaining over a redundancy affecting 500 employees. In particular there was concern over the allegation that under the threat of withdrawing the redundancy payments on offer the employer had put pressure on employees to sign individual settlements under which they would waive their right of access to an industrial tribunal.

The ACAS obligation under the law is quite clear. If the employer and an employee wish ACAS to assist towards an individual settlement in cases of this kind, the Service is under an unqualified obligation to comply. Equally it is not part of ACAS policy deliberately to undermine the negotiating position of the trade unions (or, come to that, of employers).

ACAS tried in this case to reconcile these conflicting interests by assuring the TUC that it was ACAS policy:

> to inform relevant unions at the outset in situations of this kind, and to keep unions informed of developments as they occurred. In addition, it was ACAS's policy to await the exhaustion of grievance or disputes procedures before commencing individual conciliation procedures. In some circumstances, however, it could be necessary to issue COT3 forms [this is the reference number of the ACAS form on which conciliated settlements are recorded] to individuals who wished to leave early to go abroad or take up other employment, but in such cases, ACAS would alert those individuals to the legal rights being waived and to the need to consult the relevant union officers or representatives.[37]

The TUC welcomed these assurances but another issue which concerned them was that the waiver clause in individual settlements was so widely drafted as to exclude the right of an employee to submit a claim over any employment right to an industrial tribunal and not just one relating to the original complaint (usually unfair dismissal). The TUC thought that this could be unduly wide. Arising from a subsequent review of its role in individual conciliation ACAS decided that in cases leading to 'all-embracing' settlements ACAS conciliation officers, when counselling the parties as to the implications of any agreement, would draw specific attention to a list of the statutory employment rights that would be waived.

But a much more serious problem over ACAS's individual conciliation role arose in the course of the long-running dispute between News International and the print unions.

After months of discussion this dispute reached crisis point in 1986 when negotiations over arrangements for the printing of a proposed new London evening paper broke down, the unions called some 5000 members out on strike, and the management responded by dismissing the strikers and, virtually overnight, moving all four of its existing titles from Fleet Street and Grays Inn Road to Wapping.

Subsequently, negotiations took place twice between News

International and the TUC's Printing Industries Committee but on both occasions, proposed terms for the settlement of the dispute were rejected by a majority of the dismissed workers. At the end of October 1986 the company decided to make available to ex-employees on an individual basis the compensation terms that had been contained in its final offer to the unions. The offer was subject to the condition that those accepting it would withdraw all claims against the company and take no further part in the dispute. Naturally, the company required every individual settlement to be concluded under ACAS auspices and by the end of November, when the offer lapsed, some 1700 ex-employees (out of an original total of about 5300) had concluded settlements on this basis.

But the print unions still regarded themselves as in dispute with News International, and in November 1986 the National Graphical Association (NGA) wrote to the TUC expressing concern at the impact of the process of individual conciliation on the print unions' efforts to pursue their dispute with News International collectively. The union was particularly concerned that ACAS should have decided to act so soon after the offer incorporated in the individual conciliated settlements had been collectively rejected in secret ballots, and when the unions were continuing their efforts to achieve a negotiated settlement of the dispute. The NGA considered that in acting as it had ACAS had exceeded its statutory duty.

The TUC concluded that the News International dispute once more highlighted the potential conflict between the collective and individual conciliation roles of ACAS and decided that the issue should be included in the work being done by the TUC on future employment legislation.

Within the constraints imposed by reason of its statutory obligations, ACAS gave the TUC what assurances it could regarding the procedures it would follow in future. But when News International later decided to re-offer compensation terms to those who had not previously settled, and again requested ACAS assistance, the Service considered it had no option but to provide it. A further 3509 ex-employees decided this time to accept the offer, bringing to a total of 5264 those who concluded settlements under ACAS auspices.

Cases of this kind impose a heavy administrative burden on ACAS. Legal representatives on both sides are almost inevitably involved and have to be consulted; ACAS has to prepare a meticulously balanced explanatory statement for the employees (or ex-employees) involved; a special telephone enquiry point may be opened; and conciliation officers must also be on hand to deal with the considerable number of queries that inevitably arise.

The General Council of the TUC may well be right that further problems of this kind could have an adverse effect on ACAS's standing with trade unions, but it is not easy to see what can be done that would be of practical help to them. If in future the law was changed and ACAS was debarred from exercising its individual conciliation role in these cases, its neutrality might be confirmed in trade union eyes. But employers would still negotiate individual settlements but now without ACAS involvement. And without that involvement the employee might lack the objective advice he needs in order to make up his mind that he is not being bounced into an unsatisfactory deal.

Research into Individual Conciliation

In this chapter some indication has been given of the problems which confront the ACAS individual conciliation officer. To these can be added the fact that his work is more frequently exposed to the spotlight of research and analysis than that of his colleagues.

The research and analysis is sometimes conducted on behalf of organisations and individuals concerned with what they perceive to be the need for social justice or advancement. Inevitably therefore progress in this field will always be thought by some to be too slow and the blame is heaped not just on government, employers and trade unions, but also on those responsible for trying to ensure that the law, as it stands, is properly and sympathetically applied, namely industrial tribunals and ACAS. With equal inevitability therefore, ACAS does not emerge from research and analysis with universal approbation and an unblemished record. Perhaps this is no bad thing. It keeps the organisation on its toes and it acts as a useful counterbalance to the embarrassingly favourable results of research in other areas of its work.

There are three other points to bear in mind in considering the research work. The sizes of some of the samples used tend to be small; the time span involved in initiating the research and publishing the results is often lengthy, and by the time the results are available ACAS may have instituted changes to its systems and procedures such that the original criticisms although forcefully made, are no longer justified.

Thus in June 1986 the Equal Opportunities Commission commissioned some research the central aim of which, in the words of the authors, Cosmo Graham and Norman Lewis, was 'to examine individual conciliation in equal pay and sex discrimination cases in order to consider its impact on ultimate case outcomes. Our primary concern was to try to explain the reason for so many cases being withdrawn'.[38]

The research was conducted between September 1981 and June 1982. The sample eventually comprised 95 applicants who had submitted tribunal applications between January 1980 and October 1981 and 69 respondents. The results were published in June 1985. In their report Graham and Lewis noted that there was overwhelming evidence from the applicants that ACAS conciliators did not tell applicants about the existence of 'supportive agencies'. To point out that in September 1982 ACAS had issued a leaflet explaining the conciliation officer's role, which, amongst other matters, covered this very point, is not a criticism of the authors but is an indication of how the time-lags involved in research of this kind can invalidate some of the conclusions. Perhaps it also indicates how earlier research with similar findings may have been a catalyst to ACAS action.

Graham and Lewis reached the very firm conclusion that 'the mere context of lodging a complaint in a world of unequal resources and unequal access to information is the *clearest single explanation* for applicants withdrawing their complaints'.[39]

In their view:

> the primary explanation for the relatively large proportion of withdrawals and the relative failure of the conciliation process in gender cases lies outside the performance of ACAS conciliation officers. The criticisms of the officers made by applicants (and, very occasionally by respondents) seemed to have been largely based on a misinterpretation of the role of ACAS.[40]

In all, Graham and Lewis were 'impressed by the general performance of ACAS officers and firmly convinced that it was not a significant influence on the pattern of case outcomes'.[41] They ended their report with the timely reminder that as other research had indicated that most employers were receptive to the advice they received on the advisory visits of ACAS officers, this was a resource that ought not to be ignored in advancing the aims of the discrimination legislation. They could have added that in its advisory work ACAS does not have to work under the same legislative constraints that are involved in discharging its individual conciliation responsibilities.

Despite the relatively clean bill of health given to ACAS in this report, the Service cannot duck its share of the criticism that applicants in equal pay and sex discrimination feel themselves so overwhelmed by the system as a whole that many of them throw in the towel. The report refers, for example, to how the mere fact of conveying a full summary of the employer's statements, accompanied by explanations of the law, the onus of proof and the limited success rate at tribunals, can totally overwhelm the applicant. The antagonism of some women to ACAS conciliation officers certainly ran deep.

A report (*Industrial Tribunal Applicants under the Race Relations Act 1976*) written by Vinod Kumar, in which ACAS came under greater criticism, was published by the Commission for Racial Equality in February 1986. The fieldwork for this report was carried out between November 1981 and the spring of 1982. The final sample that was chosen covered 377 applicants to industrial tribunals in England and Wales during the two-year period July 1978 to June 1980.

In the words of the report itself it:

> draws attention to the powerful effect of good professional assistance on the outcome, not only of tribunal hearings but also of conciliation, for it can help to redress the imbalance between the applicant and the employer. Yet the study finds that there were huge gaps in the availability of professional assistance to complainants in industrial tribunals, and the Commission strongly urges the Government to extend legal aid to them . . .[42]

ACAS was specifically taken to task about the timing of its contact with the applicant. It was argued that an approach within a few days of receipt by ACAS of the tribunal application was:

> too early from the applicant's point of view for he or she would not have received any information from the respondent and, for the most part, would not have a representative available, so that his or her bargaining position would be at its weakest.[43]

More seriously perhaps, it was contended that ACAS was 'likely to be judged by the Government according to the extent of its sucess in conciliating cases. By the same token, this is also likely to be a vital element in appraising the performance of individual conciliation officers'.[44] In fairness it has to be said that the ACAS response to this charge was also published in the report, namely that 'ACAS regarded the indicator as just one factor which had to be taken into account when assessing performance. In respect of discrimination cases ... sensitivity in handling such matters was an important element in the satisfactory performance of its duties'.[45]

The fact that ACAS, although not expected to take a view on the merits of a case, might advise about the risk of costs being awarded by a tribunal against an applicant was taken as implying that the conciliation officer had taken such a view. It was questioned whether the number of cases withdrawn was entirely due to misunderstanding on the part of the complainants. Was it the case that some conciliation officers tended 'in their zeal to cross the dividing lines between impartial advice and undue pressure?'[46]

The author of the report suggested that ACAS should 'institute a thorough review of their role and actual practices at least in race relations cases'.[47] He went on to say that:

> since the period to which our survey relates, ACAS tells us they have taken steps to refine their approach to individual conciliation such as the provision of an information leaflet about the ACAS role, particularly for unrepresented parties. A review has led to changes in the specialist training arrangements for conciliation officers involved in discrimination cases. However, we feel that there is need for a detailed racial awareness training of all Conciliation Officers and a more comprehensive understanding of the Statute ...[48]

Although it may be felt that the changes ACAS has made to its procedures do not go far enough, they do at least indicate a measure of flexibility and responsiveness to the criticism it receives. For one reason or another (some of them probably due to a failure to understand the ACAS role), 54 per cent of the applicants covered by the survey regarded the role of ACAS as having been either of no help at all or not very helpful. Thirty-five per cent of them felt that in his general attitude the conciliator had been more on the side of the employer. Clearly there is no reason for complacency here.

A thorough piece of research into dismissals which sought the views both of applicants and of employers (and their representatives) was carried out as part of the Warwick Survey with the assistance of Social and Community Planning Research. From a structured sample of 1339 cases from the registers of applications dated 1 October 1976 to 30 September 1977 interviews were achieved with 979 tribunal applicants and 1013 respondents. The interviews were held in the first half of 1978. The results were subsequently analysed by Dickens *et al.* in *Dismissed*, first published in 1985.

In the words of Dickens *et al.* the parties' assessment of ACAS conciliation:

> was obtained by seeking whether they regarded the conciliation officer's intervention as helpful and to what extent they thought that the same outcome could have been achieved without such intervention. Also . . . the parties were asked about the impartiality of the conciliation officer . . .[49]

Dickens *et al.*'s conclusions were clear:

> There is no doubt that the general view of both applicants and respondents is that ACAS conciliation officers are impartial and helpful. It is also clear that, not surprisingly the parties' assessments are, to some extent, influenced by the outcome of their particular case. About two-thirds of all applicants and employers who had contact with a conciliation officer considered he or she was 'not on one side or the other'. Although the proportion of applicants regarding the conciliation officer as neutral remains at 66 per cent, the distribution of perceived bias varies according to the outcome.[50]

As to the possibility of settlement without ACAS, 79 per cent of applicants and 42 per cent of employers in cases stated to have been settled through ACAS said that without ACAS a settlement would have been either definitely not possible or probably not possible.

Representatives apparently had a less flattering view about the effects of ACAS. 'Three-quarters of self-represented applicants found the conciliation officer helpful' reported Dickens *et al.*:

> compared with 59 per cent of those who had legal representation and personal contact with the conciliation officer. A similar picture is found among employers, with 73 per cent of lay-represented employers finding the conciliation officer helpful compared with 58 per cent of those with external legal representation.[51]

Dickens *et al.*'s explanation for this was that unrepresented parties were satisfied relatively easily but that the represented parties were likely to be more demanding. Success was seen as achieved through the representatives rather than any effort on the part of ACAS.

The individual conciliation staff at ACAS can draw little comfort from another point revealed by the research, namely that trade union and employers' association officials often 'using their experience of other forms of conciliation – notably that provided by ACAS in collective disputes – as a yardstick against which the individual conciliation was measured'[52] in some respects found it wanting. One official complained about lack of initiative or 'only good listeners and messenger boys'.[53]

Individual Conciliation and the Courts

Because the duties of the conciliation officer are prescribed in the statutes it follows that if, in the view of the complainant or respondent, an officer has failed to act in accordance with the law, ACAS is liable to action in the courts. Between 1975 and 1988 ACAS received some 600 000 cases for individual conciliation but only a handful ever found its way to the courts – a tribute to the way in which conciliation officers have at least stuck to the letter of the law.

With the exception of the *Keys* v. *Courage Take Home Foods* case, the courts have taken a supportive view of the way in which ACAS has applied the law – perhaps surprisingly so. Thus in the case of *Slack* v. *Greenham (Plant Hire) Ltd* the Employment Appeal Tribunal, in affirming that a conciliation officer was not obliged to follow any specific formula and that his only obligation was to try and promote a settlement, declared that he was not under a statutory duty to inform an employee of his right to claim for future loss of earnings or, indeed, to explain the law or his rights. The nature of a conciliation officer's function depended on the circumstances of the case. Mr Slack had been anxious for an immediate monetary settlement and it might have defeated the conciliation officer's function if he had told the employee that he might receive considerably more money because of his right to claim future loss of wages.

The case of *Moore* v. *Duport Furniture Products Ltd* (in which ACAS was joined as a party) dealt with the important question of whether the duty of a conciliation officer went beyond that of simply recording an agreement, that is, satisfying himself that the agreement was fair to both sides.

Mr Moore had been suspended by Duport on suspicion of having stolen company property and subsequently agreed under protest to accept £300 and resign. A conciliation officer was then called in (this was a non-ITI case) and asked to record the settlement, which with appropriate explanations to both sides, he duly did. Mr Moore was subsequently informed by the police that he was not going to be prosecuted and he then claimed that he had been unfairly dismissed. Duport counter-claimed that an industrial tribunal was not empowered to consider the complaint as it had already been settled through conciliation.

At the House of Lords hearing, Mr Moore's contention that it was the duty of the conciliation officer to try to promote a settlement that was fair to both sides and that he had failed in the duty was expressly abandoned. In delivering his judgement Lord Russell of Killowen stated:

> In my opinion the conciliation officer in this case, faced with an agreement as to the amount of compensation, and faced with the fact (as was obvious) that reinstatement or re-engagement was not practicable, fulfilled as much of his duty as was open to him by ascertaining that the parties had truly agreed and reducing the agreement of form COT3 into clear writing for signature by the parties.

In response to other propositions advanced on behalf of Mr Moore their Lordships stated:

- that it was not necessary for Mr Moore explicitly to claim that he had been unfairly dismissed – it was sufficient for the conciliation officer to have inferred an implied claim from the employee's 'overt acts or attitudes';
- where action to promote re-employment was not applicable, the conciliation officer was not under any duty to take it;
- where the parties had already agreed on a sum by way of compensation there was no room for the conciliation officer to seek to promote agreement between them as to an appropriate sum.

Mr Moore's appeal was accordingly dismissed.

The case of *Hennessey* v. *Craigmyle* and ACAS raised the interesting point as to whether economic or physical duress could provide grounds to make an agreement void.

After a dispute with his employer, Mr Hennessey was told that he could either sign a document to be prepared by a conciliation officer 'in full and final settlement' and be made redundant (with certain payments) or be summarily dismissed without pay in lieu of notice and without a reference. In any event he would be dismissed in eight days' time. Mr Hennessey was advised by his solicitor to sign, which after an unsuccessful attempt, through ACAS, to negotiate with Craigmyle, he duly did. But he then went on to file an unfair dismissal complaint both on the grounds that various statutory requirements had not been met and that he had been forced to sign under economic duress.

The Court of Appeal found that the statutory requirements had been met and declared that the fact that employees received independent advice from skilled ACAS officers did not rule out the possibility that duress could make a settlement void but it did make that possibility more remote. In the particular case the Court decided that the industrial tribunal had come to a proper conclusion, that is, that it had no jurisdiction to hear the employee's complaint of unfair dismissal.

In the case of *Gilbert* v. *Kembridge Fibres Ltd* the relatively simple principle of whether an agreement, for it to be binding, had to be in writing and signed by the parties came before the Employment Appeal Tribunal. Mr Gilbert was dismissed by Kembridge and his complaint of unfair dismissal was subsequently the subject of an oral settlement reached through ACAS. The terms of the settlement were set out by the conciliation officer on the usual form COT3. Mr Gilbert signed it but then had second thoughts and returned the form to ACAS with his signature crossed out. The industrial tribunal decided that an offer to settle had been made and accepted with the assistance of ACAS and that an enforceable agreement had been set out on form COT3 even though the form had not been signed by both parties. Mr Gilbert was therefore not entitled to have his complaint of unfair dismissal heard.

The Employment Appeal Tribunal dismissed Mr Gilbert's appeal. Legal agreements could be made without their terms being reduced to writing.

So far the attitude of the courts has not unduly restricted the way in which conciliators set about their work. There is, of course, a point of view that ACAS should be much more proactive in support of the applicant. Dickens *et al.*, for example, have said that in practice, 'by acting in a neutral way in a situation of inequality, ACAS conciliation officers perpetuate the inequality rather than redressing it'.[54] But neutrality between employer and employee is so much part of the ACAS philosophy that short of changes to the law or of judgements by the courts, there is no prospect of ACAS conciliators acting differently.

Some Conclusions

We have noted in this chapter the considerable extension of statutory employment rights during the past 20 years; the valuable but difficult role performed by ACAS in filtering out (either through conciliated settlement or withdrawal) cases that would otherwise proceed to an industrial tribunal; and the way in which the ACAS process is prescribed by statute and case law.

The conciliation officer involved in seeking a solution to a collective dispute has exactly the same objective as his colleague engaged on individual conciliation but despite recent changes to employment law the former still works within a less restricted legal framework. Perhaps too, he works with more sophisticated users. The battle-scarred management and the trade union official accustomed to the cut and thrust of collective bargaining are well aware of the advantages, disadvantages, scope and limitations of the conciliation process. But the employee who thinks he has been unfairly dismissed or the applicant who believes that failure to get the job was due to sex or racial discrimination is likely to feel much more deeply and, even at times, irrationally about the issue. A sense of optimism that an injustice will be remedied leads to an unjustified level of expectation as to what the conciliator will or can do. Just when he needs a friend and ally he discovers that this is not supposed to be the conciliator's role. Perhaps in these circumstances it is surprising that there is not more resentment and misunderstanding about the ACAS role than there is.

And of course, the individual conciliation officer is as human as the rest of us. Perhaps at times he does press too hard for settlements either because of the personal challenge or out of a belief that his performance and that of the organisation will be judged by the number of settlements that are reached. And perhaps, at times, he is too diffident and cautious to the extent that he acts as little more than a channel of communication between applicant and employer; and perhaps at other times he goes further than he should in spelling out the detailed consequences of a claim pressed too far or of a response inadequately made.

But even allowing for these frailties a record which shows that year in, year out, some two-thirds of all the applications submitted to industrial tribunals are disposed of (a) without the need for a tribunal hearing, and, (b) with a minimal amount of litigation on the part of either applicant or respondent is not one of which ACAS should feel ashamed.

5 The Statutory Minimum Wage Question

The Early Background

Employers and trade unions in the UK were at one time united in their opposition to the concept of a statutorily-fixed national minimum wage, this despite pressure for its introduction from those speaking on behalf of the low paid. Employers were concerned that any form of state regulation would interfere with the freedom of the labour market and that any minimum that might be established would be fixed too high. This would lead to an unsupportable increase in labour costs in organisations directly affected and to pressure for the maintenance of differentials elsewhere. Trade unions were concerned either that the statutory minimum would be so low as to be meaningless or that its very establishment would weaken potential employee commitment to trade union organisation and collective bargaining.

Historically, therefore, the UK initially approached the low pay problem by providing statutory minimum wage protection only to those employed in specific industries in which employees were considered to be exceptionally lowly paid. This was done through the medium of trade boards, subsequently retitled wages councils.

Not that Parliament, in a *laissez-faire* Victorian age, was quickly persuaded to the need for statutory protection for the underpaid. Winston Churchill was credited with piloting the first legislation through Parliament (the Trade Boards Act of 1909), but the pressure for legislation had started 30 years earlier when public attention was drawn to the practice of 'sweating' of which the payment of very low wages was just a part. In 1891 a forerunner of what eventually became the Fair Wages Resolution was approved by Parliament without a division. This stated:

> In the opinion of this House it is the duty of the Government in all Government contracts to make provision against the evils which have recently been disclosed before the House of Lords' Sweating Committee, and to insert such conditions as may prevent the abuse arising from sub-letting, and make every effort to secure the

> payment of the rate of wages generally accepted as current for a competent workman in his trade.[1]

As Phelps-Brown wrote:

> the Resolution ... marked the acceptance of a principle, and the invention of a procedure: government could hardly itself fix wages, but where in a given trade and district certain wages were recognised as reputable, it could require that they be paid by employers.[2]

The same principle, on a basis wider than just government contracts, was subsequently extended elsewhere, for example, in the wartime arbitration orders, the Terms and Conditions of Employment Act, 1959, and the Employment Protection Act, 1975. But none of these requirements had the compulsion of a national minimum wage that had to be observed by all employers.

The awakening of the public conscience in the last decades of the nineteenth century owed a great deal to the efforts of Sir Charles Dilke, MP for Chelsea. It was Dilke who persistently kept the issue of sweating before Parliament. In 1886 his political career was apparently in ruins following his involvement in sexual behaviour of a kind that the Victorians found intolerable, namely, it was not so much what he did that mattered as the fact that he was caught doing it. But, with the support of Joseph Chamberlain, he returned to Parliament six years later where, although debarred from office, he steadfastly advocated the need for the establishment of trade boards. The draft of his first bill was first printed in 1900 and was thereafter printed annually but never received a second reading.

But as the nation gradually moved towards measures which tackled some of the problems of poverty, the mood changed and under Churchill's Act of 1909 four trade boards were set up – for ready-made tailoring, paper-boxmaking, chain-making and machine-made lace and net finishing, where current wages were considered to be below subsistence level. The Act gave the boards the strictly limited function of fixing minimum time rates of wages; at the same time a wage inspectorate was set up to enforce compliance with the boards' decisions. The constitution and procedures of these first four boards set the basic pattern for all the boards and wages councils that were to be established over the following 50 years.

The trade boards got off to a slow start – it was not until 1913 that the first order was issued. Nevertheless, in 1917 the Whitley Committee recommended that the scope of the trade boards should be 'extended to cover, in addition to industries in which low wages were prevalent, those industries in which there was a lack of organisation, particularly on the side of the workers, resulting in an absence of collective bargaining arrangements'.[3] A second Trade Boards Act that reflected this principle, was passed in 1918 and, as a result, by 1938 there were some 50 boards in existence covering over a million workers.

In 1945 the Trade Boards Acts were repealed and replaced by the Wages Councils Act. The wages councils, as they were now called, were given the power, not just to fix minimum time rates, but guaranteed weekly remuneration and holidays with pay as well. Under an Act of 1948 the existing statutory basis of fixing pay in the road haulage industry was replaced by a wages council and in 1959 the Terms and Conditions of Employment Act brought the existing provisions for regulating the remuneration and conditions of employment in the catering industry within the scope of four new wages councils. By 1964 the number of Wages Councils stood at 57 with 3.5 million workers in scope.

But by 1988 the number of wages councils had dropped to 26 covering 2.5 million workers aged 21 and over. Retailing, clothing manufacture and hotel and catering covered an estimated 94 per cent of all workers covered by wages councils. About two-thirds worked part-time and the majority of workers were female. To those numbers should be added the nation's agricultural workers who since 1948 in England and Wales, and since 1949 in Scotland, had been covered by two agricultural wages boards operating in a similar manner to wages councils.

Problems of Enforcement

Ever since the establishment of the first trade boards there has been machinery for the enforcement of statutory pay orders. A wage inspectorate was set up under Winston Churchill's Act of 1909. It continues to operate today although the 1988 total of 71 inspectors was considered by many to be totally inadequate.

Wage inspectors are appointed by the Secretary of State. Establishments are supposed to be inspected at regular intervals and the inspectors are also charged with the responsibility of investigating any complaints from workers who think they are not receiving the statutory minimum remuneration to which they are entitled. Where an offence has been committed, legal proceedings may be taken. Thus, for example, an employer is liable to be fined for:

- failing to post notices or to keep proper records;
- paying less than the statutory minimum remuneration;
- obstructing an inspector.

Civil proceedings may also be taken by or on behalf of a worker for the recovery of arrears of remuneration.

The present-day methods used by the inspectorate to check the pay of workers were described in the Department of Employment's 1988 consultation document, *Wages Councils*. The aim is to check not less than 30 000 establishments each year:

- where a firm has a formal pay agreement a check is made to ensure that its provisions are at least as favourable as those in the wages orders. Provided this is the case and a satisfactory grievance procedure exists, compliance is assumed;
- in the case of 'multiple firms' which have five or more branches, and which hold their wages records centrally, the records are examined at head office and a sample of the branches is chosen for confirmation visits. Where the results are satisfactory compliance throughout the firm is assumed;
- for smaller firms an initial check is normally made by postal questionnaire. If the reply indicates that there may be under-payment, or if no reply is received, an inspection visit is carried out. Where the reply shows that no workers are underpaid, no visit is made except to a 5 per cent sample in order to monitor the validity of the postal enquiry method;
- all other checks, such as routine investigations put in hand without the questionnaire procedure, or the following up of confidential complaints from workers, are carried out by visit.

In total, the consultation paper stated, 'about two thirds of inspections are carried out by visit and one third by other methods'.[4] It was also stated that although the inspectorate 'has power to prosecute employers for offences ... it has always followed a policy of securing compliance by advice and persuasion. The great majority of employers respond to this approach'.[5]

In its evidence to the Donovan Commission the Ministry of Labour produced a table showing the extent of inspection and enforcement. Table 5.1 is an extract.

Table 5.1 Wages councils: inspection and enforcement

Numbers Covered	*1938*	*1954*	*1964*
Number of wages councils	47	65	57
Estimated number of workers within scope	1 000 000	3 500 000	3 500 000
Number of establishments in employers' lists	83 378	513 995	507 438
Inspections during year	18 671	53 300	48 606
Inspections during year as percentage of employers' lists	22.4	10.4	9.6
Establishments where arrears of wages paid	2518	6 638	6 010
Establishments where arrears of wages paid as percentage of total inspections	13.5	12.5	12.4
Workers underpaid as percentage of workers' wages examined	2.9	3.9	3.8

These figures were noteworthy:

- for the way in which, over the years, the proportion of inspections to the total number of establishments had declined;
- for the fact that in each of the three years 1938, 1954, and 1964 about one establishment in every eight inspected was failing to pay the statutory minimum remuneration;
- the consistently low percentage of workers actually found to have been underpaid.

By 1987 the inspectorate had tightened its policy by gearing its visits to establishments *likely to be underpaying* (two-thirds of all checks). Figures published by the Department of Employment in its 1988 consultation document are not, therefore, strictly comparable with the figures presented to the Donovan Commission in 1965. Nevertheless, they showed that in 1987 the percentage of workers underpaid as a percentage of workers' wages examined ('a more reliable indicator',[6] it was claimed) was still low (about 3 per cent). This seems reasonable, for even in establishments covered by voluntary collective agreements, it is safe to assume that as a result of genuine error in the pay office or elsewhere, a number of errors of underpayment will always be found. This does not mean that the collective agreement is being totally flouted or ignored. But Brian Doyle, without adducing any specific evidence to support his contention, has suggested that the resources of the inspectorate 'are not sufficient to undertake comprehensive policing of employers covered by the legislation and diverse evidence . . . suggests that as many as 40 per cent of employers are underpaying about 16 per cent of workers'[7] covered by wages councils.

Establishment, Variation or Abolition

Under the Wages Councils Act of 1979 (a consolidating Act which replaced the earlier legislation), the Secretary of State could establish a wages council either on his own initiative or after an inquiry and recommendation by ACAS. Under earlier legislation inquiries were carried out by *ad hoc* committees or, between its formation and demise, by the Commission on Industrial Relations. He could act on his own initiative if he considered that adequate machinery for the effective regulation of the remuneration of any group of workers did not exist and should be established, having regard to the remuneration of the workers concerned. He was required to refer a question to ACAS if an application for a wages council was made by trade unions, employers' organisations or joint bodies. He might also refer a question to ACAS on his own initiative. ACAS could recommend the establishment of a wages council either when it considered that adequate machinery did not exist, or that any existing machinery was likely to cease to exist or be adequate and a reasonable standard of remuneration would not be maintained.

Similarly, a wages council could be abolished or its scope varied by the Secretary of State, either on his own initiative or following an application by trade unions, employers' organisations or joint bodies. Any application had to be on the grounds that the wages council was no longer necessary to maintain a reasonable standard of remuneration for the workers concerned. Before deciding whether to abolish or vary the scope of a council the Secretary of State could refer the question to ACAS for inquiry and report.

Once the Secretary of State had considered any recommendations and allowed sufficent time for objections to be made and considered, he was required to lay any order for the establishment, abolition or variation of a council before Parliament. An order could be annulled by resolution of either House of Parliament.

One of the problems in connection with either the possible establishment or abolition of a wages council was that the statute did not define what was meant by the term 'reasonable standard of remuneration'. In its annual report for 1980 ACAS expressed the view that it seemed appropriate:

> for the purposes of the legislation, and bearing in mind the economic environment, to consider positive recommendations only if the workers were very low paid in comparison with workers generally. The benchmark adopted was the median of the lowest minimum rates of pay for adults set by the existing wages councils'.[8]

The Role of the Independent Council Members

Like the trade boards before them, each wages council consists of equal numbers of employers' and workers' representatives together with three independent members one of whom is the chairman.

Within each council, every member has a vote, but in practice voting is generally by sides. When the two sides disagree, the question is decided by the majority of the independent members or, if only one is present, by his vote. The role of the independent members is thus vital. In effect, they first act as conciliators trying to bridge the gap so that the employers and the workers can reach their own agreement. But failing agreement, each independent must vote either for the workers' claim or the employers' offer, either of which may have been modified during the preceding conciliation process. In other words, the independents become arbitrators – and pendulum arbitrators at that. It is reasonable to suppose that their votes will go to the side that has taken either the most reasonable or the least unreasonable position. In their conciliation role they may have suggested some kind of compromise but in their arbitration role, whatever their wish, further compromise is not allowed. Hence the occasional howls of protest when the independents combined with the employers to produce a proposal which the workers regarded as miserably low or with the workers to produce one which the employers regarded as disastrously high.

At one time each wages council was required to formulate changes in remuneration or holidays in the form of proposals. These would be published so that those affected could make representations about them. After possible amendment the council would then submit its proposals to the Minister (now the Secretary of State) for the making of an order to give them legal effect. The Minister had no power to amend or reject proposals put to him by a wages council. His only alternative to approval was to refer them back to the council for further consideration. If the council sent them back unchanged the Minister then had no alternative but to make a wages regulation order giving the proposals legal effect.

This procedure was a trifle embarrassing to governments during times of statutory pay policies, and since 1975 wages councils have been empowered to issue their proposals and orders without the need to refer them to the Secretary of State. Thus the government still has no powers to amend or overturn a council's decision.

The Case for Total Abolition

The case for wages council abolition has taken some strange twists. Typically it was the trade unions that pressed for their establishment, but in the first 30 post-war years of full employment it was also the trade unions that pressed for their abolition, basically because they were no longer seen to be so vital as a means of protection against low pay and because their very existence, far from paving the way towards the establishment of collective bargaining, positively inhibited its development. This was a view that was shared by the Donovan Commission. But at the time when trade unions were pressing for abolition it was the employers, so resistant to the establishment of wages councils in the first place, who were pressing for their retention largely on the grounds that without legal enforcement of minimum rates of pay there was a risk of undercutting of both wages and prices.

The policy of the Labour Government which came to power in 1974 was to encourage the abolition of wages councils. In its Wages Councils Act of 1979 it tried to ease the process by making provision for the conversion of a wages council into a statutory joint industrial council (SJIC) – a body similar to a wages council but without independent members. An SJIC was intended:

> to operate as a half-way stage between a wages council and a voluntary joint industrial council, for example, in an industry where the independent members on the wages council are not

normally called upon to vote, but where organisation amongst workers is not yet sufficiently developed to dispense with the enforcement services of the Wages Inspectorate.[9]

Disputes within an SJIC could be settled by compulsory arbitration at the request of either side.

Between 1974 and 1979, 12 wages councils were abolished, and in 1979 another nine were merged to form a single council for the retail food and allied trades. But not a single SJIC was formed. In its annual report for 1980, however, ACAS reported an investigation which it had carried out into a trade union request that the Licensed Residential Establishment and Licensed Restaurant Wages Council should be converted into an SJIC. In the words of its report, ACAS confirmed that the:

main condition ... was that the employers' and workers' sides of the wages council should have shown that normally they can reach joint agreements without the intervention of the independent members of the Council. Other relevant considerations ... were the willingness of the two sides to operate in a SJIC, the level and spread of membership of the trade unions and employers' associations concerned, their ability to negotiate and the extent of voluntary collective bargaining in the industry.[10]

On the basis of these criteria the conversion of the wages council into an SJIC was not recommended, and despite appeals by the trade unions to the Secretary of State for Employment, no change was made.

In retrospect it can be seen that the criteria for the conversion of any wages council into an SJIC were unlikely to be met. There was little likelihood of the two sides getting into the habit of concluding voluntary agreements if one side felt that the involvement of the independent members could produce a more satisfactory outcome.

As the country moved into the Thatcher years the mood changed and trade union pressure for the abolition (piecemeal or totally) of the wages councils diminished. Chris Pond described how much industrial relations and trade union opinion was moving back 'to a position of acceptance of the wages councils as a necessary form of safety net protection.[11] He quoted some words of ACAS in its annual report for 1980 that:

the retention of the councils has been necessary partly as a result of lack of progress in the development of collective bargaining, and

> partly because surveys of pay in wages council industries have indicated that there remain significant numbers of low paid workers who would be vulnerable if statutory protection was to be removed.[12]

Against the background of these statements it was hardly surprising that, in 1980, ACAS recommended the extension of the scope of one existing wages council and the establishment of a new one. A possible extension arose in the case of the Laundry Wages Council. ACAS recommended that statutory protection should be extended to 'launderette cleaners and attendants, laundry receiving shop staff, process workers and unit shop counter staff in dry cleaning establishments, and textile repairers in rental firms'.[13] The possibility of a new wages council arose in the contract cleaning industry when, after investigation, ACAS recommended that if there was no possibility of setting up some form of industry-wide collective bargaining on a voluntary basis, 'a wages council should be established to cover general cleaners and working supervisors in contract cleaning'.[14]

The Secretary of State never took any action on these recommendations and in 1986 the law would be changed so that he would be empowered entirely on his own volition, namely, without any prior need to refer the issue to ACAS for investigation, to set up, vary or abolish a wages council.

The attitude of Mrs Thatcher's government to wages councils was one of hostility. The pay levels they set, particularly for younger workers, were considered to be so high that they were holding back employment in the industries and services concerned. The government thus announced that it was denouncing Convention No. 26 of the International Labour Organisation to give it the freedom it needed either to abolish on substantially reform the wages council system. It is this Convention which:

> requires the creation and maintenance of machinery for fixing minimum wages in manufacturing and commercial trades (and in particular home-working trades) when no arrangements exist for the effective regulation of wages by collective agreements or otherwise and wages are exceptionally low.

The tone of the government consultative document suggested that it favoured abolition but in the light of the widespread representations it received, including some from employers' organisations that might normally have been expected to give their support, it decided instead on a policy of reform.

And so in 1986 the Wages Act was passed which, amongst other provisions:

- repealed the Wages Councils Act of 1979 but left in being the councils already established;
- empowered the Secretary of State at any time by order to abolish or vary the scope of any wages council. The provision for a prior inquiry by ACAS was thus removed. Before making an order the Secretary of State was required to have regard to the current levels of remuneration and 'such other matters as appear to him to be appropriate'.[15] In other words, any reference to collective bargaining, *per se*, was eliminated;
- empowered the Secretary of State to exclude specified employers from the scope of a council;
- restricted the wages councils (a) to workers aged 21 and over, and (b) to fixing a single minimum basic rate, a single overtime rate and a limit to any charge which an employer could make for providing accommodation with the job;
- debarred the councils from fixing other conditions of employment.

The councils were also required to consider the employment effects of their decisions in areas where workers were generally paid below the national average for their trade or occupation.

In 1988 the government returned to the attack and in the Department of Employment's consultation document *Wages Councils* comments were invited on its view 'that the time has come for the councils to be abolished'.[16] In support of this view it was suggested that:

- the system of national statutory rates of pay was inconsistent with the need for flexible pay determination;
- in some crucial respects the 1986 changes had not had the desired effect and had also left untouched the anomalies and anachronisms with which the system was 'shot through';[17]
- the world of the 1990s would be very different from that of 1909. The facts did not suggest that if abolition did take place, cases of extremely low wages, imposed against workers' wishes, would become 'endemic or widespread'.[18]

TUC and Labour Party Policy

Meanwhile, the TUC and the Labour Party had moved in the opposite direction. In July 1986 a pre-election statement, *Low*

Pay: Policies and Priorities was adopted by the General Council of the TUC and the National Executive Committee of the Labour Party for submission to the 1986 TUC and Labour Party conferences. Included in the proposals was one for the introduction of a national minimum wage backed by the force of law. The precise level of the wage was not mentioned but statements like 'a large number of national and international bodies have agreed that a level of earnings close to two-thirds of average earnings represents the lowest level for a decent living standard',[19] and 'the consensus of [union] replies . . . points in the direction of an initial £80 per week, in current terms, equivalent to about half average male manual earnings'[20] surely gave a clue as to the intention. In its 1989 Policy Review the Labour Party committed itself to a starting level of 50 per cent of male median earnings.

In their 1986 document the TUC and the Labour Party admitted that the problem of low pay could not now be solved by the traditional mix of a TUC target for negotiators, effective industry-wide agreements with statutory enforcement provisions, and wages councils where industry-wide collective bargaining was not so well developed. This approach was not even adequate to prevent the continual undermining of the collectively-bargained pay structure and of organised unionism. It was certainly not adequate to raise pay to the collectively-bargained level.

It was envisaged that collective bargaining would be the main vehicle for implementing the national minimum. Provision would, however, be made for the external enforcement of the minimum standards, first through conciliation by ACAS, followed if necessary by a reference to the CAC. In the words of the statement: 'The CAC would be empowered to make a declaration as to whether the national minimum wage was being paid and to make an award specifying what changes were necessary and providing for back pay where appropriate'.[21] The terms of CAC awards would become terms in the contracts of employment of the workers concerned. The CAC would also be empowered 'to give advice where appropriate about the implications of an award for the rest of the pay structure in question'.[22]

Enforceability would also be secured through 'a greatly expanded, strengthened and properly resourced wages inspectorate, renamed the minimum wages inspectorate'[23] whose responsibility would be to monitor observance and to ensure compliance with the national minimum wage 'as well as continuing to enforce Wages Councils orders'.[24] These words are of significance because of their implication that the concept of a national minimum wage and the wages council system would exist side by side.

The inspectorate would have three principal methods of enforcement:

- to refer complaints of underpayment to a trade union in the case of workers for whom a union was recognised;
- to refer other cases to the CAC for determination;
- to prosecute employers in the event of persistent or deliberate underpayment. 'This approach to enforcement', according to the statement, 'will ensure a high degree of union control and minimise the risk of the effectiveness of the minimum wage strategy being undermined by excessive legalism, appeals to the courts, and adverse case law'.[25]

The TUC and the Labour Party were pretty dismissive about the possible consequences of introducing a national minimum wage. Although accepting the need to give 'tapered pay increases' in existing pay structures which 'straddle the level of the minimum', and to provide 'appropriate differentials for responsibility and skill', the conclusion was unequivocal. 'Our conclusion is that implementation of a national minimum could be carried through without undue repercussions in terms of "particular" differentials and relativities'.[26] Trade unions would 'be expected to undertake not to quote in claims for higher paid workers that element of general percentage increases in earning specifically related to the general move to attain the national minimum wage'.[27]

Sadly these no doubt sincere expressions of intent at the national level are not inevitably shared by workpeople themselves. However much lip service may be paid to the need for a redistribution of income by means of statutory pay regulation, our experience shows that the principle has a pretty short shelf-life, and that before long the old arguments emerge with new force: 'My job has always been regarded as worth some differential over his. In my view, it still is'. No statutory incomes policy has ever been able, other than for a relatively short period, to overcome that very natural feeling.

The Future

By the end of 1989 the Conservative Government had not made any pronouncement that it intended to legislate on its 1988 proposals and abolish wages councils. Perhaps it had had second thoughts.

If there were grounds for retaining a modified system in 1986, it seemed difficult to justify total abolition in 1989. Certainly, there had been no great public clamour from the affected employers. The 1988 consultation paper referred to 'several requests for the abolition of particular councils, the exclusion of individual firms, or the release of particular sectors of a trade from regulation'[28] but the number of requests was not specified. As for 'the anomalies and anachronisms with which the system is shot through', it is reasonable to point out that given the will, these could have been addressed. The exclusion of launderettes from the Laundry Wages Council could, for example, have been remedied if the government had been willing to act on the recommendation contained in the 1980 ACAS report that statutory protection should be extended, amongst others, to 'launderette cleaners and attendants'.[29]

The underlying reason for the government's wish to abolish wages councils in their entirety was based on the conviction that any system of pay determination at the national (multi-employer) level is thoroughly bad. Certainly the arguments used in the consultation paper were not confined to the wages councils alone:

> National agreements and concepts such as the 'going rate' and 'annual pay round' need to be replaced by systems which respond more readily to local labour market conditions, the profitability of the enterprise, and differences in performance, merit and skills.[30]

The consultation paper drew attention to the consequences of national increases in wages council rates of pay, namely, their national uniformity regardless of local circumstances, the 'knock-on' effect on the pay of other workers higher up the scale, the practice adopted by the higher-paying employers of adjusting the pay of their workers as well, and the financial constraints on employers' ability to recognise or encourage extra effort or skill. The paper clearly inferred that these consequences also applied to national increases negotiated through the voluntary collective bargaining process.

Sadly for the sake of objectivity, the consultation paper failed to draw attention to what many employers perceive to be the disadvantage of determining minimum rates of pay at the local level, for example, the management time involved in getting the balance right between, say Newcastle upon Tyne, Leicester and Cardiff; a sense of unfairness amongst employees because different rates could be paid to people doing an identical job; the opening of the door to trade unionism in the case of those companies that get it wrong; and the danger of local strikes.

The determination of minimum rates of pay at the national level has certainly outlived its usefulness in some sectors (but not all), but the consultation paper signally failed to discuss the options that fell short of the total abolition of the wages councils. If, as the paper suggested, there was a need in 1986 for the provision of 'a safety net for a vulnerable minority',[31] it is difficult to see what change of circumstances had occurred over the ensuing two years to remove that need. It is certainly difficult to accept without detailed evidence which the consultation paper failed to produce, that rates of pay which fell at the time within the range of £73.32 to £92.82 for a 39-hour week (the end-1988 figures for the wages councils) were inhibiting job creation.

Thus at the end of 1989 it seemed politically more likely that a Conservative government would retain the wages council system for the time being. But the Labour Party in its Policy Review (*Meet the Challenge Make the Change*) was committing an incoming labour government to the establishment of a Fair Wages Commission (presumably another role for the independent third party) charged not just with the task of implementing the national minimum wage but with the promotion and encouragement of fair wage policies more generally, including the work traditionally carried out by wages councils.

6 From Bridlington to Bournemouth

The TUC and Inter-union Conflict

More bile and venom can be squeezed into a trade union letter that starts with the words 'Dear Sir and Worthy Brother' and ends up with 'Yours fraternally' than any other piece of business correspondence. So it has been said, but not altogether fairly, for there have been plenty of cases in which company boards, too, faced with a hostile bid from an unwelcome competitor, have used language not exactly noticeable for its temperance.

The competitive analogy is chosen deliberately, for trade unions themselves operate in a highly-competitive environment. Every union is in the competitive business of attracting recruits to its ranks and of persuading union members and potential members of the superiority of its officials' achievements at the negotiating table. Every union official is in the competitive business of persuading the membership that he possesses the best credentials for office and that it is only his brand of politics that will produce the best results for working people.

But as long ago as 1939 the TUC was stating that 'we condemn competition as practiced in the economic life of the nation, and we extol the virtues of co-operation. As a Movement we must still further apply the principle of co-operation to our business in the work of Trade Union organisation'.[1]

It is to the independent role of the TUC in trying to foster this co-operation and to settle inter-union disputes that we now turn.

The TUC's task is made no easier by reason of the unplanned way in which British trade unionism has developed. In the words of a recent TUC report, trade unions:

> emerged with little theory or design and without any agreed view about the development of overall trade union structure, thus giving rise to a pattern of trade unionism with no overall or common plan. Thus each union has determined for itself whether it should confine recruitment to one particular industry, occupation or skill or whether it should extend its membership to other groups. Each

union has decided whether it shall amalgamate with other unions. Because of history and democratic choice, unions have developed different structures.[2]

Nowadays, where differences between unions arise, they are normally over membership, recognition for purposes of collective bargaining, demarcation of work and matters of policy. In cases where an inter-union dispute also involves an employer, any third-party assistance required will probably be provided by ACAS, but when the issue is one which substantially affects the unions alone, it is to the TUC they turn for help if they cannot sort out the problem themselves.

The TUC's procedure for resolving inter-union disputes has been modified in detail over the years, but the principles have remained basically unchanged. If unions cannot settle their differences directly the question may be referred to the TUC, where after assembling all the facts and contentions of the parties, an attempt is first made to achieve a settlement through conciliation. Where he considers it appropriate, however, the General Secretary of the TUC may refer a dispute to a Disputes Committee consisting of not less than three persons who are either members of the General Council or experienced union officials. A member of the General Council always acts as chairman.

In the words of a 1988 explanatory TUC document:

> The basic approach of the Disputes Committee shall be to seek to obtain an agreed settlement, whether of a permanent or an interim character, which is acceptable to all the disputants, and the Disputes Committee may at any time make such recommendations as it sees fit. But whenever the Disputes Committee considers it to be necessary, it shall make an award. In deciding the dispute the Disputes Committee shall have general regard to the interests of the trade union movement and to the declared principles or declared policy of Congress but shall in particular be guided by the Principles Governing Relations Between Unions ... as amended by the General Council and adopted by the Congress from time to time.[3]

In this way every trade union that is affiliated to the TUC gives it the authority to resolve the disputes between them. The TUC puts it this way:

> As in any system of binding arbitration, for that is what this amounts to, it is hard on the losers. They often have to give up

members, or back out of agreements. But in all cases they must do so. The whole system depends on the fact that the awards are implemented.[4]

The branch secretaries of all affiliated unions are required to apply the TUC procedure (the so-called Bridlington principles) when dealing with applications for membership. The recruitment form of every trade union includes an enquiry form which has to be used if an applicant for union membership indicates that he is or was a member of another union. On average, about 100 disputes involving demarcation, allegations of membership poaching and recognition are referred to the TUC each year. The majority of these disputes are disposed of through conciliation but about 20 each year are referred to a TUC Disputes Committee for determination. The TUC makes a major effort to operate the procedures as quickly and efficiently as possible and regards it as a major objective to avoid industrial action because of inter-union conflict. The TUC prides itself on this aspect of its work and believes that its success is to be measured by the absence of pressure for legislation.

It is not very often these days that the TUC can find anything favourable to say about the law lords, but in the information note which it issued over the suspension of the EETPU the TUC pointed out that the Bridlington principles had 'received formidable support'[5] from this quarter and that, in a case challenging the operation of these principles, the House of Lords had upheld the TUC's rules with Lord Diplock commenting as follows:

> I know of no existing rule of public policy that would prevent trade unions from entering into arrangements with one another which they consider to be in the interests of their members in promoting order in industrial relations and enhancing their members' bargaining power with their employers; nor do I think it a permissible exercise of your Lordships' judicial power to create a new rule of public policy to that effect.[6]

Suspension from the TUC – Near Misses

Prior to the EETPU case only one union had left the TUC as a result of defying a TUC Disputes Committee award, but there have been some 'near misses'. In 1984 'SOGAT came within days of being suspended before they finally excluded a group of Fleet Street electricians who had sought transfer from the EETPU to membership of SOGAT'.[7] And an even more spectacular case, because it involved the seemingly all-powerful TGWU, occurred in 1977, when at the TUC annual congress taking place at Blackpool a vote was actually passed to suspend the union from membership.

The opening day of the 1977 Congress at Blackpool was much like any other. The mayor welcomed the delegates. The president delivered the presidential address, and was duly thanked for it. Fraternal delegates and visitors were welcomed and gold badges for long and devoted services to the trade union movement were awarded. But after lunch, when Harry Shindler of the National Association of Licensed House Managers (NALHM) went to the rostrum, the mood changed.

In July 1976 (that is, 14 months previously) a TUC Disputes Committee had considered a complaint by the NALHM that draymen members of the TGWU were refusing to recognise the card of, and were taking industrial action against, a member of NALHM by refusing to deliver supplies to a Birmingham pub, the Fox and Goose, owned by Ansells, the brewers. As a result the individual concerned was being prevented from taking up his appointment as the pub's manager. The Disputes Committee awarded that the TGWU should recognise the NALHM membership card of the newly-appointed manager and that there should be an immediate resumption of delivery of supplies to the Fox and Goose.

The award was not honoured.

When he got to the rostrum Mr Shindler moved a resolution which invited Congress to use its authority and suspend the TGWU from membership of the TUC until the award of the Disputes Committee was implemented. Against the advice of the General Secretary, Len (now Lord) Murray, the resolution was narrowly approved. The unthinkable was about to happen. The TGWU was going to be suspended from the TUC.

But salvation in the surprising shape of Hugh (now Lord) Scanlon, president of the Amalgamated Union of Engineering Workers (now the Amalgamated Engineering Union) was at hand. He pleaded that due to the absence of his executive council at the time the card vote was taken, his union's vote had been wrongly cast. After a short adjournment, the TUC's General Purposes Committee agreed to declare the vote null and void and to recommend that a new vote be taken. Despite the dissenting voice of Joe (later Lord) Gormley, president of the National Union of Mineworkers, the vote was taken once more and this time the resolution to suspend the TGWU was defeated.

A number of the votes cast for the NALHM probably reflected the desire of some unions to settle old scores with the TGWU. But the vote probably reflected, too, the very strong feeling in the trade union movement that, whatever their terms, TUC Disputes Committee awards must be observed both by the humble and the mighty.

The Bridlington Principles

The TUC procedure under which inter-union differences are handled is widely believed to have first been laid down in the Bridlington agreement, so called because it was at the annual congress held at Bridlington in 1939 that certain principles were approved. It was, in fact, at an earlier congress held in Hull in 1924 that the following four basic principles (all relating to matters of membership) were first approved:

- the application for membership form of the Union should contain an enquiry to be answered by the candidate as to whether he is or has been a member of any other Union and, if so, what his financial relationship to that Union is;
- as a general principle, no member of any Trade Union should be accepted into membership in another without enquiry from the Union concerned;
- no member should be allowed to escape his financial obligations by leaving one Union while in arrears and by joining another;
- under no circumstances should a Union accept members from any other Union which is engaged in a trade dispute. It should be a general understanding that both national and local officials of Trade Unions should refrain from speaking or acting adversely to the interests of any other Union during any period in which the members of the latter Union are participating in a trade dispute. Much trouble could be avoided if Unions about to participate in a trade dispute would take care to inform other unions whose members would be likely to be affected thereby.[8]

In a paper to the Bridlington congress 15 years later, the TUC stated that the principles had had some effect in regulating relations between unions, but that 'good trade union practice'[9] should now be more clearly defined. Congress was invited to approve six proposals, which it duly did. Like the 1924 principles, these proposals were still concerned with problems of membership, but one proposal in particular (which had in fact already been previously endorsed at the 1938 Congress in Blackpool) was of far-reaching significance, namely, that no union should 'commence organising activities at any firm in which another union has the majority of the workers employed and negotiates wages and conditions, unless by arrangement with that union'.[10]

Nearly 50 years later the TUC was able to state that the Bridlington principles had been:

> drawn up because trade unionists recognised that, in situations where more than one union was capable of representing a particular grade of worker, it was necessary to prevent the indiscriminate proliferation of unions if stable and rational trade union structures and collective bargaining machinery were to be developed. Their existence has also prevented the instability that would occur if breakaway unions were formed, or if groups of workers were able to move on a whim from one union to another.[11]

This approach to trade union organisation has one great disadvantage. Even if workpeople, for reasons more substantial than a mere whim, wish to transfer their membership from one union to another (assuming that both are TUC affiliates), they can find it extremely difficult to do so. However ineffective the union may have become in representing their interests, however out of touch its officials may be with the grassroots, however unacceptable its political views, however attractive the policies of an alternative union, the Bridlington principles impose a rigidity which is not easily broken. It is easier today for an individual worker to terminate his union membership in a closed shop than it is for all the workers in that closed shop to transfer their membership from one union to another. Arrangements in the USA are very different. Under US law, workers can ballot for a trade union to become a certified bargaining agency to act on their behalf. They can also vote for a change of bargaining agent or for complete decertification, that is, no bargaining agent at all. But in fairness it has to be pointed out that if workers are free to switch their membership from one union to another, a union's position at the bargaining table can never be secure. The achievements of one union may be criticised by another and the members may be told how much better they would do by transferring their loyalties elsewhere. As a result, employers would find that trade unions would be less reliable at the bargaining table.

From time to time the TUC has adjusted or supplemented the Bridlington principles to take account of changing relationships both within the trade union movement and between trade unions and employers. Thus at a special congress held at Croydon in 1969 the General Council of the TUC was given further responsibilities to intervene in disputes between employers and workpeople. (This was at a time when the country was bedevilled by strikes that either did not carry official union approval or were in breach of the procedure agreed between employers and trade unions.) It was at this Congress that the TUC was for the first time given powers to become involved in inter-union disputes over recognition, demarcation and wages and conditions of employment.

Minor amendments were made to the principles in 1973, and further changes were made in 1979. But in 1985 a potentially more far-reaching change was made. As a result of a resolution adopted at that year's congress concerning single-union agreements, the General Council agreed an amended note to the first Bridlington principle to provide 'that no union should enter into a sole negotiating agreement where another union(s) would be deprived of their existing rights of recognition or negotiation except by prior consultation and agreement of the other union(s) concerned'.[12]

Single-union Agreements

By 1985 single-union agreements, their arbitration provisions and associated problems concerning the right to strike (or the sacrifice of it) were beginning to assume crisis proportions within the British trade union movement. By the end of 1988 the EETPU, having first been suspended, would have been expelled from the TUC and the TUC itself would have instituted a more thorough and detailed examination of the Bridlington principles than they had received in their almost 50 years of existence.

The irony of the situation is not just that single-union agreements have existed for a long time, but that even those unions which were most outspoken over recent developments had not been averse themselves to concluding these agreements when they were able to do so. Although employers who had recognised trade unions for generations had had to accept multi-unionism as a fact of industrial life that could not be avoided, many of them had cursed the disadvantages it could bring in its train, for example, fragmented bargaining, and had speculated how much easier relationships would be with their employees if they were all represented by a single union possessed of a single style, philosophy and approach. It was no wonder that any employer considering recognition for the first time, particularly when setting up on a greenfield site, would insist on the recognition of one union only.

And in the 1980s employers were in a more powerful position to impose their will than they had been for decades past. Trade union membership and influence were in decline; many workers were more concerned about their jobs than trade unionism; new industrial relations laws were in place; and the recognition provisions of the 1975 Employment Protection Act had been repealed. The alternative to recognising one union was not recognising two but recognising no union at all. Employers opening up on greenfield sites were free to pick and choose which union they would recognise ('beauty contests', they were called by at least one union official) even before the first employees had been recruited. Given this freedom it was hardly surprising that they preferred a trade union which was considered likely to be less constrained by old attitudes and to be more understanding about the efficiency and productivity imperatives of the day.

Problems with the EETPU

And if they did have any doubts as to which union to recognise it would not be very long before the EETPU would be brought to their attention, probably by the union itself. Here was a trade union that had ridded itself of communist domination in the 1950s and was now vigorously marketing a new form of trade unionism of which the most attractive feature to employers was its assertion that perpetual strife was outdated and unrewarding for all concerned. Co-operation with employers was available on the right terms and as far as the EETPU was concerned these were:

- a single-union agreement;
- single status for all employees;
- an advanced system of employee involvement;
- a participative or consensual style of management;

- a final procedural stage of pendulum arbitration for the settlement of all unresolved claims and grievances.

In return, the union would accept such labour efficiency measures as full labour flexibility and facilities for training and retraining.

At times the EETPU seemed to act in a deliberately provocative manner. Perhaps it could not be blamed for the fact that its policies drew plaudits from ministers of a government considered hostile to the trade union movement. But its principal officers did little to conceal their contempt for the union's erstwhile political allies; it marketed itself vigorously not just among prospective members but among employers as well (even to the extent of the union's general secretary addressing a fringe meeting on the occasion of the CBI's 1984 national conference); it used the new role of the electrician in an age of enormous technological change as justification for declaring that no putative bargaining unit was 'off limits' to the EETPU; it was willing to negotiate terms with employers which were quite contrary to union policy generally, for example, private health care; and it was prepared to question some of the fundamental tenets of trade unionism, eventually to the point of challenging the Bridlington principles themselves.

The 1985 amendment to the principles came about as a result of growing trade union concern and anger over single-union agreements that had been negotiated by the EETPU. One agreement with Toshiba Consumer Products (UK) Ltd has already been mentioned in Chapter 2. Another was with Eddie Shah's *Today* newspaper. And a third was with Hitachi to cover the company's plant at Hirwaun (South Wales). This was not a true greenfield site because Hitachi and GEC had previously operated the plant on a joint-venture basis. In 1984 GEC had pulled out but Hitachi, instead of doing the same thing, decided to take over the business and to instal Hitachi conditions and standards as quickly as possible. But in place of the six unions that had previously been recognised, Hitachi decided that in future it would recognise just one, the EETPU.

The excluded unions protested, and to cut a long story short, the issue eventually came before a TUC Disputes Committee. The EETPU was charged not just with being in breach of the Bridlington principles, but with having collaborated with an employer to try and destroy the negotiating rights of other union members. The EETPU denied the charges. They protested that they had not tried to poach the members of other unions and committed that they would not do so in future. But they argued, faced with an intransigent employer, if they had refused to enter into a single-union agreement, Hitachi would have withdrawn recognition from all unions and established a non-union plant.

In the light of subsequent events, the findings of the Disputes Committee were surprising. The EETPU was told that it should not have signed the sole recognition and negotiating agreement until the dispute had been settled, if necessary by TUC adjudication. But the union was not ordered to abandon the agreement. Instead, it was required to meet three conditions:

1. New employees at Hitachi should be told that they might join a union other than the EETPU.
2. Where a grievance arose affecting a member of one of the unions not recognised, an official of the union concerned should be enabled to take the issue up with the company.
3. The EETPU should establish a body which would allow the displaced unions to pass on to the company via the electricians their views on issues affecting them.

Naturally the EETPU was delighted with the findings. The other unions were appalled.

But single-union agreements continued to be negotiated, and not just by the EETPU. In April 1988 Nissan signed an agreement with the Amalgamated Engineering Union. In 1987 Orion Electric (UK) Ltd, Port Talbot, and the EETPU, negotiated a single-union agreement in the face of strong objections from the TGWU which claimed substantial membership in the plant. And, despite objections from three unions, the EETPU also negotiated a single-union agreement with Christian Salvesen (Food Services) Ltd, Salstream Division. And in 1988 the AEU was able to secure a commitment from Ford of USA that when a new electronics plant was opened in Dundee the union would be granted sole negotiating rights, this despite the fact that for its automotive plants in the UK, Ford of Britain already recognises a number of trade unions. (In the event, and with much inter-union recrimination, Ford decided not to proceed with its Dundee plan.)

It was the Orion and Christian Salvesen agreements which were eventually to lead first to the suspension, and then to the expulsion of the EETPU from the TUC. This disciplinary action was not taken because the union had negotiated a couple of single-union agreements, but because it had committed the unforgivable offence of refusing to accept two Disputes Committee awards of the TUC. In the words of a TUC statement:

> The issues now at stake do not amount to a choice between modern trade unions and some outdated approach to industrial relations. Nor are single union or 'no strike' deals the issue. The TUC's rules do not preclude single union agreements – only agreements that ignore the reasonable interests of other unions. And in the two cases concerned whether or not the agreements were 'no strike' was totally immaterial.[13]

In the Orion case the Disputes Committee ruled that the EETPU should withdraw from its agreement, and that with the TGWU it should 'formulate a common approach to the company for joint recognition and negotiating rights and work together at Orion Electric to eliminate competition for members'.[14] In the Christian Salvesen case the Disputes Committee decided that 'all the unions should meet and make an agreed common approach to the company for recognition ... The Committee also decided that the EETPU should terminate its sole agreement and exclude the members they had recruited at Warrington and West Cross'.[15]

The EETPU refused to comply with either award and so at Bournemouth on Monday, 5 September 1988, the union was expelled from the TUC, not with much visible sign of rancour but perhaps with an underlying feeling that if it had not been on the technical grounds of failing to comply with Disputes Committee decisions, some other issue would soon have arisen which would have led to the same result.

Reviewing the Situation

The British trade union movement is said to be divided between the fundamentalists and the reformers. The fundamentalists cling to the old belief that conflict between capital and labour is inevitable, that other than for reasons of short-term expediency there can be no compromise and that there must certainly be no sacrifice or modification of the right to strike. The reformers, including the EETPU, believe that the environment within which the trade unions operate has now so changed that unless the trade union movement is prepared to change its traditional conflict-oriented approach, it has no long-term future at all. But by 1987 the fundamentalists and reformers had agreed on one thing – on the need for a comprehensive review of the future direction of trade unionism. And so at the TUC's congress that year, that is, twelve months prior to the EETPU's expulsion, this review had been put in hand. Eight motions and amendments had been tabled by individual unions for debate at this conference and most of them were noticeably short, although not entirely devoid, of the normal anti-Thatcher polemics. They all reflected trade union concern for the future.

Thus in its motion the National Union of Public Employees referred to the need for 'a major initiative to promote a positive image for trade unionism'.[16] The motion submitted by the General, Municipal, Boilermakers and Allied Trades Union contemplated that 'over the next decade our overriding priority will be the recruitment and organisation of new groups of workers into trade unions'[17] and called on the TUC's General Council 'to develop and implement a programme to expand the frontiers of trade unionism'.[18] Amendments to this motion put forward by other unions referred specifically to the need to target women workers and part-time and temporary employees. The Engineers' and Managers' Association asked Congress to 'affirm the need for a strategy to deal not only with ideologically based attacks on trade unionists such as those mounted by the present Government but also with the challenges presented by social and economic change.'[19] It went on to invite Congress to recognise:

> that the role of the TUC can and should go beyond the resolution of inter-union disputes to assisting in the avoidance of such disputes, promoting trade unionism among current and potential members, helping to co-ordinate the organising efforts of unions and generally providing the means for unions to deal more effectively with changing labour markets and new employment practices.[20]

The Association of Scientific, Technical and Managerial Staffs invited Congress to call upon the General Council 'to take steps to transform the TUC into a campaigning organisation on behalf of trade unionists and employees everywhere'.[21] The National Union of Hosiery and Knitwear Workers proposed that Congress should call upon the TUC General Council to give urgent and further emphasis to the objective of assisting 'in the complete organisation of all workers eligible for membership of its affiliated organisations'.[22] And the Inland Revenue Staff Federation asked Congress to instruct the

General Council 'to commission, as priority requirements, a series of analytical reports into the condition of modern Britain'[23] and then to use the results of the research to 'contribute to a basis for an agreed strategy for trade union regeneration'.[24]

Even the EETPU submitted a motion which, after referring to 'considerable friction between unions and, in some cases, to major conflicts', invited Congress to call on 'the General Council to conduct a full examination and re-evaluation of trade union structure'.[25]

The only motion that referred expressly to single-union agreements came from the Transport and General Workers' Union. Congress was invited to express its concern:

> at the increasing use by employers of a strategy involving the disavowal of basic trade union rights in return for recognition and sole negotiating rights ... Congress believes that the use of 'no strike' clauses and compulsory arbitration clauses which deny the right to strike should be strongly resisted by all affiliated unions.[26]

The General Council should therefore be called upon:

> to establish a special review body to report to the 1988 Congress on measures to prevent the use of such clauses, and lay down proper procedures for achieving union recognition in addition to the present Bridlington principles, with a view to maximising unity in the TUC and the trade union Movement.[27]

An amendment to this motion put forward by the Amalgamated Engineering Union suggested that the lines for entering into single-union agreements had now been clearly laid down. The amendment went on to say that 'Congress believes that the imposition by Government or employers of no strike clauses and compulsory arbitration clauses which deny the members' right to strike, should be strongly resisted by all affiliated unions'.[28] (What this amendment did not say is what the unions should do if their members were prepared without government or employer coercion to accept these agreements.)

The TUC General Council had prepared itself well and seemed determined to avoid a highly-publicised debate that might serve only to sharpen up the differences between the fundamentalists and the reformers. The delegates were accordingly invited to approve a long statement entitled 'Promoting Trade Unionism and Union Organisation'. The statement:

- emphasised that the need for unity within the TUC and the trade union movement had never been greater;

- pointed out that major tasks for Congress were 'projecting a positive image of trade unions in the wider community and extending trade union organisation';[29]
- welcomed the creative thought given by the unions to these issues in their motions and amendments;
- proposed the establishment of a Special Review Body (SRB) to consider all the issues that had been raised.

The tasks of the SRB would be to:[30]

- report to the General Council 'on the scope for change and with recommendations of proper procedures for achieving union recognition in addition to the present Bridlington Principles';
- examine 'the scope for promoting a more positive, outward-looking image for trade unionism';
- continue 'the General Council's consideration of a programme to give further emphasis to organising and to expand the frontiers of trade unionism';
- to widen the scope of a planned General Council review 'to include the committee structure of Congress, the role for the TUC in campaigning, and to consider priorities for the allocation of resources'.

And so to Bournemouth

The General Council's statement was adopted by the 1987 Congress on the understanding that the issues raised in the motions and the amendments would be considered by the Special Review Body. It was part of the understanding that after six months the SRB would report on the issues surrounding single union or 'no strike' agreements.

A TUC document stated:

> Subsequently the SRB reported to the General Council and the General Council decided that a Code of Practice could play a useful role in improving inter-union relations in regard to organising and seeking recognition on new sites. The terms of the Code of Practice would be taken into account by Disputes Committees when considering cases of dispute or disagreement between affiliated organisations.[31]

The Code seemed to have as its objective the need to impose an element of discipline and constraint on any trade union's ability in future quietly to seek out single-union agreements and to enter into whatever terms were thought necessary to convince the employer that he wouldn't do better elsewhere.

Thus the Code provided that a union in the process of making a single-union agreement would have at an early stage to notify the General Secretary of the TUC who would 'aim to tender advice within two weeks'.[32] The TUC would be required to take into account factors such as whether another union had a significant membership at the site (like Hitachi) or whether another union was recognised by the employer for similar groups of workers elsewhere (like Christian Salvesen).

As for 'no strike clauses' and arbitration, the Code stated very clearly that unions 'when making recognition agreements, must not make agreements which specifically remove or are designed to remove, the basic democratic lawful rights of a trade union to take industrial action'.[33] Clearly this provision was intended to rule out compulsory arbitration as the final means of dispute resolution. Unfortunately, for the sake of clarity the Code later seemed to qualify this statement with another one. 'Unions must not make any agreements which remove, or are designed to remove, the basic democratic lawful rights of a trade union to take industrial action *in advance of the recruitment of members and without consulting them*'[34] (author's emphasis). The implication of the words (and it is on these that the observer has to reach his conclusion) seemed to suggest that if workpeople had been recruited on a greenfield site, had been consulted and would like compulsory arbitration, a trade union could then agree. But if this was not the intention and TUC policy prevails, there will be no more agreements negotiated by affiliated unions which contain compulsory arbitration provisions. The EETPU is, of course, free to negotiate what it likes.

The third provision in the Code would prevent any trade union from using its representative position on any of the inward investment authorities to its own advantage. 'Unions are expected to co-operate with any procedures, which have been approved by the General Council of the TUC, which are operated by the TUC, STUC, Wales TUC or TUC Regional Councils in relation to inward investment authorities'.[35]

The final provision of the Code dealt with the difficult problem of terms and conditions of employment. The first report of the SRB acknowledged frankly that on issues like new technology and flexible working patterns it was inevitable that the employer would expect any new plant to have a competitive edge over existing plants. It was also possible that 'employers may wish to take account of variations in regional wage levels and this can pose a difficult problem for unions'.[36] The best advice the Code could offer was that:

> unions should have regard to the general level of terms and conditions of employment which are already the subject of agreement with the company concerned, or which have been set through recognised arrangements, and take all possible steps to avoid undermining them.[37]

National trade union policy of this kind cannot be easily reconciled with what might be seen as the overriding local priority in an area of high unemployment, of securing additional jobs even though the price might be that the terms and conditions would be different from those observed by the same employer elsewhere.

The first instalment of the SRB's work was not confined to the preparation of a Code of Practice.

A particular cause of criticism of single-union agreements negotiated on the 'beauty contest' basis has been that until the first employees were recruited, it would not be known whether there was any commitment to the recognised trade union (or even to trade unionism itself). Rumours were widespread that the level of union membership in some companies where recognition had been secured on the 'beauty contest' basis was disappointingly low. But there was also a widespread union belief that even in this kind of situation the Bridlington principles were a pretty sure guarantee against subsequent 'raiders' from other unions.

The SRB was of the view that the Bridlington principles already were specific enough, but to remove any possible doubt it proposed textual amendments to the principles which would make it clear that in cases of this kind the TUC Disputes Committee would be required to have regard not just to the efforts of the recognised union to secure or retain a majority membership and to the new Code of practice, but to 'the efforts which the union seeking entry is prepared to make in trying to secure a majority membership and negotiating rights and prospects of success in this regard'.[38] The purpose of this textual change was obviously to make it clear that at least in the context of new style, single-union agreements, the successful union could not rest on its laurels. Its entitlement to a continued monopoly in terms of negotiating rights would depend on proof of its ability to maintain or expand the membership base.

These then were the results of the SRB's first discussions, and when Congress met at Bournemouth in 1988 the proposals for a Code of Practice, and for the amendment of the Bridlington principles, were duly adopted.

Early reports after Bournemouth suggested that with TUC guidance, further conflict over the process of sole union recognition had been avoided. Press reports in late 1989 indicated that even on the potentially explosive issue of a demand by the AEU for sole recognition at a new engine plant which it was anticipated Vauxhall Motors would be building at Ellesmere Port, the TUC had been able to secure an inter-union agreement that the unions currently recognised by the company at Ellesmere Port would have rights at the new plant. Clearly the TUC was determined that there would be no re-run of the Dundee affair.

Past history has shown a willingness on the part of the trade unions to accept the revision of the Bridlington principles from time to time. But in its evidence to the Donovan Commission, the TUC stated explicitly that these principles were 'not an instrument for achieving trade union reform'.[39] We now have to wait and see whether the trade unions will be prepared to accept any recommendations from the SRB which do not involve the Bridlington principles but which would lead to greatly enlarged responsibilities and the necessary financial resources for the TUC itself.

Conclusions

For over 100 years the independent third party has been a familiar figure in British industrial relations. But not uniquely so. The trade union official who sees it as his responsibility not just to represent his members but also from time to time to persuade them to moderate their more extreme or unachievable demands is not unique to the United Kingdom. No more so is the employers' association that accepts a responsibility not just to ensure that its members honour the agreements negotiated on their behalf but that they conform to certain standards of industrial relations behaviour as well.

In probably every industrialised country, conciliation, arbitration and mediation – provided either by the state or by collective agreement – are available for the settlement of industrial disputes.

Pendulum arbitration may have been 'invented' in England, but its principles have been applied elsewhere.

Even ACAS, which is regarded by many as a unique British institution, bears some similarities to the Federal Conciliation and Mediation Service in the USA.

The Future of ACAS

In the years 1978–88 ACAS conciliated in no fewer than 18185 collective disputes or threatened disputes between employers and trade unions – with an 80 per cent success rate; arranged 2469 voluntary arbitrations; and conciliated in over 500 000 cases involving an alleged breach of one or other of the statutory employment rights – with a disposal rate (that is, cases settled or withdrawn) of about 70 per cent.

From such figures as these it might be assumed that the future of ACAS as an effective industrial peacemaker was never in doubt. Certainly during the years of the Labour Government that established ACAS, the Service was able quietly to build up its acceptability and its reputation – this despite the view of some employers that a body charged at that time with the responsibility of inquiring into and making recommendations over union recognition issues was bound to be pro-union. But when a Conservative administration took office in 1979 there was some speculation whether ACAS would survive.

Mrs Thatcher was, after all, ushering in an era in which the labour market was to be deregulated and in which employers would be encouraged to stand on their own feet and place less reliance on the state and its agencies.

But survive ACAS has – and there seems to be no disposition on the part of any of the major political parties to abolish it. Why should this be so?

Probably because there is now a realisation among politicians of all parties that there is as much criticism as kudos to be gained from personal involvement in a major industrial dispute. If a settlement isn't reached it may be all due to the fumbling of the conciliators; if a settlement is reached, its terms are either too high or could have been picked up weeks ago. How much better for the government to distance itself from direct involvement in any dispute and then from the sidelines, either compliment or criticise like everybody else.

Certainly this seems to be the policy of a Conservative government. But the relationship between the Labour Party and the trade unions is very close, and it will thus be interesting to see whether any incoming Labour administration could discipline itself in the same way. If it made a practice of closer direct involvement in industrial disputes the hard-earned credibility of ACAS would be sorely tested.

There have, nevertheless, been developments which should give rise for concern for the future of ACAS.

Thus, whilst the statute as it stands states specifically that the Service shall not be subject to directions of any kind from any Minister of the Crown as to the way in which it does its work, there is nothing to prevent central government, if it feels so disposed, from either duplicating or taking unto itself responsibilities already discharged exclusively by ACAS. The ACAS powers to issue codes of practice have not been changed, but under the amended law the government has issued its own codes as well, and ACAS has been deprived of its responsibility for inquiry before a wages council is established, modified or abolished. The Secretary of State for Employment can now take this decision without the need for external inquiry of any kind.

There were even those who whispered in 1987 when a senior civil servant from the Department of Employment was appointed as chairman of ACAS that this would be a way of ensuring that in future ACAS would dance more readily to the government tune. Happily, for ACAS, these critics would not have been aware of the experience, skill and, above all, integrity of the individual concerned. That

ACAS retains its sturdy independence of the government machine was amply confirmed in 1989 when the Service submitted its strong criticism of the Department of Employment's draft code of practice on pre-strike balloting.

Industrial Relations and the Third Party

Good industrial relations are not synonymous with the need to keep strikes and other forms of industrial action to a minimum. They are not an end in themselves but one of the means – perhaps the most important – whereby the corporate or business objectives are achieved and, through their achievement, the customers are satisfied, the future of the business is assured, employees' job security is increased and their living standards are improved. Business objectives embrace everything from sales generated and profit earned, to patients 'processed' through our hospitals, children properly educated in our schools and taxes gathered by our civil servants.

Good industrial relations are certainly not synonymous with the need to avoid strikes at any cost. Indeed there are occasions when it is far better for the long-term future of the business if the short-term consequences of a stoppage of work are accepted. Equally there are occasions when a management may have so abused its 'managerial prerogative' that for the sake of long-term stability in the employment relationship neither employees or their trade union can afford to compromise.

Collective Conciliation

There is, therefore, no case for asserting that every dispute which can't be settled directly between employer and trade union should automatically be referred to conciliation. Indeed, employers and trade union should have such an abiding concern for the integrity of their own procedure agreements that if concessions are to be made, offers to be tabled or compromises reached, this should be done during negotiations within the procedure and not afterwards as a result of third-party involvement.

Employers, in particular, always have to bear in mind that, once they have been pressurised into a conciliation, the same thing will be expected of them in future. The agreed procedures will become nothing more than stepping stones towards an expected dénouement in the ACAS building. Trade unions, in contrast, may feel able to take the opportunistic view, namely, they have nothing to lose by agreeing to conciliation and may end up with something better than the employer's last offer in direct negotiations.

In theory, therefore, employers and, to a lesser extent, trade unions, should always look askance at the prospect of conciliation whenever it is proposed. But the fact remains that, in practice, in a great number of disputes both sides do agree to conciliation.

Why should this be so?

Perhaps despite all the calls for a tougher or more determined style of management there is still an under-lying belief that reasonable compromise is preferable to confrontation, and should at least be sought. Perhaps, too, there is a greater willingness for third-party involvement when one side or the other begins to appreciate that an error of judgement has been made, for example, the strike is not being supported as enthusiastically as the union had expected, or the consequences of the strike are much more serious than the employer had anticipated. And, maybe, the more sophisticated trade union official or management negotiator is aware of how the conciliation procedure differs from direct negotiation and how, as a result, settlements can sometimes be achieved in apparently the most unpropitious circumstances.

An industrial dispute can easily destroy the mutual trust which is the essential basis for satisfactory long-term relationships. In these circumstances the conciliator may be the only trustworthy channel of communication that is left. And ACAS could certainly quote occasions in which a dispute seemed inevitable, communication between employer and trade union had completely broken down, and yet a timely telephone call or two by the conciliator pulled both sides back from the brink.

The conciliation workload of ACAS is to some extent a reflection of the prevailing level of industrial peace in the country. The more strikes, the greater the number of conciliations handled. Even though there may be increasing provision in procedure agreements for automatic ACAS conciliation after direct negotiations have broken down, this will in no way compensate for any decline in the demand for conciliation brought about by a reduction in the number of disputes during a period of relative industrial peace.

Given the high success rate of the conciliation process it is sometimes suggested that whenever direct negotiations break down, the process should be obligatory. This would be entirely wrong. For its success, conciliation depends on the willing participation of the parties. Even if one side (or both) were obliged to attend a conciliation, there is no power on earth that could compel them to enter into constructive discussions against their will. But the process itself would rapidly become discredited.

Arbitration

The new-style agreements with their built-in provision for arbitration are so relatively few in number that their impact upon the arbitration workload will be negligible. But should governments change the law, for example, by making collective agreements enforceable at law, by restoring pay provisions like the Fair Wages Resolution or Schedule 11 of the Employment Protection Act of 1975, by introducing the concept of a national minimum wage (with appeal mechanism for non-compliance), by reintroducing union recognition provisions, or by legislating for wider use of arbitration in dismissal cases, then the arbitration caseload would increase substantially.

Of these six possibilities five could realistically happen only if a Labour government were to take office. From which it must be deduced that any substantial increase in arbitration will only take place if and when that event occurs. So far as voluntary arbitration is concerned the realistic conclusion must surely be that, apart from relatively narrow fluctuations, the annual demand is unlikely to increase over disputes of interest or even, despite its greater theoretical attractions, over disputes of right.

For their different reasons employers and trade unions have never liked arbitration as a regularly-used system for settling their disputes, and for all the publicity that pendulum arbitration has received in the context of the new-style, no strike agreement, it is unlikely that this form of arbitration, any more than the conventional kind, will prove widely acceptable in the future.

For reasons which were developed in Chapter 2, there is certainly a stronger case for arbitration in those areas of the non-trading part of the public sector not covered by pay review bodies, for example, the lower echelons of the Civil Service, and a number of occupational groups in the National Health Service. We have noted that in the new-style Civil Service agreements provision is at least being made for the possibility of arbitration on a jointly-agreed basis – a step in the right direction – but we have yet to see whether, in practice, the Treasury will ever agree to its being used. Any similar arrangements in the National Health Service seem unlikely.

It also seems unlikely that we shall see the introduction of any system whereby problems affecting the police, the firemen, school teachers, civil servants and National Health Service employees will all be handled on the basis of reasonably principled consistency.

Pay Review Bodies

But at least the notion of the pay review body for professional occupations who are covered only at the margin by conventional collective bargaining seems to be gaining acceptance probably because, so far, the government has been wise enough, apart from occasionally requiring an element of staging, to accept the salary increases recommended.

Pay review bodies, for the occupations they cover, offer a more sophisticated form of inquiry than the government-appointed *ad hoc* courts of inquiry that became so discredited in the 1960s. It is difficult to envisage many situations today in which the government would wish to revert to the old courts even though the relevant section of the Industrial Courts Act which provides for their establishment, remains in force.

Individual Conciliation

One area of considerable government activity over the past 20 years has been in the field of statutory employment rights – their introduction or modification. Almost without exception any complaint over an alleged breach of these statutory employment rights requires ACAS to try conciliation before an industrial tribunal hearing takes place. The ACAS conciliation workload in this area has remained consistently high, largely because of the number of cases of alleged unfair dismissal (nearly 90 per cent of the total). With the variation of the qualifying conditions that have to be met before an unfair dismissal claim can be lodged, and with the reduction in the total number of dismissals for all reasons (particularly redundancy), it might be thought that the total number of complaints would decline. But in 1988 the total number of cases received was 3626 higher than in 1987 – due in large part to the number of cases arising from the Wages Act of 1986. The caseload will probably remain high and some kind of filter will continue to be necessary so as not to overload the industrial tribunals with cases that are either capable of settlement or are unsoundly based, but can be handled more economically elsewhere. Despite some criticism as to the way ACAS discharges its responsibility for individual conciliation in the area of statutory employment rights, its reputation, on the whole, is pretty good. There is certainly no case for transferring the responsibility elsewhere.

The Final Conclusion

For more than a century the independent third party has made an enormous contribution to the working of the British industrial relations system. There is no reason to suppose that this contribution will not continue in future. But one of the essential ingredients of continuing success is that the processes of conciliation, arbitration and mediation are used as infrequently as possible. In other words, they should only be used as a last resort and not as a regular substitute, either for the imaginative planning of sound relationships between employer and employed, or for effective in-house procedures for dealing with whatever claims or grievances may arise.

But that does not mean that conciliation, arbitration and mediation should never be used. There are certainly some occasions when long-term considerations dictate that the temptation to use the third party should be resisted. But neither employers nor trade union should ever become so proud or arrogant as to believe that there will never be any circumstances, or that there will never be any dispute, in which the third party will not be able to be of some assistance.

Notes and References

Introduction

1. H. Phelps Brown (1959) *The Growth of British Industrial Relations*, Macmillan, p. 126.
2. Quoted in Ministry of Labour (1967) *Industrial Relations Handbook* revised edition, HMSO, p. 134.
3. Ibid., p. 21.
4. Ibid.
5. ACAS (1980) *Industrial Relations Handbook*, HMSO, p. 57.

1 Collective Conciliation

1. A. Marsh (1965) *Industrial Relations in Engineering*, Pergamon Press, pp. 13ff.
2. Employment Protection Act 1975, SS2 (3).
3. ACAS (1975) *Annual Report 1975*, HMSO, p. 10.
4. S. Weighell (1983) *On the Rails*, Orbis Publishing, p. 83.
5. I. MacGregor (1986) *The Enemies Within*, Collins, p. 250.
6. P. Wilsher, D. Macintyre and N. Jones (1985) *Strike*, Deutsch, p. 136.
7. I. MacGregor (1986) op. cit., p. 288.
8. Ibid.
9. Ibid.
10. ACAS (1984) *Annual Report 1984*, HMSO, pp. 24–5.
11. Ibid.
12. Ibid.
13. Ibid.
14. M. Edwardes (1983) *Back from the Brink*, Collins, p. 151.
15. ACAS (1984) *Annual Report 1984*, op. cit., p. 25.
16. N. Jones (1986) *Strikes and the Media*, Blackwell, p. 26.
17. M. Edwardes (1983) op. cit., p. 151.
18. P. Hall (1983) *Peter Hall's Diaries*, Hamish Hamilton, p. 305.
19. S. Weighell (1983) op. cit., p. 82.
20. ACAS (1982) *Annual Report 1982*, HMSO, p. 29.
21. Ibid.
22. H. Phelps Brown (1959) *The Growth of British Industrial Relations*, Macmillan, p. 338.
23. B. Tillett (1912) *History of the Transport Strike 1911*, p. 30.

2 Arbitration

1. H. Phelps Brown (1959) *The Growth of British Industrial Relations*, Macmillan, p. 187.

2. C. Jenkins and B. Sherman (1977) *Collective Bargaining*, Routledge & Kegan Paul, p. 77.
3. *Fourth Report of Whitley Committee* HMSO, 1918.
4. C. Barnet (1986) *The Audit of War, Britain as an Industrial Society*, Paper given to RSA, 23 April.
5. Sir Harold Emmerson (1968). Written evidence to Donovan Commission set out in Commission's Report, HMSO, pp. 340–1.
6. Ministry of Labour (1967) *Industrial Relations Handbook*, revised edition, HMSO, p. 145.
7. B. Doyle (1986) *'Essay on Legal Regulation of Collective Bargaining'*, in *Labour Law in Britain*, Blackwell, p. 121 fn.
8. C. Jenkins and B. Sherman (1977) op. cit., p. 142.
9. CAC (1977) *Annual Report 1977*, p. 22.
10. ACAS (1980) *Annual Report 1980*, HMSO, p. 26.
11. L. Dickens and D. Cockburn (1986) *'Essay on Dispute Settlement Institutions and the Courts'* in *Labour Law in Britain*, Blackwell, p. 537 fn.
12. R. Lewis (1983) *'Essay on Collective Labour Law'*, in *Industrial Relations in Britain*, Blackwell, p. 374.
13. CAC (1978) *Annual Report 1978*, p. 22.
14. L. Dickens and D. Cockburn (1986) op. cit., p. 537.
15. HM Treasury undertaking quoted in Ministry of Labour's (1967) *Industrial Relations Handbook*, op. cit., p. 122.
16. Civil Service Arbitration Agreement (Clause 2).
17. Council of Civil Service Unions (1984) *The Bulletin*, September/October, p. 120.
18. Statement by the Minister for the Civil Service, quoted in *The Bulletin*, September/October 1984, p. 121.
19. D. Winchester (1983) *'Essay on Industrial Relations in the Public Sector'*, in *Industrial Relations in Britain*, Blackwell, p. 172.
20. S. Weighell (1983) *On the Rails*, Orbis Publishing, pp. 27–32.
21. W. Ashworth (1986) *The History of the British Coal Industry*, vol. 5, Clarendon Press, p. 291.
22. P. Bassett (1986) *Strike Free*, Macmillan, p. 110.
23. CAC (1981) *Annual Report 1981*, p. 14.
24. CAC (1976) *Annual Report 1976*, p. 14.
25. Shakespeare, *King Henry IV*, Part 1, Act 2, Scene iv.
26. Ministry of Labour (1967) *Industrial Relations Handbook*, op. cit., p. 139.
27. Report of Donovan Commission, HMSO, 1968, p. 73.
28. CAC (1977) *Annual Report 1977*, p. 21.
29. G. Cyriax and R. Oakeshott (1960) *The Bargainers*, Faber & Faber, pp. 178–9.
30. P. Bassett (1986) op. cit., p. 111.
31. From the Agreement set out in Trever (1988) *Toshiba's New British Company*, Policy Studies Institute, p. 245.
32. Wickens (1987) *The Road to Nissan*, Macmillan, pp. 150–1.
33. Ibid., p. 152.
34. Trades Union Congress (1988) *Meeting the Challenge*, First Report of the Special Review Body, p. 10.

35. Agreement of August 1987 between IBC Vehicles Ltd. and six trade unions.
36. TUC (1988) op. cit., p. 19.
37. ACAS (1986) *Annual Report 1986*, HMSO, p. 22.
38. CAC (1984) *Annual Report 1984*, p. 19.
39. Quoted in Seyforth, Shaw, Fairweather and Geraldson (1968) *Labour Relations and the Law*, University of Michigan, p. 120.
40. Ibid.
41. Ministry of Labour (1968) *Evidence to Donovan Commission*, HMSO, p. 109.
42. Ibid.
43. Ibid.
44. *Report of Donovan Commission*, HMSO, 1968, p. 72.
45. *Report of an Independent Committee of Inquiry under Sir Jack Scamp to the Joint Secretaries of the NJC for Local Authorities' Services (Manual Workers)* (1970) pp. 12, 13, 16.

3 Mediation, Inquiry, Investigation and Review

1. ACAS (1981) *Annual Report 1981*, HMSO, p. 26.
2. ACAS (1987) *Annual Report 1987*, HMSO, p. 31.
3. Ibid.
4. ACAS (1986) *Annual Report 1986*, HMSO, p. 29.
5. Ministry of Labour (1967) *Industrial Relations Handbook,* revised edition, HMSO, p. 141.
6. Ibid.
7. Ministry of Labour (1965) *Evidence to Donovan Commission*, HMSO, p. 109.
8. Engineering Employers' Federation (1965) *Evidence to Donovan Commission*, EEF, p. 36.
9. Sir Jack Scamp (1968) *Report to the Minister of Labour on the Activities of the Motor Industry Joint Labour Council*, HMSO, p. 6.
10. Department of Employment and Productivity (1969) *In Place of Strife*, HMSO, p. 14.
11. Ibid., p. 13.
12. Industrial Relations Act 1971, Section 121 (1).
13. J. Purcell (1981) *Good Industrial Relations Theory and Practice*, Macmillan.
14. *Hansard*, 2 November 1970.
15. Ibid.
16. Ibid.
17. Ibid.

4 Individual Conciliation

1. International Labour Organisation (1963) *Recommendation 119*.
2. Report of Donovan Commission, HMSO, 1968, p. 268.

3. M. Redmond (1986) 'Essay on Women and Minorities', in *Labour Law in Britain*, Blackwell, p. 472.
4. EC Directive on Equal Pay, Article 1.
5. Redmond (1986) op. cit., p. 496.
6. CAC (1977) *Annual Report 1977*, p. 16.
7. Redmond (1986) op. cit., p. 496.
8. CAC (1979) *Annual Report 1979*, p. 14.
9. Report of Donovan Commission, op. cit., pp. 155–6.
10. Ibid., p. 155.
11. L. Dickens *et al.* (1985) *Dismissed*, Blackwell, p. 140.
12. ACAS (1987) *Individual Employment Rights – ACAS Conciliation between Individuals and Employers*, p. 6.
13. Dickens *et al.* (1985) op. cit., p. 180.
14. Ibid.
15. Ibid.
16. ACAS (1987) *Individual Employment Rights – ACAS Conciliation between Individuals and Employers*, op. cit., p. 10.
17. Ibid., p. 6.
18. ACAS (1983) *Annual Report 1983*, HMSO, p. 22.
19. ACAS (1984) *Annual Report 1984*, HMSO, p. 65.
20. ACAS (1984) *Annual Report 1984* HMSO, p. 65.
21. ACAS (1984) *Annual Report 1984*, op. cit.
22. Dickens *et al.* (1985) op. cit., p. 190.
23. Dickens *et al.* (1983) op. cit., pp. 159–60.
24. ACAS (1983) *Annual Report 1983*, op. cit., p. 62.
25. Lord Chief Justice Goddard, quoted by Wedderburn (1965) *The Worker and the Law*, Pelican, p. 52.
26. Dickens *et al.* (1985) op. cit., p. 114.
27. TUC and Labour Party Liaison Committee (1986) *People at Work: New Rights, New Responsibilities*, p. 12.
28. ACAS (1986) *Annual Report 1986*, HMSO, pp. 86–7.
29. ACAS (1987) *Annual Report 1987*, HMSO, p. 58.
30. Ibid.
31. ACAS (1985) *Annual Report 1985*, HMSO, p. 39.
32. Ibid., p. 86.
33. ACAS (1987) *Annual Report 1987*, op. cit., p. 59.
34. ACAS (1982) *Annual Report 1982*, HMSO, p. 38.
35. ACAS (1983) *Annual Report 1983*, op. cit., p. 61.
36. ACAS (1985) *Annual Report 1985*, op. cit., p. 80.
37. TUC (1987) *Report of 118th Annual Trades Union Congress*, p. 39.
38. C. Graham and N. Lewis (1985) *The Role of ACAS Conciliation in Equal Pay and Sex Discrimination Cases*, Equal Opportunities Commission, p. 7.
39. Ibid., p. 48.
40. Ibid., p. 58.
41. Ibid., p. 65.
42. V. Kumar (1986) *Industrial Tribunal Applicants under the Race Relations Act 1976*, Commission on Racial Equality, p. (iii).
43. Ibid., p. 21.

44. Ibid.
45. Ibid.
46. Ibid., p. 22.
47. Ibid.
48. Ibid.
49. Dickens *et al.* (1985) op. cit., pp. 164–5.
50. Ibid., pp. 165–6.
51. Ibid., p. 167.
52. Ibid., p. 169.
53. Ibid.
54. Ibid., p. 179.

5 The Minimum Wage Question

1. Quoted in Ministry of Labour (1967) *Industrial Relations Handbook*, revised edition, HMSO, p. 214.
2. H. Phelps Brown (1959) *The Growth of British Industrial Relations*, Macmillan, p. 202.
3. Ministry of Labour (1965) *Evidence to Donovan Commission*, HMSO, p. 114.
4. Department of Employment (1988) *Wages Councils*, Consultation Document, p. 7.
5. Ibid., p. 8.
6. Ibid.
7. B. Doyle (1986) *'Essay on Legal Regulation of Collective Bargaining'*, in *Labour Law in Britain*, Blackwell, pp. 124–5.
8. ACAS (1980) *Annual Report 1980*, HMSO, pp. 59–60.
9. ACAS (1980) *Industrial Relations Handbook*, HMSO, p. 66.
10. ACAS (1980) *Annual Report 1980*, op. cit., p. 63.
11. C. Pond (1983) *'Essay on Wages Councils, the Unorganised, and the Low Paid'*, in *Industrial Relations in Britain*, Blackwell, p. 199.
12. ACAS (1980) *Annual Report 1980*, op. cit., p. 58.
13. Ibid., p. 61.
14. Ibid., p. 62.
15. Wages Act, Section 13 (2) (b).
16. Department of Employment (1988) *Wages Councils*, op. cit., p. 2.
17. Ibid., p. 4.
18. Ibid., p. 5.
19. TUC and Labour Party Liaison Committee (1986) *Low Pay: Policies and Priorities*, p. 11.
20. Ibid.
21. Ibid., p. 13.
22. Ibid.
23. Ibid., p. 14.
24. Ibid.
25. Ibid.
26. Ibid., p. 18.
27. Ibid.

28. Department of Employment (1988) *Wages Councils*, op. cit., p. 3.
29. ACAS (1980) *Annual Report 1980*, op. cit., p. 61.
30. Department of Employment (1988) *Wages Councils*, op. cit., p. 4.
31. Ibid., p. 4.

6 From Bridlington to Bournemouth

1. V. Tewson (General Secretary of the TUC) (1939) *Disputes Machinery of Congress*, adopted by the Bridlington Congress.
2. Trades Union Congress (1988) *Meeting the Challenge*, First Report of the Special Review Body, p. 8.
3. Trades Union Congress (1988) *TUC Disputes Principles and Procedures*, p. 21.
4. Trades Union Congress (1988) *The EETPU Suspension*, p. 6.
5. Ibid., p. 5.
6. Ibid.
7. Ibid., p. 7.
8. Quoted from V. Tewson (1939) *Disputes Machinery of Congress*, op. cit.
9. Ibid.
10. Ibid.
11. Trades Union Congress (1988) *TUC Disputes Principles and Procedures*, op. cit., p. 5.
12. Ibid., p. 6.
13. Trades Union Congress (1988) *The EETPU Suspension*, op. cit., p. 8.
14. Ibid., p. 6.
15. Ibid., p. 7.
16. Trades Union Congress (1988) *Meeting the Challenge*, op. cit., p. 29.
17. Ibid., p. 30.
18. Ibid.
19. Ibid.
20. Ibid.
21. Ibid.
22. Trades Union Congress (1988) *Meeting the Challenge*, op. cit., p. 31.
23. Ibid.
24. Ibid.
25. Ibid., p. 30.
26. Ibid., pp. 30, 31.
27. Ibid.
28. Ibid., p. 31.
29. Ibid., p. 29.
30. Ibid.
31. Trades Union Congress (1988) *TUC Disputes Principles and Procedures*, op. cit., pp. 6–7.
32. Ibid., p. 14.
33. Ibid., p. 15.
34. Ibid.
35. Ibid.

36. Trades Union Congress (1988) *Meeting the Challenge*, op. cit., p. 20.
37. Trades Union Congress (1988) *TUC Disputes Principles and Procedures*, op. cit., p. 15.
38. Trades Union Congress (1988) *Meeting the Challenge*, op. cit., p. 21.
39. Trades Union Congress (1965) *Evidence to the Donovan Commission*, p. 184.

Index